'This particular study is not based upon so-called 'revelation', but upon actual documents, hitherto unpublished, and discoveries made in different parts of the world. It derives from research into manuscripts kept secret or hidden away in the dusty pigeon holes of libraries, and from information provided by authentic Masters . . .'

In 1968 Robert Charroux covered 25,000 miles travelling all over Mexico, Libya and Tunisia checking sources of information for this book. Readers will find his immense documentation, ideas and proofs will open new vistas of time—past, present and future . . .

The Mysterious Unknown

Robert Charroux

Translated from the French by
OLGA SIEVEKING

CORGI BOOKS
A DIVISION OF TRANSWORLD PUBLISHERS LTD
A NATIONAL GENERAL COMPANY

THE MYSTERIOUS UNKNOWN

A CORGI BOOK 0 552 09392 0

Originally published in Great Britain
by Neville Spearman Ltd.

PRINTING HISTORY

Neville Spearman edition published 1972
Corgi edition published 1973

Copyright © Robert Laffont 1969

This book is set in Plantin 10/11 pt.

Corgi Books are published by Transworld Publishers Ltd.,
Cavendish House, 57–59 Uxbridge Road, Ealing,
London, W.5.

Made and printed in Great Britain by
Richard Clay (The Chaucer Press), Ltd., Bungay Suffolk.

**NOTE: The Australian price appearing on the
back cover is the recommended retail price.**

'No sooner had I completed the course of study at the end of which one would normally be admitted to the degree of Doctor, than I changed my views completely because I found myself beset by so many doubts and errors that I felt that nothing had accrued to me from my efforts at learning but the discovery that I was more ignorant even than I had supposed . . .'

DESCARTES

CONTENTS

Foreword by André Bouguenec: The Author and
the Unknown Masters   13
Unknown Masters help Robert Charroux—The Master
of Villeneuve—Contact with the Unseen—Suggestions for
an Unbeliever

THE FANTASTIC

1   Unsolved Enigmas   20
1529, a Rocket launched into Space at Sibiu, Rumania—
Three Tiers, Solid Fuel—Flying Machines of Monte Alban
—26 April 1967: St. Brendan's Isle—Not a Mirage—An
Image from the Depths of Time? We know Nothing

2   Fantastic Science   29
The Philadelphia Experiment—The Moebius Strip—The
Russian Version—P. Earth-bound—P. Airborne—The
Mystery lies in the Pyramid

3   Ancient Science   37
Hermes and Aesculapius—Who were the Teachers?—
Stone Spheres in Guatemala—Mysterious Diagrams at
Nazca—Writing or a Message from an Extra terrestrial
Source?—The Lexicon: Telescopes 1,000 Years ago—A
Plant to make Granite Malleable—The Secrets of Christos
Mavrothalassitis—The Astronomical Clock of Antikithira
—Space Rockets 3,000 Years ago?

THE HIGHER ANCESTORS

4   Memory Chromosomes   52
Desire-Images—The Stupendous Chromosomes—The
Mystery of Dreams—Remembrance of Past Lives—The
Mechanism of Reincarnation—Animal Migration—A

Panorama of the West—Dolmens, Cathedrals and Rugby Matches on other Planets—The Bible in A.D. 3000—Two Extra-terrestrial Visits—Hyperboreans and Atlanteans—Aryan Dispersals—Aryans, Sanskrit and the Vedas

5 Tradition and the Mystery of Megaliths   69
Druidic Sanctuaries and the Religious Life of Brittany—Carnac and the Mysterious Menec—Carnac and the Trojan War—Temples as Transmitting and Receiving Stations—Radio-active Pyramid at Couhard—An Accumulator 5,000 Years old—The Phalli of Filitosa—The Serpents of Gavr'inis

6 Celtic Civilisation: the Mother of all Civilisations   79
No Pyramids in Mexico—Celtic Pyramids made of Concrete—Tumuli, Pyramids and Barrows—The Brown Book—The Lady of the Hills—Celts discovered America 10,000 Years before Columbus—The White Lady of the Leni-Lenapes—The Popol Vuh—The Mexicans came from Europe—An Eagle perched in a Tree—Some Mayas return to Europe—Initiators from the East—Celtic Megaliths at La Venta—Thule—Were the Incas Celts?—Amerindians have European Ancestors—All Humanity is One—The Evidence of Pythagoras, Herodotus and Aristotle

7 Vanished Civilisations   103
France = 30,000 Years—Glozel = 15,000 Years—No Coffee Pots carved on the Rocks—Denis Saurat's Giants—Daniel Ruzo's Giants—The 'Mater' of the Forest of Fontainebleau—The Land of the Hills—Dream Days

8 Atlantis   114
The Story according to Critias—Atlantis swallowed up—Proofs of the Existence of Atlantis—Secret Archives—From Seneca to Paul Lecour—The Hebrews, were they Bretons?—The Mystery of the Guanches—Did Jesus visit the Guanches?

9 Other Sites for Atlantis   127
Atlantis in the Caspian and Heligoland—Atlantis in the Mediterranean—The Mystery of the Labyrinth—The Myth of Pasiphae—The Labyrinth and Pyramids of Clusium—The Atlantis of Christos Mavrothalassitis—Atlantis in Mongolia—The Land of Mu and Gondwana

10 Hyperborea and Egypt   140
    Hyperborea—Was Apollo an Extra-terrestrial Being?—
    Thule, The Gateway to . . . ?—Celts were Sea-farers—
    The Mighty Pharaohs were Kings only in Name—Staking
    Everything on a Future Life—Golden Keys to the Truth
    —Primeval History Falsified by False Gods—The Mystery
    of the Uraeus—The Mystery of 'Solar' Barques—The
    Calendar of Sothis (Sirius)—Atlantis and Egypt—The
    Land of Punt

11 Barbarian Civilisations   157
    The Cradle of the Aryas—Civilisation of Lake Titicaca—
    The Bible of the Black Races: Zimbabwe and the
    Foggaras of Adrar—History begins at Chatal Hüjük—
    Lepenski-Vir—The Celts of San Agustin—The Oldest
    Civilisations in the World, Summary of Dates

                    DEEPER MYSTERIES

12 The Mystery of the Pyramids   168
    An Atlantean Form—Earth's Vital Forces—The Saqqarah
    Pyramid—The Royal Burial Chamber in the Pyramid of
    Cheops—Usurpers of the Tombs—The Curse of the Dead
    —The Neutralising Djed—The Forbusch Effect—Earth, a
    Privileged Planet—The Sign of the Phoenix—Hibernation
    at Minus 196°C.—Travelling in Time—Predictions for the
    Years 1970 to 2100—What Use should We be in 2100?—
    The Land of Sleepers—Resuscitation according to
    Genetics—Pyramids for the Year 3000

13 The Mystery of Phantasms   189
    The Initiate Must Speak—Cerebral Waves in Man—
    Messages from Other Worlds—The Mystery of Spheres—
    Phantoms do Exist—The Ghost which Tula Followed—
    The Ghost of Eva J.—Phosphenes—How to See Flying
    Saucers

14 Words, Apes and Dolphins   202
    Heredity transmitted by Words—The Language of
    Animals—Apes are descended from Man—Hanuman, the
    Friend of Rama—The Yeti, is it Hanuman?—The
    Mystery of Dolphins—Dolphins talk with Men—When
    Dolphins tell the History of Man

15 The Water of Life   213
Hallucinogenic Couch-Grass—The Great Chinese Initia-
tion—The Power of Rain-water—Plain Water is Deadly—
The Water of Life—No Evolution, no Initiation—Man in
Regression—Extra-terrestrial Man

16 Ancient Mysteries   224
The Egyptian God Asari—The Legend of Eleusis—Greeks
did not believe in their Gods—The Secret of Eleusis—The
Rites of Eleusis—Cyceon—The Cabirian Mysteries—The
Mystery of Delos—The Mystery of the Celestial Ship

17 The Mystery of Agartha and of Shamballah   239
Light in Darkness—The Vault of Zalmoxis—The Vara
of the Iranian Plateau—Shamballah—The Luminous Race
—Mount Merou—Vril

18 The Universe   248
The Law of Hermes—Time and Speed—From the
Infinitely Great to the Infinitely Small—Imaginary
Calculations—Ancient   Cosmogonies—Cosmogeneses—
Development: The Abbé Lemaitre's Universe—Creation
is Continuous: The Universe according to Fred Hoyle—
An Explosion: The Universe of Sir Martin Ryle—The
Oscillating Universe of Allan Sandage—The Cosmo-
genesis of Oscar Klein—The Cosmogenesis of Andrei
Sakharov—The Cosmogenesis of Gustav Naan—Anti-
Matter—Who Created the Universe?

CURIOSITIES

19 Oddments and Oddities   262
Bonaparte's Pentacle—Napoleon, Breton or Charentais?—
Dashing One's Head against a Wall—American Curiosities—Mazdak, the Communist Prophet—A Determined
Messiah, Sabatai-Sevy—The Forest of Broceliande: Eon
de Lestoille—Tanquelin, God the Father—John of Leyden
and Robespierre as Messiahs

20 Predictions and the End of the World   274
False Prophecies—Predictions about the End of the World
—The Mess of Pottage—Jacob takes another mean Advan-
tage—Esau, a Seir—The Antichrist of the Hebrews—The
End of the World as Scientists see it—Electronic Astrology

THE SCIENCE OF LUCIFER

21 Sorcery   288
    The Bardo Thödol—Never eat Beans (Pythagoras)—
    Erotic Inspiration—The Witches' Weighing Machine at
    Oudewater—Ghosts may know the Future—Necromancy
    —Ritual Sacrifice by Alchemists—The Great Work of
    Gilles de Rais—Oracular Figures

MYSTERIES OF THE SKIES

22 Extra-terrestrials and the Journey to Bâavi   302
    The Paris Observatory, 1 December 1967—Life on Mars
    —Extra-terrestrial Alphabets—Mn. Y. returns—Parch-
    ments in a Pottery Container—Documents 1 and 2—'I
    went to Bâavi'—Guessing at the World—Conclusions of
    Mn. Y.—Vaïdorges: Mn. Y's Description—Light From
    the Skies

ILLUSTRATIONS

Two 16th century rockets
Two pages from *The Sibiu Manuscript*
Mysterious machine engraved on a rock in Mexico
The Moebius Strip
Two Maya Wheels
Huge drawings traced on uninhabited mountains at Nazca
Message from outer space, found in Nazca
The finest French Dolmen
The largest French Dolmen

Serpents engraved on the wall of the crypt at Gav'rinis
Fallen Menhir outside the tumulus at New Grange, Ireland
The great 'pyramid' of Teotihuacan
Monte Alban, Mexico
The pseudo-pyramid of Cholula, Mexico
Celtic Monuments?

A crucifix raised on a dolmen
Precious tablet from the museum at Glozel
The 'Mater' of the Forest of Fontainebleau
The sacred uraeus
The mystery of the solar barques and serpents
Extra-terrestrial drawing and writing
A specimen of Baal handwriting
Section of a vaïdorge
The six possible results of the movement of the titanium ring

FOREWORD

THE AUTHOR AND THE UNKNOWN MASTERS

Robert Charroux's books have always given readers a stimulus to deep thought and to further investigation; this one is no exception. It reveals unsuspected vistas, especially of the hitherto unpublished history of our Celtic ancestors: a history unpublished, actually interdicted, because it runs counter to some of the statements made in the Bible, in Sumerian and other Scriptures, as also by historians and prehistorians.

The whole history of the West has, in fact, been deliberately distorted in order to develop a mental outlook encouraging particular modes of thought, of behaviour and of social structure.

Unknown Masters help Robert Charroux

Robert Charroux is not the sole author of this book. True, he has written it, he has carried out the research, selected and planned the material, laid the foundations, argued his points. He has scoured the archives of the world in search of original and unpublished documents. But he has had a great many collaborators.

Some of these fellow-workers are very far out of the ordinary. He has been instructed by exalted Beings, some of whom may be the unknown Masters of the World. They have taught him little by little, one thing at a time, disclosing their secrets as it were on a pre-determined plan.

The 'Master of Angles', for instance, is not a myth. He

really exists, and lives in France. But he does not wish his name to be published.

The High Priest Anubis Schenouda is an Egyptian initiate. Robert Charroux has been the absolutely exclusive recipient of certain revelations which only a few adepts of the highest grades are entitled to learn. Why? The Master does not give his reasons.

Stranger still, the unknown Masters of a College of Initiates into the Hindu Mysteries, of which only the initials, C.P., may be given, are from beyond the veil helping our friend and suggesting to him ideas that are rich in potentialities.

'We have been commissioned by the Master of the World,' says a C.P. spokesman, 'to give to Robert Charroux the directions for his mission. Whether or not he is a believer is immaterial. Things will come to him without his being obliged to search for them consciously. . . .'

The 'Centre for Study and Research into the Unknown Elements of Civilisation' (CEREIC) at Nice, which also directs other Seekers, such as Guy Tarade and André Millou, has put its archives at the disposal of Robert Charroux.

Then, too, certain authentic Druids, such as the mysterious Mn. Y, who is said to be a representative of Masters from beyond our planet, and Gregori B., who has re-established the Inca Religion of the Sun, have spoken of the author of this book to their Superiors in the highest terms, a fact which is the more significant since Robert Charroux is not a member of their brotherhood.

It is collaborators such as these who have helped Robert Charroux to add a new ingredient to his discoveries which should help to promote a spiritual revival.

The Master of Villeneuve

Initiation is not the prerogative of a single Master. All Masters, according to information issued by the Society of the Rose Croix, are mandated by a central organisation of High Initiates ruled over by the Master of Masters—the Maha.

The Maha is believed to be the highest of all Initiates working in Paris, Cairo, Bombay, Pondicherry, and in the secret sanctuaries of Mount Merou and Asgard.

Several centres of initiation have been established in France, the most famous of them being that of the Rose Croix.

Since the fifteenth century—In reality since the dawn of human existence—members of the Rose Croix have been the highest Council of the Unknown Masters through whom the secrets of our Great Ancestors have been transmitted.

The Head of the French Rose Croix is Raymond Bernard, supreme Envoy in Europe, and Grand Master in all French-speaking countries. Above him is the Imperator of the Rose Croix, Dr. Ralph Lewis. Above even the Imperator are the Unknown Superiors with, at their head, the Maha.

Contact with the Unseen

The Master of Villeneuve met the Unknown Superiors at Istanbul on 24 December 1966.

In a restricted publication he described the interview. Or, to put it more accurately, he published what the Unknown Superiors allowed him to divulge.

The title of the book is *Meeting with the Inconceivable*. It is a work of the highest importance, because it proves with absolute certainty that the 'Invisible' of which men have spoken for centuries is not the invention of charlatans and visionaries.

The Master of Villeneuve tells that, like Saint Yves d'Alveydre, he is permitted to make certain revelations.

The name of Agartha, of which d'Alveydre speaks, has been changed, and within the High Council itself certain modifications are taking place, to bring it into accord with the speeding up of history and of time. Agartha's new name may be communicated only to 'the few'.

The High Council consists of a dozen human members who know 'the ultimate point to which this world will attain in its

15

evolution'. They are in a position to influence the politics of the day, although men still enjoy free will. Above these twelve men, on a yet higher level, are Invisible Beings in a superior hierarchy.

No earthly politician is a member of this High Council, and the 'Synarchy', that mythical monster of occultism, does not exist.

In his book, the Master of Villeneuve also reveals that the Unknown Superiors read the works of Robert Charroux, among others. He has the following to say about these writers.

'Valuable work has been done by them; problems are well presented, and answers are suggested if not actually given. Among contemporary authors in this sphere, Robert Charroux is on the highest level.'

Suggestions for an Unbeliever

This writer believes that Robert Charroux is 'helped'. Perhaps by 'mysterious influences' (or whatever people like to call it when they are faced with a miracle of thought: inspiration, the Muse or God), unknown forces which guide and stimulate him, even if he does not realise it, to evolve theories, make discoveries and give explanations, which are in fact dictated to him from 'the invisible'.

Yet he is neither clairvoyant nor even receptive to what people call 'revelation'. In fact, he does not believe in revelation. Yet, it does exist and so, as C.P. says, it does not matter whether Robert Charroux believes in it or not.

In Robert Charroux's normal 'conscious' life, the preparation of a book is a serious matter, to be undertaken in a spirit which allows nothing to be shirked or neglected, and for which he dedicates himself to world-wide research. In 1968, for instance, he covered 25,000 miles, travelling all over Mexico, Libya and Tunisia. Few writers show such professional integrity in checking their sources.

His readers—there are over 100,000 of them—are getting

16

full value. Whether as professional writers or as intellectuals, students will find in his immense documentation ideas and proofs that will open new vistas of time, of history, of the world.

André Bouguenec

THE FANTASTIC

CHAPTER ONE

UNSOLVED ENIGMAS

Initiates have their mysteries; scholars, ancient magi, occult practitioners their scientific dreams; history, past and future, has been falsified, distorted.... These, in brief, are the problems which are to be discussed in this book.

At the same time, it would be a bold man who would insist that what historians usually call pre-historic events ('primeval' is perhaps a better word), necessarily happened exactly in the supposed way, whatever may be the evidence believed to have been found.

This particular study is not based upon so-called 'revelation', but upon actual documents, hitherto unpublished, and discoveries made in different parts of the world. It derives from research into manuscripts kept secret or hidden away in the dusty pigeon holes of libraries, and from information provided by authentic Masters.

Wherever possible, photographic proof is given of any statement or discovery.

A space-rocket in the Middle Ages? Yes, indeed!

Aeroplanes four thousand years ago? Everything seems to point to it.

A rational, scientific explanation of strange phenomena, of dreams, of so-called supernatural appearances, of pyramids which up to the present have defied the efforts of seekers? Yes!

Files will be opened, photographs published, proofs presented!

A three-tiered, solid-fuelled space-rocket, of the same type as those launched at Cape Kennedy, was actually invented in 1529.

It was launched in 1555 at the city of Sibiu in Rumania.

Thousands of witnesses were present at the experiment, which was crowned with success, as was also the case at the Portuguese court in 1709, when Gusmao demonstrated his flying machine.

Historians have never referred to this 'unimportant' episode, which has therefore been lost in the mists of time.

During the past sixty years thousands, in fact tens of thousands, of books have been written about aviation and the conquest of the air.

Two or three of them have briefly alluded to Gusmao's machine, but not a single one has mentioned the earlier space-rocket—which makes one wonder whether historians are really honest investigators!

The honour of making the invention belongs to Conrad Haas, a pyrotechnician or Master Gunner ('Fire-Master'), whose drawings and description were discovered in 1961 by Doru Todericiu, Professor of Science and Technology at the University of Bucharest, when he stumbled across an old manuscript in the archives of the Sibiu library and published it in a Rumanian Historical Review in 1967 under the title 'The Sibiu Manuscript'.

The whole work was bound into a single volume at some time after 1570, and consisted of manuscripts by three authors. The first was by Hans Haasenwein, whose section dates back to 1417; the second was written in 1460; the third was by Conrad Haas, head of the Artillery Depôt of Sibiu between 1550 and 1570.

The last part of the manuscript contains a detailed report of the launching in 1555 of a multi-tiered rocket, and of a 'flying javelin' with a considerable effective range.

There is even mention of a 'little house' which might be

propelled into the air by a rocket. Although this was in fact never built it is a primitive, but real, anticipation of the spacecraft used by cosmonauts of the twentieth century.

Three Tiers and Solid Fuel

As the picture facing page 96 shows, Conrad Haas' rocket was built in two tiers with different diameters, one fitting inside the other. The rocket used in the experiment of 1555 had three tiers.

Solid fuel was used in both types and was made up of specially prepared powdery substances, though these could be replaced by a mixture whose base was ethyl acetate ammoniac, with other chemical components. The manuscript makes it clear that ethyl acetate was obtained from vinegar and alcohol; the ammonia was distilled from urine.

Conrad Haas also used delta wings, which have become a modern solution to the problem of steering and stabilising rockets.

The list of inventions mentioned in the Sibiu Manuscript is as follows:

two-tier ignition rocket 1529
three-tier rocket 1529
rocket fuel 1529
'flying cabin' 1536
tests for type of ignition needed in multi-tiered rockets 1555
use of delta-wings for stabilisation 1555

All these details are strictly accurate and come from the best possible sources: Professor Doru Todericiu, the discoverer of the manuscript at Sibiu, and from the Rumanian Historical Review.

The Flying Machine of Monte Alban

The site of Monte Alban is one of the most impressive in Mexico.

Some two thousand years ago the mysterious Olmecs settled

there. Nothing is known about the Olmecs except that they were sculptors of enormous statues—colossal heads—and steles on which are represented men with stern faces, wearing the same sort of headgear as modern cosmonauts.

They appeared on earth and disappeared again, leaving no trace except possibly that of the biblical legend that 'there were giants in those days'.

Their knowledge was very advanced, and an exciting detail connects them with those other, equally unknown, civilising influences who built Tiahuanaco in Bolivia and carved on the Puerta del Sol (Gateway of the Sun) motifs showing flying machines which some Amerindians identify with space-men and space-rockets.

An even more astonishing bas-relief of the same type is to be seen in the temple of Palenque, which seems to give similar information. It is of a space-rocket, piloted by an individual wearing an inhaler and heading for the planet Venus, if one may so interpret the marks engraved on the engine.

At Monte Alban a piece of rock-sculpture has been found, which makes one think that, if interplanetary travel was impossible for the ancient Mexicans, it probably was not for their Initiators; and that at all events their scientific achievements left a profound impression on the pre-Incas, the Olmecs and Mayas, since these peoples were evidently determined to perpetuate the memory in their traditions, in their laws and on their finest monuments.

How may the stele of Monte Alban be interpreted?

This is what Robert Carras, a member of CEREIC (an institute at Nice which researches into unknown elements of civilisation) has to say:

This is a technical drawing, and reminds one of an aeroplane stripped of its outer shell to show the structure and the engine. It has a screw propeller. It is easy to imagine a cockpit over the engine which would turn it into a flying machine. An extension to the propeller is no doubt intended to be the rudder.

The propeller is clearly distinguishable, and has three blades turning on an axis; it is prolonged to the foot of the sculpture.

This drawing is of a type seen only at Tiahuanaco, at Palenque and at Monte Alban, but its description is also found in Mayan manuscripts, and is written in a style completely different from normal Mexican calligraphy.

This abnormality is of obvious interest, as showing the exceptional character of the event.

There seems to be no doubt whatever that the Mexicans themselves were incapable of inventing the Tiahuanaco engine, the fire-belching rocket of Palenque or the screw-propelled machine of Monte Alban.

If they carved pictures of these machines, it was either because they saw them with their own eyes, or because they had heard of them as having been seen by others—with, no doubt, some inevitable errors or omissions due to misunderstanding or forgetfulness.

It is fair to deduce, therefore, that at some unknown epoch, men from another planet landed on American soil.

This theory is supported by dozens of drawings in the Troano manuscript, and in the codices of Perez, of Dresden and the Cortesianus.

The documents agree with the Mexican and Inca traditions which state that their Teachers—that is to say, their gods Quetzalcoatl, Kukulcan, Orejona and Viracocha—came originally from the planet Venus, and that they travelled in flying machines.

In addition it is most important to be able to study, in the Codex Cortesianus, the map of the route taken by an earthman on his way to the planet Venus where he was going to consult the Masters, whom he naturally referred to as gods.

26 April 1967: St. Brendan's Isle Again

This unexplained story, which has been ignored by most prehistorians, has always fascinated people who refuse to be put

24

off by false interpretations of history.

It would seem only logical to suppose that those whom the ancients called 'gods' were a more highly evolved race of men.

What could be more reasonable than to say that interplanetary travel existed in the past, as it surely will in the future?

One thinks of thousands of legends still current on earth which, it seems most probable, will in a very short while reveal the grain of wheat among the chaff.

What about the Atlantis of our Higher Ancestors? And the Hyperboreans who are our direct forebears? And St. Brendan's Isle, which stirred men's imaginations during the Middle Ages? Are they all only legends? Not, one must believe, for very much longer.

Curious happenings, which one might suppose to be inspired by invisible but rational beings, are shaking the assurance of materialists.

St. Brendan's Isle, vainly sought in the Atlantic during the Middle Ages, is forcing itself on people's attention once more.

This allegedly mythical island was seen by some thousands of flabbergasted inhabitants of Hierro, in the Canaries, on 26 April 1967. It was an amazing sight, which ended when it disappeared again, as it has done from time to time for the past three centuries.

Some explanation is due and it is here that an 'unknown factor' comes into play. This unknown factor is the same as those which enter into what is called initiation, magic, parapsychology and other unexplained phenomena, which spiritualists and other 'experimentalists' say are caused by invisible, but conscious, forces emanating either from the subconscious ego, or from some Other World. They have to be taken into account, because they are for ever coming up to jolt us out of our complacency.

Not a Mirage

From time to time a glorious island appears to the north-west of Hierro in the Canaries—a phenomenon peculiar to this part of the world.

In the eighteenth century its appearances were so frequent and so clear that the authorities in the Archipelago several times organised expeditions to take possession of the land which had risen from the ocean bed.

Was it no more than a mirage?

A mirage normally occurs in hot places, on land or sea, where the air is warmed perpendicularly by the sun. Atmospheric density varies with height, and rays of light are reflected in their entirety from distant objects, so that an inverted image is produced. But, according to the disposition of layers of density, such as if several warm strata are separated by layers of cold air, the opposite effect might occur.

This explanation does not, however, fit the case of St. Brendan's Isle.

Actually, Hierro is situated at the eastern extremity of the Archipelago, and there is no island in the neighbourhood which could cause a mirage.

The nearest islands in the direction in which the apparition is seen are the Azores to the north-west, and the Cape Verde Islands which lie over 900 miles to the south-west.

This distance, which is also affected by the curve of the earth's surface, seems much too great to justify the mirage theory. Added to which, it must be remembered that 26 April is not, by a long way, a date when the heat of the sun is strongest in that part of the world.

Moreover, if the 'mirage' had been that of a known Atlantic island, it was bound to have been identified, even if the image had been reversed. So where do we go from there?

If St. Brendan's Isle is not the reflection of any island existing on this earth, one is inclined to wonder if the original may not exist in some other world?

An Image From the Depths of Time?

Whatever the truth may be, it comes under the heading of Mystery and, that being the case, one might venture the hypothesis that it is a reflection from a parallel world or a world of the future.

Flying saucers may be a phenomenon of the same kind.

Science has made such strides that, if our civilisation continues to exist for a few more centuries, there is no doubt that time-machines will become a possibility for our descendants.

Ideas upon the nature of time propounded by philosophers make one think that past and future are concepts which attach only to our visible, dynamic universe, and not to absolute reality.

In short, as most theologians say of God, Time is an eternal Present.

In this sense, it is no longer an impossible idea that generations already living in the twenty-third or twenty-fourth century, may have found a scientific way of taking temporal observations of our epoch—which would be an exciting explanation of the mysterious UFO's and of the fabulous Saint Brendan's Isle.

Finally, it is extremely curious to note that the 'mirage' appears in the North Atlantic shallows, at the very spot where Plato and other traditionalists placed Poseidonis, the capital of Atlantis.

In fact it looks as though from time to time, and from the earliest days of our history, Atlantis has been resurrected before our eyes to prove its existence in spite of those who continue to question its authenticity.

We Know Nothing

Everything must have a beginning, and that beginning, according to accepted truth, is the creation of the world.

You may remark: 'It's a fine day,' or 'Well, I suppose Spring's on the way,' but these little every-day phrases involve the deepest mysteries of time and the cosmos.

'The acorn is the fruit of an oak-tree' is another obvious truth which is right every time without fail, yet it may rouse an infinity of speculation about the universe, evolution, free

27

will or the invisible forces of Nature.

Obviously, in every-day life it would be absurd to refer every statement back to its ultimate causes; but on a higher level it would seem impossible to understand a part of the whole, if the whole itself were not known.

All things are interdependent; nothing begins at any moment in time; everything begins in the infinite past; in other words, it has no beginning.

CHAPTER TWO

FANTASTIC SCIENCE

Even in these days, there are 'more things in heaven and earth ... than are dreamt of in (our) philosophy', but no doubt at some not too distant date these things will come to be accepted as a part of conventional science. At any rate, their study encourages the spirit of research and competition and prepares us to receive the thrilling discoveries which are hinted at in astrophysics and biochemistry.

What seems preposterous to us is more often than not simply due to our ignorance of what is possible: for example, the story of the Dutchman in the West Indies who told a Javanese that in Holland the water sometimes got so cold and so hard that you could walk on it. The man burst into a shout of laughter at what he thought was a joke.

The Philadelphia Experiment

George Langelaan, in his book *Terrifying Facts*, tells the extraordinary story of an American convoy ship which in November 1943 suddenly vanished from its moorings in Philadelphia and then reappeared before the astonished eyes of casual spectators and sober official witnesses.

While it was out of sight, the vessel was not simply absorbed into some invisible world, but was instantaneously transferred in space, for its 'ghost' was seen at the same moment in the harbour of Norfolk, Virginia, nearly 1,000 miles away. In short, the ship was said to have vanished from Philadelphia, to reappear at Norfolk, and then disappeared from

Norfolk to return to its point of departure.

Furthermore, George Langelaan says that Dr. Morris K. Jessup, who was one day found dead in his car, knew the real story behind what came to be called 'The Philadelphia Experiment', and that it was for this reason that he, according to the Police, committed suicide.

The explanation published in America, as related by George Langelaan, is as follows:

In 1942 Dr. Jessup, an up-and-coming young scientist, was understood to have submitted to the Naval Research Office a scientific thesis based on one of Einstein's theories, which would enable them to make ships invisible by using certain combinations of metals to create a powerful source of electricity, strong enough to displace any object.

The experiment was made on the open sea in the year 1943. The ship disappeared and re-appeared, not once but a number of times, over a great distance, and no one could stop it. At length the terrifying sequence came to an end, but most of the members of the crew had vanished, either by being 'consumed in a great fire', or by passing into another state of existence.

Some of those who survived died raving lunatics. The facts were published in a newspaper article over the signature 'Allen'; the F.B.I. enquired into this and finally tracked it down to Dr. Jessup—which might explain the young scientist's 'suicide'. After one other newspaper report, all documents relating to The Philadelphia Experiment were lodged among top-secret files by the American Navy and an embargo placed on the subject. Consequently, the mystery cannot now be solved, since the documents that might shed light on it are not open for public inspection.

Although Einstein was invoked to explain the transference of matter by the action of a specific magnetic field, no scientific theory, no laws, observations or physical data can be instanced that would allow the slightest credit to be given to the affair.

That is the American version of The Philadelphia Experiment, and it must be admitted that it was greeted with only very limited credence, until a Russian version turned up which showed that behind the Iron Curtain considerable interest was being shown in it.

Before retelling this, but in direct relation to the explanation put forward, it is worthwhile to consider the odd geometrical figures obtained with what is called the 'Moebius Strip', the study of which relates to a branch of science that has nowadays reached considerable importance and is known as topology.

The Moebius Strip

The Moebius Strip is a well-known geometrical curiosity. It consists of a narrow length of paper, AB–CD, the ends of which are joined, after a half-twist in the paper, so that AB is not joined to CD but to DC.

This gives a ring of paper, with one surface and one edge— neglecting, of course, the thickness of the paper.

If the paper strip is now cut lengthways, half-way through its width, a single twisted strip is obtained, twice as long as the original piece, and with four half-turns in it. If it is cut anywhere except half-way through, two twisted and interlaced strips result, of different lengths and widths.

The strip and its properties have raised some curious hypotheses touching upon the mystery of parallel worlds. For instance, one may speculate upon the situation of a humanity living in a two-dimensional world like the Moebius Strip. If the strip were cut lengthwise, one part of that humanity would pass into another world, which thereafter would have only a single, very slender point of contact with the other part, although would still be linked with it.

According to whether the paper is cut at one-third, one-quarter or half-way along its width, other and unfamiliar two-dimensional worlds will result from the first world.

This hypothesis, built up as an analogy, may, it is thought, help to explain The Philadelphia Experiment.

The Russian Version

It was in the course of luncheon with a friend that Doru Todericiu told the version of The Philadelphia Experiment current in the U.S.S.R.

In this version, a remote-controlled ship pursues a circular course on the water outside Philadelphia, and is powered by a form of electric current, the exact nature of which is not known, but which is obviously very strong and holds the vessel as it were a prisoner in the electro-magnetic field in which it functions.

This particular ship could have been a submarine which, at a given signal, submerged to sail upside down, then surfaced, turning on its side, then sailed round again in the normal position. So, if it did two rounds, it would sail half a turn in the normal position, then half on its side; half upside down, and again half on its side. At least, that is how one can imagine it, no official report of the operation and its results having been published by the American authorities.

At a given moment the electro-magnetic current, like the Moebius Strip, would be cut in two, a buoy perhaps acting as the hypothetical scissors, so that the single-dimensional world in which the evolution takes place becomes the same world in duplicate. Hence the submarine would have been lost to view at Philadelphia, and the vessel itself instantly (that is to say with no passage of time measurable on any clock) would have found itself in a different world, without the time factor coming into play at all, although the displacement in space was considerable.

The known result was dramatic in the extreme: of the twenty-two crew-members, sixteen died and six went mad.

The experiment was never repeated.

These are the strange events told by Professor Doru Todericiu, who had the information from official reports published behind the iron curtain. The Professor explains the phenomenon of quasi-ubiquity, or rather, of instantaneous displacement in space, by another and more scientific analogy borrowed from the behaviour of atoms.

You are asked to imagine two atoms orbiting round a nucleus, one small, with, say, a force of fifty, the other larger, powered with a hundred ergs.

If the smaller corpuscle's energy is increased to a hundred, one would expect it to rush instantly into the orbit of the larger—not by simple transference, but by a sort of spontaneous irruption, without the intervention of time or space.

Frankly, the whole affair is most mysterious, and would seem to be quite impossible, were it not that The Philadelphia Experiment appears to provide it with some authenticity.

In that experiment, the Americans would appear to have translated the ship from one line of force to another and more powerful one. The properties of the Moebius Strip, together with considerable intensification of the electric power, would have made it impossible for the ship to function in its original orbit, and would by its very nature have integrated it into the field of the other orbit.

It seems interesting to give the facts and the explanations, but, for what they are worth, they must be added to the file which is labelled 'Unproven'.

P. Earth-bound

This is an experiment easy to make, which, though it throws no light on The Philadelphia Experiment, at least shows that the inexplicable is a factor in our unexplored universe and in our daily lives.

The experiment may be called 'diminution of weight' or 'the pyramid of hands'. To carry it out, five people are needed: one man simply to sit on a chair, and four others (men, women or children) to lift the man, who shall be called P. The important point is that P. is to be lifted solely by means of two fingers of each of the four 'lifters', that is to say, the weight of his body will rest entirely upon the two top phalanxes of the four pairs of index fingers.

The first attempt is made quite simply by each of the four

lifters placing their two index fingers under P.'s knees (which, of course, are bent, as he is seated) and under his shoulders. Synchronising their efforts, they now try to lift P. off the chair. Nothing happens—especially if P. is a heavy-weight! Obviously the thing is impossible, at any rate for men and women of average strength.

P. Airborne!

The next step is to proceed to the real experiment, although it is to be carried out by the same people. For example, by two men and two women, with P. weighing, say, fourteen or fifteen stone.

He can be lifted perfectly easily.

The fingers are, as before, placed under P.'s knees and in his armpits. But, and herein lies the mystery: before attempting to lift him, the four people will pile their hands one above the other, the first touching P.'s head. The hands, it should be noted, must be so placed that no two consecutive hands belong to the same person.

All eight hands are now resting on P.'s head. No pressure need be exerted; contact alone is sufficient. The important thing is that the contact should last for a certain time, at least twelve seconds, and it is helpful to count up to, say, twenty-five or thirty. Then, at a given signal, the four lifters as quickly as possible take their hands off P.'s head, put their index fingers under P.'s knees and shoulders, and lift: he rises like a bird!

This experiment is successful ten times out of ten, a hundred times out of a hundred. However frail the lifters may seem in comparison with P.'s weight—it can even be done by children—he is raised into the air, can even be tossed up to the ceiling if the lifters are strong enough!

What is the explanation?

It cannot be explained by physicists any more than by meta-physicians.

One may imagine that P. is somehow 'conditioned' by hypnosis, by the magic of the pyramid of hands, which puts him into a state of semi-levitation. Not a bit of it! The experiment can be made with a heavy block of stone, with a big steel girder, with a large piece of furniture, and the result will be the same. This does away with any idea that the weight to be lifted can have been 'influenced'.

In appearance, and possibly in truth, it would seem that the pyramid of hands acts as an accumulator of energy.

Although the lifters make a much smaller effort than at the first attempt, they raise the weight with quite astonishing ease, or so it seems. The weight of the 'victim' does not change, so whatever happens takes place only in the lifters, even if they are unaware of it, by the addition of some unknown force which, though it does not increase their strength tenfold, certainly multiplies it by two or three.

It will be remembered that at the first attempt, before the laying on of hands, the lifters' effort was synchronised, but at the second attempt it was made with some loss of time, which should complicate the task. But, actually, it does not!

At all events, the fact remains—something happens! But what?

Possibly the phenomenon has something in common with an athlete's concentration. Very probably the effect of using the unknown powers of the ego may be apt to develop muscular strength or even to generate some buoyancy.

No doubt there is a scientific explanation of this mystery which has not yet been discovered simply because it has not yet been studied; it would also seem to have some bearing on the levitation of Saints, and the transportation of immense blocks of stone to, say Baàlbek, or Cuzco, or Stonehenge.

The ancients certainly had some secret force for raising menhirs, putting in position the slabs over dolmens, hoisting enormous blocks of stone in building the temple at Baàlbek, the Egyptian pyramids and the Peruvian fortifications, which they seem to have managed by somehow doing away with the weight of the objects.

That secret force is known as *vril*, and is believed to be an element in transcendental science which makes it possible to annihilate completely the weight of anything, or indeed to annihilate all active forces in the universe.

CHAPTER THREE

ANCIENT SCIENCE

It seems highly probable that civilisations flourished on earth in antediluvian times, and that some kinds of science—whether similar to ours or of a different type—were known, especially among the Incas, Mayas, Celts, ancient Egyptians and Greeks.

Although many refuse to agree with this heretical view, because it contradicts statements made in the Christian Bible and in the Hebrew Torah, nevertheless the study of certain events, the discovery of unexpected inventions and perhaps of scientific instruction given in Schools of Initiation, leaves no doubt that, in some unknown distant past, everything we now know was already familiar to our forebears, terrestrial or extra-terrestrial.

Hermes and Aesculapius

In the old days the priests of Aesculapius (Asclepios in Greek) were guardians of the sacred teachings of the Gods of Healing.

Fasting, dreams and visions, played a great part in the therapy members of this sect, who were known as Asclepiads (or sons of Aesculapius).

It was believed that Aesculapius himself had been taught by Hermes Trismegistus, the Egyptian god Thoth.

The following extracts are taken from one of the books attributed to Hermes, and seem to be very much in line with scientific ideas of our own days.

Something cannot grow from Nothing, the nature of which

is its inability to exist. The nature of what does exist, on the other hand, is that it cannot cease to be.

... Thus, O Aesculapius, man is a great marvel, a creature worthy of respect and veneration; for he is merged in the divine nature as though he were himself God.

... All things are bi-sexed, positive and negative.

In his book *The Secret of Hippocrates*, Anaxagoras says to Hippocrates of Cos, the successor to Aesculapius:

All things are infinite and eternal, even matter, for through it and by it are engendered innumerable worlds, which exist simultaneously and consecutively in space and time.

Not only is the whole of Nature infinite, but all that is comprehended in it is infinite in number and dimensions.

You should also know, O Hippocrates, that the macrocosm is contained in the microcosm, and that absolute disintegration is impossible, since everything is a part of the whole.

Nothing is born and nothing dies; but all things that exist can be amalgamated and redistributed. Or, if you prefer to put it this way: all substances can be broken down into their components and so they seem to change; the quantity of every element is incalculable and always remains constant, equal to itself.

Who Were the Teachers?

Nicetas of Syracuse, a Greek philosopher and a disciple of Pythagoras, had already accepted the truth of the theory of the revolution of the earth, which had long been known to the Aryans of India.

Cicero, in the first century B.C., set up a model of the universe, in which the earth occupied a very minor position. He maintained that unknown stars of immense size existed in the Milky Way (*The Dream of Scipio*).

According to Lucretius, the cosmos was full of worlds like

our own, where life manifested itself in various ways.

So-called 'pre-historians', learned and distinguished men, solemnly aver that the Mayas of Mexico did not know the use of the wheel. Are they trying to fool us, or are they really ignorant?

How can such a statement be made when the Mexican museums are full of representations of wheels, of mill-stones, of blocks and pulleys, and so on.

A magnificent stone wheel is to be seen in the museum of Oaxaca, pierced for the axle, and there are bobbins and the wheels of pulleys with axle-holes and deep grooves.

Mayan ornaments are often made of wheel-shaped pieces, strung together through the axle-holes.

In a jungle at Coba, near Quintana-Roo, a huge stone roller, weighing nearly five tons, was found. In a museum at Jalapa (Vera Cruz) a pre-Colombian whistle may be seen made in the form of a dog standing on four little wheels.

The Incas paved the roads in their Peruvian empire.

Of what use would be roads, roller, wheels and pulleys if, in fact, the inhabitants of ancient America did not use harnessed horses and carriages?

It is a difficult subject to study, because so many of the road-surfaces have been disturbed and the evidence destroyed.

A baffling enigma, in view of the fact that these people 'who never knew the wheel' invented a drainage system, diving suits, machinery and screw-propellers!

Is one perhaps interpreting too liberally the unknown past of the human race?

Undoubtedly one is liable to make plenty of mistakes in trying to reconstruct history. But how can anyone avoid making them when the truth is systematically suppressed by those whose official duty it is to teach it?

Stone Spheres in Guatemala

It is known that the Mayas, who were the ancestors of most of the peoples of Mexico, also settled in Yucatan and Guatemala.

In the Guatemalan jungle quantities of stone balls have been found, made of a kind of rock very rare thereabouts, with diameters varying from an inch or two to several yards. The stones were arranged in a way which puzzled archaeologists.

When the site was thoroughly examined and a few of the smaller stones which had been shifted in the course of the centuries were put back where they belonged, it was found that they had been arranged so as to represent our solar system and the principal constellations of the cosmos.

It was an astonishing discovery, which makes it abundantly clear that the Mayas had a knowledge of astronomy—which, indeed, is also shown in their monuments and their almanacs.

Furthermore, the geographical situation must have been considered to be exceptionally suitable for them to have taken the trouble to transport stones weighing anything up to several tons into the jungle and over a considerable distance.

Mysterious Diagrams at Nazca

Somewhere along the fifteenth parallel in the Peruvian savannas of Nazca and Palpa, to the north and south of the city of Nazca, certain mysterious gigantic figures cut in the rocks have also given archaeologists something to rack their brains over.

The country is mountainous and arid, and the valleys are watered only intermittently by torrents in the rainy season; the population is sparse and poverty-stricken.

Yet, in these desolate regions, enormous works have been carried out—designs have been carved in the rocks; the ground has been broken up in a geometrical system of trenches, so accurately aligned that they might have come directly from an industrial architect's drawing office.

These furrows, dug in the earth and the rocks, cross valleys and ravines and mountains, and extend over a distance of thirty miles.

Seen from the air, they make an absolutely clear pattern. Every now and then the shapes of plants and animals may be distinguished; tortoises, three-headed serpents, birds, spiders ... and an anthropomorphic divinity, with a halo round its head, is faintly discernible.

About three quarters of a mile from Nazca, at the bottom of the narrow Puquio valley, a number of such designs are to be seen, outlined in white on a red ground.

In general the lines are parallel or radiate from a central point, but there are also other figures, trapezoid or triangular in shape.

The parallel lines, seen at close quarters, look like roads with raised kerbs made of stone blocks. But they are quite obviously not roads; they lead nowhere and have no conceivable purpose as lines of communication.

In addition to all these, there are rectangles, spirals and some designs that are completely inexplicable. One of these shows a slender rod with line and reel, such as might be used by a fisherman.

The fascinating problem is: what is the meaning of the furrows which run dead straight towards the four cardinal points of the compass?

The archaeologist Paul Kosos thinks he has found the key: the designs were laid in order to show the paths of the stars, so that the agricultural work of the year might be organised in due season.

'There you have,' he says, 'the largest book in the world on astronomy.'

But what is the meaning of all the other lines and of the figures?

Paul Kosos also noticed that some of the radial centres were formed by small mounds, upon which could be seen vague structural outlines, undoubtedly of great antiquity.

Were they contemporary with the linear tracings? Or were they built later to give the place a sacred character? No one knows.

Most of the furrows are wide enough for a procession to pass along them, which suggests that they might have been used for ceremonial purposes.

41

Writing or a Message from an Extra-terrestrial Source?

Actually, none of the suggestions made by archaeologists nor the conclusions they have drawn can be taken as conclusive, for if some few lines on the Nazca site have an astronomical significance, what about the vast majority that radiate in all directions? At the same time, it is worth noting that about 180 miles further south, lying between the volcanoes Ampato, Chachani and Misti, to the east of Arequipa, thousands of gigantic rock sculptures have been found, showing snakes, deer, jaguars, birds, suns and stars; it may be that there was some connection between these and the ones at Nazca.

Was there a mysterious civilisation here? Not a very probable idea. The region would appear always to have been poor and backward.

The geometric precision of the marks and their size suggest, on the contrary, technical work by giants or a demiurge coming from a great distance, who used the sculptures as a sort of marker-buoy, or perhaps to deliver a message to humanity.

This is a solution which cannot be proved, it is purely hypothetical; but it seems to fit the essence of the problem as a non-human, therefore probably extra-terrestrial, phenomenon.

A curious fact is that the site of Nazca lies in exactly the same latitude as Tiahuanaco where tradition says Orejona, the Mother of the human race, landed on her journey from Venus. And Orejona arrived in a flying machine 'more dazzling than the sun', wrote Garcilaso de la Vega.

The 'extra-terrestrial messages' at Nazca are to be seen at a place exactly half-way between the Atlantic and Lake Titicaca, so that they are quite near the spot where, according to Andean tradition, she touched down. Could they have been meant specifically for Orejona's country?

On the other hand, the fact that both the direct and the oblique lines point towards the horizon, running straight over heights and depths without troubling to deviate, seems to indicate that the diagram was intended for someone viewing it from a great height, such as an observer in an aeroplane or on some other planet.

In 1962 mankind sent signals to the moon and to the cosmos at large by means of powerful lasers, of which the accuracy, range and strength were known.

The mystery of Nazca would be to a great extent solved if one were to suppose that scientists from outside the earth had used a laser or similar means to trace the enigmatic symbols, which might be some form of geometrical script, analogous to ogham, used in a highly advanced civilisation.

Drawings of animals and plants, of rectangles and triangles on the one side, and of unexplained figures and diagrams on the other, might be two versions of the same thing, meaning: 'This is your writing—that is ours. Try to decipher it!'

The Lexicon: Telescopes 1,000 Years Ago

The religion of the ancient Peruvians has been revived in Paris, under the title *The Inca Religion of the Sun*.

A most interesting monthly duplicated bulletin is published, the work of Gregori B., the pseudonym of Beltran Garcia, a high initiate and the descendant of Garcilaso de la Vega.

From this bulletin comes the following extract:

The *Lexicon* is a dictionary compiled in Peru in the year 1540 by Domingo de San Tomás, a Dominican Monk. It contains words in *runa-simu* (Quiché), and their equivalent in Spanish.

It was published at Valladolid in June 1560.

Many and wonderful things are to be found in the *Lexicon*, as for example on page 132 about the meaning of the word *Quilpi*. This is the word used for an article made by Incas, which is translated into Spanish as *anteojos con espejuelos curvos*.

The *espejuelos* are concave or convex mirrors or pieces of glass.

Anteojos means spy-glasses or spectacles.

Quilpi should therefore be translated as an 'optical instrument for looking into the distance'. Or, if preferred, as 'telescope'!

Furthermore, *quilpi* as etymologically connected with *quilcaquipo*, which is an adding machine, and *quilcadaricumgui*, which means to learn or to read; and with *quillaquiz*, meaning a planet, or cosmic system.

Telescopes centuries before the days of Galileo? Who would have thought it?

A Plant to Make Granite Malleable

In the museum at Cochabamba, in Bolivia, there are to be seen what they call 'moulded stones'; that is to say, pieces of rock such as granite on which the Incas were able to leave the imprint of their hands or feet by pressure only, as though the stone had been soft like butter.

Such prints are found in the mountains of Peru, and also in Tahiti, near Punaouia where, according to legend, the god Hiro, a Being of white race, first set foot on the island.

Another marvel of the same kind is that of the enormous blocks of stone which were used in building the fortified citadels of the Incas, notably that at Sacsahuaman, near Cuzco.

These blocks are amazingly accurately cut and joined, sometimes with insets which fit into one another so exactly that one might think the masons had not hewn the stones but had treated them with some chemical to make them malleable as clay.

In June 1967 it was reported that a Peruvian priest, Father Jorge Lira, had discovered how the Incas did it. They used the juice of a plant that will soften anything whatever. Father Lira claimed to have experimented successfully with pebbles steeped in the juice of this exotic vegetable. Its name has not yet been told. Gregori B. is said to know it—but there seem to be three herbs of the same name.

One plant in our own part of the world is alleged to have the same property—the herb purslane—'as long as the juice is used in a particular manner'.

44

If Father Lira's discovery can be verified, it may perhaps explain in a new way how granite is formed.

It is known that the earth's crust is broken up and reconstituted by the action of internal forces. When chalk and clay come near the magnetic pole they become schists as a result of pressure and temperature; limestone turns into marble, and since the reactions are intensified according to the depth at which they occur, new amalgams appear, until finally they crystallise to form granite.

Knowing what the natural process is, one can only marvel the more at what may truly be called the empiric science which enabled the Incas to soften granite wrought in the bowels of the earth.

The Secrets of Christos Mavrothalassitis

Some curious traditions are still current in Greece, as was gathered from what my friend Christos Mavrothalassitis told me.

At some indeterminate but no doubt extremely ancient date, the Greeks used to cut stone by using 'liquid fire', which was presumably some type of acid.

It is said that the ancient city of Ampurias, on the Gulf of Rosas, in Spain, was built by the Greeks with the help of this fire.

At Symi, one of the smaller Dodecanese islands, a peasant is said to have found a jar full of some sort of liquid, to judge by the sound it made when he shook it.

Witnesses to this are still living—but the rest of the story is only conjectural.

The peasant probably broke the jar, because an appalling explosion was heard. The unfortunate man was never seen again and a large hole was blown in the ground where the accident happened. At the same time a kind of geyser spouted there, but it disappeared again a little while later.

On the same island of Symi, somewhere about the year 1911 or 1912, a shepherd got lost in an underground cave the existence of which had not been generally known. He found a golden diadem lying on top of a tomb, which was surrounded by what appeared to be an iron railing. All around were piles of skeletons.

The shepherd was considerably startled, and told his story to the local doctor, who went and removed the iron barrier. But, fearing some trap, he had the sense not to touch the golden ornament. He excavated the ground beneath the tomb, and found two batteries in a clay container; they were no longer 'live', but in earlier times must have been capable of giving an electric shock to anyone who touched the jewel.

A legend? That will never be known; but Christos Mavro-thalassitis tells the following incredible story as gospel truth:

'It was in 1919. My father had a diving business and fished for sponges. He and his partner, Zalakhos, worked round the Greek islands. I was quite a youngster, but I used to go out with them. One day we came to a little uninhabited island. One side of it was all granite cliffs, which seemed to flow into the sea as if in the olden days something had fallen from heaven and melted the rocks.

'Zalakhos dived on the north side, swam round to the south of the little island and then got back into the boat in a state of terror.

'"Gabriel", he said to my father, "There's a fire under the sea, and if you touch a sponge, the sand it is lying in burns your hand. If you put your foot down, you're burnt by flames that you can't see. It's like some sort of radiation [sic] under the water."

'My father, of course, wondered what it all meant. He dived, taking his sponge-net with him, and found the place where Zalakhos had seen the submarine fire.

'When he came up again, I saw that he had several sponges in his net, but also a lump of iridescent metal, that varied from dark to light blue.

'The rest of the crew told him to come aboard quickly, because Zalakhos was feeling bad and said his body was on fire.

46

'All they could do was to pour water over the unfortunate fellow, who was howling with pain and kept on repeating that his body was on fire. He died during the afternoon. My father decided to return to Symi to have his partner buried.

'During the night one of the sailors went to look at Zalakhos's body, which was lying on deck covered with a tarpaulin. He gave a shout of horror and woke up everybody else, saying the corpse was phosphorescent.

'And so it was. Zalakhos's face, body, hands and feet were shining with a golden light.

'My father ordered them to tie stones on to the tarpaulin and to drop the body overboard as quickly as possible.

'In 1921 he sold the lump of iridescent metal that he had fished up to a chemist in Bordeaux.

'In 1926 he went back there to see the doctor whom he had consulted five years earlier, because ever since the day when Zalakhos died the joints of his hands had been swollen and twisted.

' "You must have come in contact with something that was stronger than radium," said the doctor. And if my memory serves me rightly, that doctor's name was Fromagé.

'When he came out of the doctor's consulting room—I was with him at the time—my father said to me: "I knew it! To the north of the island there are some jars made of this blue metal, which isn't really either metal or glass. But I don't know any more than that. People must have used the stuff a very long time ago; but goodness only knows what for." '

'And there you have my father's story,' Christos ended.

Turning to his wife, he added: 'Isn't that what I've always told you?'

She nodded. 'Yes,' she answered, 'and you even said that it might be some kind of alloy from Atlantis.'

'Maybe,' said Christos noncommittally. 'In any case, this year or next I'm going round that island with a basket. I know the exact spot. Those pots at the bottom of the sea must be worth a fortune!'

That is the extraordinary story told by Christos Mavrotha-

47

lassistis, the diver, who lives at Houm Souk on the island of Djerba.

Was he exaggerating?

'No! I swear by St. Helena and by St. Constantine,' he said, and his voice seemed to be calling on all the rest of the saints in Paradise to witness, as well as the gods of Olympus.

But Christos is a Greek, like Homer and Achilles and Ulysses. Cunning, clever and tells a good yarn.

'Everything happened exactly as I said,' he averred solemnly. 'The proof is that other divers have died in the same way. Some people say that there are active volcanoes round that island; but that isn't the real answer. . . .'

The metal, or whatever it was, has never been identified. But it is known that the Vikings used something they called a 'sun-stone' to help them steer in cloudy weather, and which they said infallibly located the sun. This has recently been discovered to have been cordierite, or iolite, which varies in colour from yellow to a dark blue. It may well be that the metal found by the Greek divers was in fact iolite.

The Astronomical Clock of Antikithira

Somewhere off another of the Dodecanese islands—if it *was* another one—some sponge divers on Easter Day in 1901 fished up a block of greenish metal, the remains of some statues and some jars.

Actually, they had just made one of the most exciting discoveries of the century. The island was Antikithira, which lies between Cythera and Crete.

When it was examined by archaeologists, after being carefully cleaned of accretions of coral and limestone, the lump of metal was found to be a box containing an astonishing collection of wheels, balances, axles, asymmetrical cylinders and delicately fashioned needles; there were also three dials in the box.

'It's a clock!' said the archaeologists. 'It must have come from an old galley.'

48

'Rubbish!' retorted the sceptics. 'It's much too accurately made to be as old as all that! You might as well say that Pericles told the time by his wrist-watch!'

It turned out to be something even more astonishing, according to official experts. It was an astronomical clock dating from between 80 and 50 B.C., and functioning exactly like one made in the twentieth century. It gave the signs of the Zodiac, the movements of tides, the orbits of Mercury, Mars, Jupiter and Saturn, the solar year, the months and the time of day. Never before had so perfect an example been seen by anyone.

Before 1901, the oldest known clock had been that of the initiate monk Gerbert, who became Pope Sylvester II. And it is still not known how that one worked.

Since the days of Aristotle the idea of inventing a clock to be worked by means of weights to turn the hands on a dial had been discussed, but no one had ever discovered how to regulate the movements.

Ancient time-pieces were either sun-dials or clepsydras (water clocks). The first clock, as we know clocks, is believed to have been the one over the Law Courts in Paris, made by Henri de Vic in 1370.

The discovery of the astronomical clock of Antikithira gave a nasty jolt to people who had thought they knew all there was to know on the subject!

Some day the world will surely learn that, long before the Antikithira clock was made, physicists had invented and used atomic clocks. . . .

Ideas that at present seem absurd and incredible will not remain so for long!

Space Rockets Three Thousand Years Ago?

Sanskrit documents discovered by the Chinese at Lhasa are said by Hindus to contain directions for building inter-planetary spaceships.

Their method of propulsion was anti-gravitational, and based upon a system analogous to that of *laghima*, the unknown power of the ego existing in man's physiological make-up, 'a centrifugal force strong enough to counteract all gravitational pull'.

On board these machines, which were called *astras*, the Aryans of old could have sent a detachment of men on to any planet, as Dr. Ruth Reyna, of the University of Chandigarth, said recently.

The Lhasa manuscripts are said also to reveal the secret of *antima* (the 'cap of invisibility'), and of *garima* ('how to become as heavy as a mountain of lead').

Hindu scientists, who were at first extremely reserved about the positive value of these revelations, have become noticeably less so since the Chinese stated that certain of the data were being studied for inclusion in their space-programme.

The manuscripts do not say definitely that inter-planetary communication was achieved; but mention is made of a trip from the earth to the moon, though without its being made clear whether this was actually carried out or only planned.

THE HIGHER ANCESTORS

CHAPTER FOUR

MEMORY CHROMOSOMES

Man is 'motivated' by his subconscious ego, by his instincts or by some biological law, without the co-operation of his intellect in the choice or progress of an action, even on the higher levels of evolution.

This is due, first to the background of his species, which is the primary reason for the difference between plants and animals; and second, to his acquired characteristics.

Desire-images

The Utopias which psychologists call 'wishful thinking', ideas that rise from the depths of the unconscious are, they think, a sort of desperate quest for an ideal, due to disillusionment and despair.

The gods, the City of God, the time of the Apocalypse, Eldorado, ghosts, visions, Atlantis, space-travel, flying saucers and so on, are all, they suggest, ideas originating in wishful thinking.

In some cases they result from the creative instinct or from the longing for security and happiness; but in others the problem lies deeper and has a more scientific explanation.

To a biologist, 'Utopias' such as Atlantis, space-travel, flying saucers, migratory birds' certainty that they will find a landing place in the Atlantic and lemmings' 'faith' in the existence of a vanished continent somewhere near Norway, are not caused by an irresistible urge nor by some kind of dream; they are unconscious memories of actual facts, of a truth for ever recorded in their unconscious racial memories. Other such memories may yet be added; but some may gradually fade or even disappear completely.

This is what agricultural scientists fear may happen to fowls and other animals bred intensively, where the selective principle is taken too far, with the risk that hereditary instincts may be lost.

In short, it is feared that natural species of animals may disappear, to be replaced by something more or less, but not exactly, the same, in which new chromosomes and genes will develop in place of the original ones.

The theory of desire-imagery is certainly not without foundation when it comes to religious beliefs.

Visions of Christ, of Saint Michael or Saint Catherine are of this nature, and to some degree also those of the Virgin Mary.

The last instance may possibly be connected distantly with a real event, or one that seems to be so: the appearance on earth in very ancient days of a feminine Initiator or 'Mother of the human race', called Orejona by the Incas, the Great Goddess by Celts, Ops or Cybele by Romans and Greeks.

Nevertheless, very frequently such phenomena do come under the heading of science, now that twentieth-century men have begun to investigate a biological mystery: that of memory-chromosomes.

The Stupendous Memory-Chromosomes

Human and animal memory exists pre-natally. Konrad Lorenz, the German scientist, has proved experimentally that a chick will recognise sounds and voices that it has heard while it was still in the egg, and that it learns the language of its kind while the hen is sitting.

What used to be called instinct (innate percept), although remaining true in the case of certain impulses and feelings sometimes called the 'sixth sense', is more often due to hereditary memory transmitted to the nervous system by memory-chromosomes. (Incidentally, some biologists even think that the phenomenon extends to all realms of nature and to the whole universe.) From this one might infer that the cosmos too has its memory-chromosomes, analogous to *akhashic* world records, which have for centuries been 'miraculously' invoked by spiritualists.

Chromosomes (from the Greek words *chroma* = colour, and *soma* = body) are elements of the cellular nucleus. They may take the form of minute particles, filaments or rods; their number is constant and equal in all individuals of the same species.

Every individual is 'controlled' by the over-all plan of his cells, which are what might be called the 'programmers' of the species.

This is why a grain of wheat will always produce straw, why an acorn always grows into an oak tree and not an elm, why a bird begets another bird and not a mammal.

Without any exception whatever.

As a result of his heredity, man speaks, builds, makes tools and has now got to the stage of inventing space-rockets, all of which have been 'programmed' in his cells.

You can take a swallow's egg from the nest, put it in an incubator and segregate the young bird so that it never sees or hears any member of its own species. In October, by which time all swallows will have departed for Algeria or the Congo, you release the bird, now a young adult. It will go and join others of its kind in North Africa, and never think of going anywhere else.

Animal instinct? Not at all: it is due to the operation of its memory-chromosomes.

The branches of every oak tree grow according to its kind; birds weave or in some other way build their nests; each of the kingdoms of nature conforms to laws that are immutable (except in the very long run) for the same reason and as a result of the same cause.

This explains why, according to Bible stories, Hebrew Initiates preached the necessity for keeping the race pure and uncontaminated amid more primitive civilisations, in order that the natural destiny of the race might be fulfilled.

This was, one might say, the real purpose of the Jewish migrations at the time of Moses.

No individual is ever solely responsible for any essential invention. His intelligence (thought, imagination, work, experiment) helps him only to evolve socially—progressively or regressively or by mutation—apparently in accordance with a design which is itself directed by universal laws that may be called God or the Law, or what you will.

Intelligence, which seems also to imply free will and creativeness, depends upon attainments resulting basically from the workings of memory.

In conclusion, one may say that the design for each species includes an initial hereditary memory, developed primarily in the chromosomes.

In 1967 the International Business Company of America organised a library arranged on a system as complex as that of our memory cells. In essentials this library consists of a multi-coloured laser with a wave-selector, which records a hundred million pieces of information upon a surface about three inches square.

The exact physico-chemical process by which memory is recorded in the chromosomes has not yet been absolutely pinpointed by biologists. Hereditary memories and those which have been acquired more recently impregnate the cells and are strengthened by repeated use. They fade if the cells are not exercised or if physical deterioration impairs their functioning.

An old person forgets things that have happened within the last few days, but probably has a vivid recollection of things that happened in the past, which were registered when his brain was able to record them easily and correctly.

The Mystery of Dreams

By means of encephalograms and other observations, biologists and physicists have clearly shown the mechanism of dreams.

55

It has been proved that babies only a few months old will dream, as also do some of the higher animals such as dogs, cats, lions, horses, monkeys, as well as birds and dolphins. It is theoretically possible that all created things dream, that all creation has a soul and an intelligence; but at present technical means of proof are lacking.

As regards animals, the physical signs of dreaming are as follows: eyes move in their sockets and extremities quiver; in the case of cats, their whiskers twitch.

During deep sleep all muscular activity ceases, but it starts up again when dreams are in progress. An X-ray photograph of the brain taken while the subject is asleep will show the exact moment when a dream begins and muscular activity recommences, by the range of vibrations in that part of the brain which tapers off into the spinal cord.

A good many hallucinations or supposedly mysterious happenings, such as some cases when flying saucers are seen, may be explained by lack of dreaming. People who do not dream or who are, for experimental purposes, prevented from dreaming, are subject to disturbances and hallucinations in their waking state. They may talk to trees, to space-travellers; they may see the Devil or an Archangel or giants; they 'recognise' people they have never met before ... and so on.

Dreams occur a number of times during sleep, maybe three or four times, the first being the shortest, lasting about ten minutes; the final one going on for perhaps half or three-quarters of an hour.

If a subject is prevented from sleeping as long as usual, but is allowed his three or four dreams, he suffers no mental upset.

Dreams, more essential than sleep, and more indispensable to our mental balance, appear to play a mysterious part in our existence, the aim of which may be to bring us in touch with the beginning of creation, or perhaps to maintain contact with the archetype of the species to which we belong.

It is difficult to find out whether a baby dreams while it is in the womb, but it seems probable that it does so. When it is only a few days old it dreams of things it wants, of its so-

56

called 'archaic' needs: drinking, passing water, the sight or touch of its mother.

Smiles, screams, tears and so on, which one is apt to think of as simply the expression of physical needs, may of course be just this, though motivated by 'archaic' memories of a previous life.

In short, a baby sucks, smiles, cries, for the same reason that a sparrow builds its nest, or white ants raise their fortifications, or migrants set out in the autumn, or a cat buries its droppings, or a dog becomes the friend of man. All these actions, these phenomena are hereditary transmissions through memory chromosomes.

Remembrance of Past Lives

Here is a very striking example to support the above argument: on a farm there was a stream which was channelled along several ditches. One of the dogs on the farm, a bitch, was accustomed to drink from one of the ditches, and never from any other; also she insisted on having her food in a blue bowl, although she was offered it in three other bowls of different colours.

She died giving birth to a litter of puppies, several of which lived. As they grew up, the puppies did exactly the same as their mother had done: they always drank at the spot where she had drunk and always liked to have their food in a blue bowl.

It must have been a hereditary memory.

In the case of a baby, the same sort of behaviour may be observed, and it can all be traced to its mother and to long-past ancestors, right back to the first created man—or rather to the original mother of mankind, as acknowledged by the Celts and shown by conclusive experiments to be a fact.

Experimental studies by Dr. Friedmund Neumann have proved that without the male hormone every living creature is fundamentally female. It is in this sense that Dr. Neumann argues against biblical statements: the first human being was not Adam, but Eve. Celts, being higher initiates than Hebrews, agree: the first human creature was feminine—Dana, or Ana, the original Mother.

Without knowing exactly how it comes about, biologists now know that memory, both of what *has* happened *and what is going to happen in the future*, is contained in the chromosomes.

Human beings reproduce by fission, and in this sense they are immortal. In other words, a part of their bodies and souls is not annihilated but persists in time and through their descendants.

Memory, transmitted through chromosomes, no doubt by some sort of energy of the same type as electricity, explains why in some cases a man who thinks he has invented something has in reality done no more than rediscover an old idea which had lain dormant in the eternal ego.

So a man may exclaim on seeing a landscape: 'What an extraordinary thing! I know this place; I've often dreamt about it! I remember it quite well!' And it's the truth, or very nearly. It may be that one of this man's ancestors lived there for a long time, or had particularly noticed it and enjoyed being there. The memory has been transmitted hereditarily.

This is what makes people say: 'I remember having lived in such and such a place ... having been that person. ...'

Things that attract or repel us can be explained in the same way—including our allergies.

The miraculous appearance of a genius such as Leucippus or Alexander, Descartes or Mozart, may be explained similarly by the memories in their chromosomes.

The Mechanism of Reincarnation

Imagination, and more particularly dreams, have a mysterious connection with the past, with our 'former lives', people often say, although one knows very well that, rationally, it is impossible that the ego with which we are familiar from every aspect could have lived as exactly the same person a century ago or ten centuries ago.

The belief is mistaken in the sense that it presupposes a continuous or intermittent series in which a 'conscious ego' always remains the same. It is true in the sense that there could be thousands of replicas of our ego, multiplied to infinity by the vicissitudes of love, of death, of chance.

In short, one might say that all men can see themselves in the primordial Eve; and, if we wander back through time, there are infinite numbers of side-tracks, which might lead to, say, King Arthur. Consequently we might be one of thousands or even millions who could claim: 'I was King Arthur!'

This little quirk on the part of memory-chromosomes gives a rational as well as an esoteric explanation of reincarnation. One must admit, all the same, that every now and then chromosome memories are transmitted with exceptional clarity to an individual; and this would be a case of almost complete reincarnation.

Descendants of people who escaped from the *Titanic* disaster of 1912, would, if they were born after the tragedy certainly have very specially strong feelings about the sea, ships, icebergs and drowning. They might never consciously think about the calamity, but it is more than likely that they would re-live events subconsciously, that is to say in dreams.

In fact, it is theoretically possible for a child born of an unknown father to discover him by a comparative study of their dreams. Both would be likely to have the same kind of dreams, since they were fixed in their chromosomes by the same salient memories.

Animal Migration

Some zoologists explain migration by a subconscious urge for natural selection or the survival of the fittest. They believe this to be true for lemmings, who go off and drown themselves when they proliferate too freely on one of their feeding grounds. It is also said to be true of swallows, who lose about fifty per cent. of their number when they cross the Mediterranean. But this explanation is not really sound.

Even though one of every two swallows may die in crossing the sea, selection does not, properly speaking, come into the question, because their numbers soon increase again since each pair breeds four to six eggs every Spring and often twice a year.

The most remarkable thing is that zoologists, however learned they may be, never seem to have noticed that animals are not really concerned about proliferation. On the contrary, their primary aim is to ensure the perpetuation of their species by any and every means. The purpose of their life is, in a word, living.

As regards natural selection, this is assured by nature itself, as the words show. If there are too many insects, birds proliferate; not enough insects, and birds, their predators, die off.

What seems to be reasonably certain is that migration is usually seasonal, depending upon temperature and the availability of food. At the same time, it seems unlikely that the little storm-petrel crosses the Atlantic in search of the food and the climate of America, when Africa has forests and fields, deserts and oases to offer. To ensure the survival of the fittest? Hardly. Storm-petrels do not breed freely; they cross the great ocean in response to a subconscious hereditary urge.

It is their memory-chromosomes which direct and guide them.

A Panorama of the West

The life-history of swallows, of lemmings, of bison, of all migrants, may therefore in some degree be explained by their biological impulses.

It seems curious that historians have never thought of using the same key to unlock the obscurities of human history.

The fact that Basques and the Irish choose to emigrate to America rather than elsewhere, that they were the first to cross the Atlantic; that Canada was discovered by Bretons; that the Incas were the first to settle in Polynesia—all these facts are, surely, highly instructive.

Migrations of peoples are determined by the same causes as migrations of animals, and the history of civilisations would seem therefore to be only the natural, logical and inevitable development of what has for thousands of years been implanted in human cells.

Starting from this premiss, it is fascinating to try to reconstruct the history of the white races as it must have developed, and to explain the evolution of their civilisations by the operation of their memory-chromosomes.

Twelve thousand years ago, the so-called 'universal' Flood destroyed the civilisations of the earth. There were, however, some people who escaped: woodcutters, hunters, mountaineers living upon the five high plateaux of the world—Iran, the Himalayas, Abyssinia, the Rocky Mountains, the Altiplano of Peru—from whence came the white, yellow, black and red races.

The white survivors from the Iranian plateau, after having overcome appalling difficulties, built up their numbers again and, impelled by some obscure attraction towards their mother country, they migrated westwards *en masse*, probably about the year 9000 B.C.

The white race was sub-divided into numerous branches, differing widely from one another despite a common origin, which complicates the study of our far-distant past; and for this reason it will be convenient to include them all under the generic name of Aryans (in the original sense of the word).

The Celts formed the largest of the subsections, and in their wanderings they turned westwards searching from Iceland to Dakar, though of course unsuccessfully, for the submerged continent of their forefathers—Atlantis. This is why Celtic megaliths (dolmens and menhirs) are found all the way from the extreme north to Senegal.

Some of the tribes settled in central Europe, others on the sea coasts in unfrequented parts of Ireland, the Isle of Man, Wales, Brittany, Poitou-Charente, Galicia, etc.—that is to say, in places where they were out of touch with other people,

61

either local inhabitants or migrants, who might have helped to enrich their civilisation. Their scientific attainments degenerated in all these places, until they lapsed into sheer rule of thumb and witchcraft.

One branch, which was opposed to the black magic of the aboriginal Bretons, turned eastward and settled in the Indies, where a most remarkable civilisation developed.

Celts who migrated to the Mediterranean lands evolved even more rapidly. They met other peoples of different races and colours, intermarried successfully and, some thousands of years before the peoples of pure Celtic stock, produced splendid civilisations, of which Egypt, Phoenicia and Assyria were the greatest.

It was left to those of pure stock—French, English, Russian, Germanic, American—to develop, to the fullest degree and to the heights once reached by Atlanteans and Hyperboreans, the civilisation based on metals, synthetic materials and the atom.

We have almost arrived at the same point as the great civilisations of the past and, like our ancestors, we are heading very surely for a catastrophe. The same catastrophe.

The evolutionary process is in tune with biological and universal laws.

Dolmens, Cathedrals and Rugby Matches on Other Planets

The cornerstone of this theory is the intervention of Beings from outside the earth, who are believed to have come at various times to teach us how to develop our higher powers.

This must have happened in the distant past, and is likely to happen again. Do not all traditions and sacred Scriptures tell us that men are descended from gods, Elohim or angels, that is to say Teachers from heaven? The word Elohim (a plural word in the Bible) suggests that it does not refer to the One God as creator of the universe, but to certain Beings who came to earth to help in human evolution.

It may be supposed, therefore, that our hereditary culture,

at its best, derives from what has been experienced to an even higher degree on other planets.

Aboriginal earth-man never invented anything much, except possibly flint instruments.

Stimulated by his memory-chromosomes, which recorded the knowledge gained from extra-terrestrial Beings, he has been unconsciously working along the lines laid down by the Elohim, building first dolmens, then huts, then houses, temples, laboratories and finally space-rockets.

On the human level, no doubt it is in this way that men will continue their endless evolution towards greater spirituality and greater complexity.

There may therefore be supposed to be other planets in the cosmos with a civilisation like our own, having, of course, discovered space-travel, but before that having also had Gothic cathedrals, steam engines, motor cars, radio and television, rugby matches, slot machines and atomic bombs.

The Bible in A.D. 3000

There are probably some planets whose sacred scriptures do not tell of angels coming down to them from heaven but on the contrary of Teachers setting off into the cosmos to disseminate the rudiments of their civilisation.

The question is, are the inhabitants of these planets, perhaps millions of miles distant from the earth, still living—or have they completed their evolutionary cycle? Do they know that their civilisation is being carried on, perhaps light years away from their own habitat, by men more or less like themselves, whose blood contains a drop of their own?

It is difficult to imagine that they went off into the blue, not knowing where they were bound for; so it is to be supposed that somewhere in the universe there exist men or superior beings who know that the earth is their colony and that we are their blood brothers. If they have the power and the wish to do so, they might try to get in touch with us; but would man—arrogant, blind and egocentric as he is—be ready to

63

accept them?

And yet, hidden forces, unexplained phenomena, perhaps even including unidentified flying objects, claim our attention.

The giant carvings at Nazca, radio signals from space, the dark mysteries of spiritualists, of mediums, of parallel worlds, might be interpreted as so many efforts by beings from beyond the earth to contact us.

The traditions of India and the Near East and of the American peoples all refer to demi-gods who came from Sirius or the Great Bear or Venus. One may imagine that a text is to be found in the Sirius Scriptures saying that the Elohim took off one day in a space-rocket to visit a planet in the solar system.

It is quite certain that a future earthly Bible will say—after the next cataclysm—that the Elohim left Earth for some other planet.

Two Extra-terrestrial Visits

The sacred scriptures of the Hindus tell that the ancestors of the Aryans were not born upon Earth, but upon a star in the Milky Way. (Note that Sirius is a star in the Milky Way.) The earliest of our forebears, says this account, was Aryaman.

'The path of Aryaman is a path leading from a star to the Earth,' says the Vedic text.

Tradition, therefore, ascribes to Aryas an origin from beyond the earth, and says that the journey from Sirius to Earth is the first of which any record exists.

There is no doubt that other races too were of extra-terrestrial origin, for African traditions speak of snakes as 'vehicles of the Ancestors', implying that flying serpents were interplanetary ships.

With some hesitation, two dates are suggested for the first of such expeditions: either 13,000 years ago, which would be during the time of the Atlantean civilisation, or 10,000 years ago, which would put it after the Flood.

The second intervention, which is vouched for by a great

many texts, was that of the Venusians about 5,000 years since.

For a long time astronomers thought that the planet Venus had been part of the solar system for many milliards of years. Thanks to the production of sundry documents, the staff of the Paris Observatory have been persuaded that the origin of this planet needs reconsideration.

Even before they acknowledged this, it is known that some astronomers were quite ready to agree that Venus irrupted into our solar system as a comet about 5,000 years ago.

Finally, as a third possibility, Mn. Y. suggests the planet BAAVI in the constellation Centaur as the original home of our ancestors.

And this is how far the genuinely scientific theory of the transmission of knowledge and remembrance by means of chromosomes has led us.

For many years it was believed that the history of man was written in the stars, then in books; and then a biological discovery upset the whole idea or, rather, extended it to the dawn of the human race, that is to say to its first, non-terrestrial ancestors ... to the primordial Adam, who was certainly not Hebrew nor Celtic nor Egyptian. It has led to the inhabitants of a star burnt out hundreds of millions of years ago, via the denizens of other stars drawn from the very ends of a universe believed to be still expanding.

Hyperboreans and Atlanteans

Starting from the Aryan migrations this panorama of the West takes us next to those Great Ancestors, the Hyperboreans and the Atlanteans.

It is always difficult to differentiate between them, and information about their origins is various.

Tradition localises the Hyperboreans, or Great White Ancestors, in the northern part of our globe, in a fertile and beautiful valley with a wonderful climate, though encircled by mountains of solid ice. The capital was Tula, Tulan or Thule,

65

as described by Plato, by Diodorus Siculus, and in the Book of Enoch.

The Atlanteans inhabited a continent, at the centre of which were the Azores, but which stretched westwards and northwards, possibly as far as the country of the Hyperboreans. This continent was Atlantis.

The Hyperboreans would seem to have constituted the highest caste in antediluvian times, the General Staff, as it were, and the rulers of a vanished world. It was to Hyperborea that Enoch went to receive his orders, to consult his Chiefs. And it was there, at Thule, that the genetic characteristics of the race were preserved intact.

The Atlanteans were a highly intellectual people, whom one might liken to the Russians and the Americans of our own day, though hybridation had apparently impaired their memory-chromosomes.

The pre-eminence attributed to the Hyperboreans is emphasised by the homage paid to the Fathers at Thule by the ancient Mayas, who were of Atlantean descent.

The investiture of the ancient Kings of Mexico could not take place, says the Popul Vuh (the sacred book of the Mayas), until they had been to Thule for confirmation of their claim.

After the Flood, it is believed that a small group of refugees returned to what remained of Hyperborea, which had become an island battered by the icy waves of the northern seas.

Aryan Dispersals

Meanwhile, the largest branch of the Celts was seeking Atlantis from Iceland to Dakar. The Aryas very probably went direct to India from Iran.

There seems, however, to be some substance in Schuré's theory that the Breton Celts, after surviving culturally for some thousands of years, with difficulty but along traditional lines, drifted little by little into empiricism, even to indulging in the grosser forms of magic and sorcery.

Another group, that of Ram, which contained high initiates,

66

migrated to India in order to safeguard the knowledge transmitted to them, choosing a well-known route, still marked by dolmens, menhirs and even pyramids.

Finally, in some out-of-the-way parts of Ireland, Wales, Poitou, the central highlands of France, Galicia and Corsica, there remained, as in Brittany, the less advanced of the Celts, and progress was for thousands of years arrested.

Statistics have been established only for France, but these show that none of her greatest geniuses have come from places which still contain large numbers of megaliths. Great soldiers, yes. But physicists, chemists, poets, writers, painters, sculptors, no. All her great men such as Rabelais, Descartes, Pascal, Rodin, Curie were born along the lines of the three great axes leading from Paris to Marseilles, Lille and Bordeaux.

That branch of the Celts which settled in the Mediterranean area evolved with great rapidity. The continental Celts—Slav, Germanic, Caucasian, Gallic—developed their brilliant civilisation later.

Aryans, Sanskrit and the Vedas

Judging from their history—though admittedly only superficially—it seems likely that some Nordics are direct descendants of the Hyperboreans, while Celts in general are more characteristically Atlantean, the offspring of aboriginal earthmen and Hyperboreans, those 'sons of God who saw the daughters of men that they were fair'.

The Aryan branch which settled in the Deccan peninsula intermarried with Dravidians, a mysterious people who may have been refugees from the continent of Mu.

The only really ancient records of our ancestors are Indo-European—the Vedas, which are older than the Eddas of Scandinavia of which, though their antiquity is undeniable, the earliest known copy dates only from A.D. 1643.

The Vedas originally told the story of our antediluvian ancestors, but they are of unequal value and contain a number of later interpolations. They have been considerably modified,

67

therefore, and the primitive teaching has been turned simply into a history of the Aryans of India.

There are four Vedas: the Rig-Veda, the Yajur-Veda, the Sama-Veda and the Atharva-Veda. Of these, only the Rig-Veda is really ancient. It gives information and instruction about cosmogony and the religion of the Aryans; about the cult of the Great Goddess, whose worship was practised among all Celts; about soma, the initiatory potion that was much the same as hydromel, the honey-drink of the Gauls; and about their mythology, which became the archetype of most European mythologies.

The Vedas are written in Sanskrit, the parent of all Indo-European languages, and probably the universal language at least among those peoples who came within the Atlantean and Hyperborean civilisation. It has been estimated that they are about four thousand years old, though actually they must be very much older. Grammarians consider Sanskrit to be the most perfect language in the world, especially for its aptness in conveying shades of meaning. Its affinities with the Celtic languages were first studied by Adolphe Pictet, a Swiss savant, over a hundred years ago.

CHAPTER FIVE

TRADITION AND THE MYSTERY OF MEGALITHS

It has been quite deliberately instilled into us that the Celts were uncivilised barbarians and that enlightenment was brought to us from the East. For 2,000 years Celtic monuments, documents and traditions have been destroyed, falsely interpreted, their original meaning distorted, so much so that it has become difficult to find the thread that leads to the truth.

By good fortune, a few vestiges remain, chief among them being those great intelligencers, the megalithic monuments. Tumuli, menhirs, dolmens, cromlechs, are found in Central Europe, in the Indies, in America and from Norway to Dakar, all along the routes of the great Aryan migrations.

Druidic Sanctuaries and the Religious Life of Brittany

It seems as though the sites of the greatest druidic sanctuaries, at Chartres, at Loudun, in the Black Forest, the Colleges of Saint-Benoit-sur-Loire, of Mont-Saint-Michel, Autun and Marseilles had been geographically fixed in order to by-pass Brittany.

It is believed that the Celts first came to Brittany during the late Iron Age. The first to invade Gaul were the Pictons, akin to the Picts of northern Britain, who settled in Poitou, well to the south of Brittany. The largest and finest Gallic dolmen exists in this part, about half a mile from Vienne.

In view of the geographic position of the various druidic shrines, it seems clear that although initiates of this cult lived in the Deccan and in most Celtic lands, they avoided Armorica (Brittany), which was never a place of high spiritual development, even in Christian times.

In the twelfth century, the famous theologian Abelard, who was born near Nantes and became Abbot of Saint-Gildas-de-Rhuis, wrote to his beloved Heloise:

'I live in a barbarian land, whose language I do not understand and dislike heartily; I see no one except savages ... the only rule my monks adhere to is that of having none. I wish you could come and visit my House; you would never think it was an Abbey: its doors are covered with the feet of deer, wolves, bears and wild boars, and the loathsome corpses of owls. I am exposed to fresh dangers every day; I feel as though I had a sword hanging over my head all the time.'

In the event, the monks used both steel and poison to rid themselves of Abelard.

'This scholar-poet,' wrote A. de Courson, 'was not meant to lead an army of Breton monks, whose disgusting habits, ferocious ways and resistance to all forms of control knew no bounds....'

This twelfth-century description of Christian Breton ecclesiastics gives one no reason to expect much of the druidic culture at Carnac some thousands of years earlier.

The dolmens were not, as the sculptor Auguste Rodin thought, our earliest cathedrals; forests were the Celtic cathedrals. The purpose of the dolmens is a mystery, but it was connected with death and burial. They formed covered passages, linking a number of graves, and acted as sub-structures for tumuli.

Carnac and the Mysterious Menec

The avenues of standing stones at Carnac in Morbihan are too well known to need detailed description.

The 'alignments' at Menec, Kermario and Erdeven are

unique in the world. Within a distance of some 3,250 yards there are 2,813 menhirs, clearly orientated in an east–west direction. The tallest stones stand about twenty feet high, and some are driven into the earth as though they were upside-down cones. The whole effect is rugged but enormously impressive, wild, but rich in magical overtones.

The etymology of the name Carnac is itself bewildering. There are various possibilities: car, ker, in Gaelic means an enclosure; carn or cairn is a landmark or a mound; ac, a Gallic suffix, indicates possession, so is really tautologous. Carnac might therefore be translated as 'a hill of stones', it is thought.

Other suggestions are: Carnac was the Goddess of health; carnarium, meaning a burial place; a piece of land belonging to the Carnutes of Chartres, the most important druidic centre; something connected with the nordic god Kar, the Lord of the Winds; or it might even refer to Kernunnos, the Father of the gods.

All this increases the mystery surrounding Carnac and its megaliths. However, the name of the largest alignment—Menec—opens new vistas, as long as one is ready to agree that the local name of a place is more important than that of the district in which it lies.

In the Breton language, mené means a hill; but in the flat marshes of Carnac it would be absurd to dignify as 'hills' a collection of mounds never more than thirty or forty feet high. The site of Menec, too, is practically flat, for the land slopes very gently, almost insensibly, so that one is tempted to equate the word Menec with the Gaelic manac, which means counting or reckoning.

Taking the notion of time and reckoning, Menec—an Arab would call it Al Menech—acquires the meaning of calendar (which seems like rather a good piece of detective work!).

Carnac and the Trojan War

In a curious book written in 1906 by the Breton pre-historian H. Hirmenech under the title *Celts and Atlanteans*, the author says that the Veneti, living on the shores of the Adriatic, who were of the same race as the Armoricans (Bretons), were a primitive type, probably Pelasgian. He calls the Pelasgians themselves 'the Celts of the East'; and, incidentally, Armorican means 'dweller by the sea'.

Hirmenech states that after the gradual collapse of Atlantis during the reign of Mena, the first King of Egypt, the central government of Atlantis, which had been in power for several centuries, was transferred to the valley of the Nile.

According to this author, the ancient Atlanteans had spread all over Europe and round the Mediterranean basin.

When the Trojan war broke out, these peoples were ruled by a supreme Aryan chief, the successor to Mena, who regenerated the human race after the Flood. They therefore quite naturally went to the assistance of Troy when it was besieged.

Unfortunately, by the time they arrived there, the city had long since fallen, and the battles of which Homer sang were those of a second war against the enemy who occupied it.

The Veneti, like other warriors, no doubt piously gathered up their dead heroes and carried them home for ceremonial burial. This, Hirmenech believes, was the origin of some of the great tumuli in Brittany.

Geoffrey of Monmouth, in the twelfth century, writes in *The Prophecies of Merlin* of Brutus and his companions fleeing from Troy when it was in flames, and journeying to the Isle of Albion, where they founded a kingdom.

In corroboration of his theory, Hirmenech quotes Hesiod who, in *Works and Days*, referring to the siege of Troy and to the heroes who fell there, says that 'Jupiter Saturninus allowed them to live apart from men; he established them at the ends of the earth, under the rule of Saturn, far away from the Immortals on Olympus. These happy warriors enjoyed peace in the midst of the turbulent ocean, in the Isles of the Blessed. . . .'

Once the funerary rites had been carried out, the Celts wrote the story of their exploits—but in their own fashion.

The celebrated and mysterious alignments at Carnac constituted a rebus and this rebus—the key to which is in the alignments at Menec—relates to the Trojan War.

'One curious feature may be observed in the great alignments: the cromlech is relegated to a position out of line with the rest, and is in the form of a testicle, thus completing the phallic design made by the adjacent lines of stones.

The idea that it is only a badly drawn circle, accidentally uneven, cannot be entertained.

Besides which, the lines which touch the outside of the cromlech represent the feminine element or, to put it more precisely, they are monuments raised to the heroines.

Each menhir indicates a burial. . . .'

Temples as Transmitting and Receiving Stations

A temple, where men commune with God, speak to him and hear his Word, may be likened to an electrical apparatus designed to ensure direct communication with heaven—in fact, a transmitting and receiving station.

A connection is established between God and man, and if our instruments are not capable of recording the full intensity of the exchange it is because our knowledge is imperfect and very likely inferior to that of the early priests and Druids.

Prayer *rises*, converted by the instrument into sound waves resonant to the universe; the Holy Spirit *descends*, and the message is decoded by a transformer-priest or by initiates.

The station consists of: first, a receiving and transmitting area (the choir), built as a power-house on the principle of the magic circle; second, an antenna—belfry, spire, obelisk, menhir; thirdly, it must be earthed—crypt, grotto, cave, labyrinth, impregnated with the water of life, as symbolised by the sacred well.

The station draws its energy from the earth-currents, and acts as an accumulator by storing the forces in condensers which, in Christian churches, are statues, the crucifix or the Host; arks, figurines, books, totems, dorjes and sundry magical

73

objects in other temples.

Collective energy can be generated by the faithful, provided that they truly believe.

In such a sanctuary, therefore, communication between God and man will be effectively consummated, upon the wavelength of the universe.

A pantheist might say that here humanity and the universe are in harmony.

To function successfully, therefore, a druidic receiving and transmitting station needed a menhir, a dolmen and a grave, and it was essential for the menhir to be close to the dolmen. When such a sanctuary no longer received any but earth-currents, the dolmen or the magic circle served only as an accumulator or storage cell, with a positive and a negative pole.

The Radio-active Pyramid at Couhard

The Master of Angles (the pseudonym of an initiate who wishes to remain anonymous) has made some staggering discoveries which throw new light on the mystery of the pyramids.

The pyramid at Couhard, which was originally 100 feet high, but of which only ruins now remain, was built of stones bonded with *radio-active mortar*, that is to say the monument itself was radio-active, which shows that the Celts had an amount of knowledge of the secret forces of nature unimaginable in these days. It was built of great masses of phyllite rock (a type of stone intermediate between clay-slate and mica-schist), very accurately oriented horizontally, and at right angles to a shaft, the opening to which was at the summit. This shaft, according to certain documents, communicated with an immensely deep geological rift, which kept humidity at the required level and supplied negative 'vital' rays. (Vital rays, or vital waves, are electro-magnetic forces which physicists used to call coulombian.)

The interior of this immense 'accumulator' contained alkaline electrolyte (limestone and caustic potash), which attacked the silicic acid in the stone. This caused double radiation, gamma rays on the one hand and 'vital rays' of very high intensity on the other, both having the same acceleration and alternating on a very long wave-length.

To sum up, the orthose mortar of the Couhard pyramid still emits K41 gamma rays and vibratory waves due to the rupture of the valence-load in the rock crystal.

It is known that strong gamma rays projected upwards into space produce ionisation of the atmosphere and cause the formation of helions immediately followed by that of water vapour. The same result may be obtained by lighting a brushwood fire, as is done in some parts of Africa for rain-making.

Radiation of such intensity makes one think that the Couhard pyramid and no doubt other Celtic edifices, not excepting the Egyptian and Mexican pyramids, might be marker-buoys on the earth's surface for the use of space-travellers. They might even be accumulators at which interplanetary space-craft could recharge their engines, though at present their method of propulsion is not known.

At any rate, the discoveries of the Master of Angles seem to show that the Celtic monuments were electrical instruments used with full understanding by initiators of the year 3000 B.C., and empirically by Druids and probably by priests in Egypt.

Guy Tarade, a writer on traditionalist subjects, thinks that 'the Celts understood the nature of many of the strange cosmic phenomena, and that they knowingly guided space-people to their tremendously radio-active monuments. Druids may have been able to create visions that would arouse religious fervour, and bring glorious, luminous Spirits before the eyes of their congregations. . . .'

75

By the time seven or eight thousand years had passed after the Flood, bringing the date to, say, between two and three thousand years B.C., Celtic priests no longer retained more than a vague memory of the original purpose of a megalith. The phallic menhirs at Filitosa in Corsica are of this period.

On the site of Filitosa, which has been discovered only recently, tombs have been found near standing stones, containing stores of food, jewellery and weapons with the bodies, clearly indicating belief in an after-life, the menhir being the symbol of resurrection, and taking the form of a phallus as the organ of reproduction.

Roger Grosjean, the historian, notes that the menhir-steles are placed farther from the actual tombs as the date of their erection approaches more nearly to our own epoch. At the same time they become more anthropomorphic, and still later they are grouped in alignments.

This is what must have happened at Carnac, where no human remains have been found among the alignments, though at another Breton site the skeleton was found of a man who would have been at least six foot six inches tall.

In Carnac times, Druids may have known the symbolic reasons for the ancient rites, but the labourers certainly had no knowledge beyond the rough fashioning of the local granite into standing stones and putting them in position beside channelled stones, to represent the phallus and the womb.

Nevertheless, the present writer does not believe that these monoliths have the great initiatory and scientific value ascribed to them by some investigators. Neither were the Egyptian temples at Karnak, at Luxor, Esna or Edfu, which date from the same period, ever sanctuaries of Higher Initiation.

Everything leads one to believe that with the passage of time the Celts gave to their rough structures a significance very different from the original purpose. They turned them into magic armies of stone warriors, to give themselves the illusion of power.

In this way their use as radar, as accumulators and other electrical apparatus, was forgotten; and with this was also lost the knowledge that had borne witness, from Ireland to the Upper Nile, to the learning of the last of the Atlantean priests.

The Serpents of Gavr'inis

At Gavr'inis, on the Ile aux Chèvres, off the western coast of Brittany, there are druidic rock carvings representing concentric circles and serpents similar to those found in Scandinavia, in the Iberian peninsula, in Malta, in Loughcrew, County Meath and on the recumbent stone beside the tumulus at New Grange in Ireland.

Druids considered the serpent to be the most sacred of all symbols for, as in Egypt, Phoenicia, Assyria, Greece, Mexico and Peru, it represented the flying machines which had brought their Initiators to earth from outer space. It signified also, and on an even higher plane, the primordial surge of creation which had brought the whole world into existence. Concentric circles and spirals were the emblems of the Infinite Being and of the universe in expansion or contraction. Another suggestion is that the figures may be *mandalas*, such as are used by Hindu initiates to promote meditation. In the Himalayan Order of Masonry, concentric circles symbolise the epitome of all knowledge.

In contrast to most other civilisations, which have left a multitude of paintings or incised pictures on rock or clay, on wood or stone, the Celtic civilisation was very sparing of graphic representations, but those which do remain have a high initiatory value.

Celtic symbols, in order of their frequency, are: concentric circles and spirals, ram-headed serpents, phalli, the horned god, the flying griffin, the winged horse, the horse, an eight-rayed star, the sword and the axe, the bull and the swastika.

It is by studying these symbols that it is possible to reconstruct the history of our western lands which have inherited

77

the civilisation of Atlantis.

For Atlantis was the true and original source of the science and the arts, the gods and the traditions of the white races, whose world was born in the West.

CHAPTER SIX

CELTIC CIVILISATION: THE MOTHER OF ALL CIVILISATIONS

Although enthusiastic amateurs often produce the wildest theories to explain the unknown, yet among those theories there are sometimes valuable ideas that are well worth following up.

It is not expected that the present study will succeed in resolving all the enigmas connected with Celtic megaliths; but some light may be thrown on them by investigating old traditions, which tend to crop up all over the world, often with astonishing points of similarity.

Scientific explanations—the only kind that will nowadays convince an intelligent enquirer—have been supplied by a man who is a high Initiate, and is known as the Master of Angles.

To put it briefly, the Master of Angles has demonstrated that the oldest Gallic tumuli were pyramids and were built of concrete.

This seems at a first glance to be an incredible idea, not to say nonsensical; but after consideration and careful analysis, his arguments have proved convincing: one felt that he must be right.

By a fortunate chance, or perhaps by some strange intuition, the present writer, together with the historian Eugène Beauvois, discovered some particulars about a 'secret' America that records of the Spanish conquest had done their best to suppress; and the history of this hidden past dovetailed so perfectly with that of the Celts, their tumuli and their menhirs, as to be indissoluble.

Hence, anyone hoping to understand Celtic Gaul and Celtic

Britain must at the same time rediscover Mexico and the Mexicans, 'the Pelasgians of America', as the great naturalist Alexander von Humboldt called them.

One's over-all view of the Celtic past suddenly opened out like a fan, to disclose an idea of which some students had already caught a glimpse—namely, that the Celtic civilisation is the oldest in the world and the ancestor of all the civilisations of the white races.

There was nothing for it but to go to Mexico, where it was believed that proofs of this theory were to be found.

No Pyramids in Mexico

Strange to say, there are no pyramids in Mexico. This is an indisputable fact, and shows to how great an extent the errors of former historians have distorted the true evidence.

To begin with, what is a pyramid?

It is a monument of geometrically pyramidal form, tapering to a point, and containing a cavity—the 'chamber of eternity' —where heroes may rest for all time. A pyramid was never meant to be climbed, only to be entered. It is seldom stepped, and carries no additional buildings.

Do such monuments exist in Mexico? Not a single one!

Most of the pseudo-pyramids of Mexico were, it is believed, intended to be burial places, just as are Celtic tumuli or the crypts of Christian churches. But in virtually every case they were built as pedestals to carry a temple or some other large edifice, access to which could be gained by means of a magnificent stairway, which might be as wide as a main street in one of our cities.

If there appear to be some exceptions, like the so-called Pyramids of the Sun and Moon at Teotihuacan, it is because they have been rebuilt quite recently, and the people carrying out the restoration did not rebuild the temples which originally towered above them.

This fact is, incidentally, agreed with by archaeologists.

So, actually, they are pedestals, which may not be more

than fifteen or twenty feet high, while the temple on the top could have been anywhere from thirty to a hundred feet tall, resting on a base larger than a football ground.

All the Mexican shrines were built as high platforms which, like those at Teotihuacan and Monte Alban, cover several acres.

One extremely important point must be stressed: any of these Mexican monuments which look like pyramids from a distance have been built either during the present century or, at most, eight to nine hundred years ago.

The surface of the so-called 'pyramids' is not smooth, and when they had wide flights of steps up them it was obviously for the purpose of facilitating ascent for the faithful visiting the temples.

An old Mexican book on local archaeology states that 'the pyramids were built at the time of the occupation and were intended as bases for the temples.'

The period of 'occupation' here referred to is dated some 500 to 1000 years B.C., and is known as Teotihuacan I.

Teotihuacan was built by people coming from 'out of the sea', possibly Mayans or Olmecs, that is to say by descendants of the Celts. Later, under the Aztecs, the pyramids probably lost their temples. When the Spaniards arrived in 1519, they were all overgrown with scrub.

They were, in fact, tumuli. The summit of the Pyramid of the Sun is still a tumulus, and its interior is packed with earth. Like true pyramids, tumuli are 'chambers of immortality' when their function is religious. (In very rare cases, as at Shansi, in China, pyramids were built to commemorate the mountain that saved humanity after the Flood.)

The pyramid at Cholula, said to be 'the largest in the world', is no more than a wooded hill, 'landscaped', with paths leading up to the Christian church of Los Remedios. It was probably originally a tumulus, for it is an artificial mound.

Five thousand years ago, thousands, indeed hundreds of thousands of earthen tumuli covered the Mexican countryside.

Shortly before the Christian era, traditions had been com-

81

pletely lost, and the Mexicans transformed the most notable tumuli into pedestals for their temples. They even built pyramidal temples, such as those at Palenque, at Chichen-Itza, Uxmal, etc.

Present-day Mexicans no longer call the monuments 'pyramids'. They refer to them as, for instance, the Palenque Temple, the Great Temple of Kabah, the Castillo (palace) at Uxmal, which last is, by the way, the nearest to being a true pyramid.

These points as well as others of still greater importance, about menhirs, covered passages and megalithic circles which have been found in Yucatan, will be discussed at the end of this chapter; they make it possible to consider the enigma of the Gallic tumuli with some hope of arriving at a rational explanation.

Celtic Pyramids made of Concrete

Long study of the problem, dozens of analyses of the earth surrounding monuments in Gaul, have led the Master of Angles to the same conclusion as that briefly touched upon by the historian Henri Martin and others, which is that tumuli were ancient pyramids that had fallen into decay.

The Master of Angles is a chemical mineralogist by profession, which guarantees not only the quality of his analyses, but also the scientific precision of his studies.

At a first glance, it seems impossible to imagine that a collection of little tumuli, dozing peacefully like sheep in the meadows of Morbihan and Poitou were, some thousands of years ago, splendid pyramids lifting proud heads heavenwards. If these pyramids had been made of stone like those at Gizeh and Saqqarah, they could have braved the rigours of the climate; but for some reason yet to be determined they were built of concrete.

The soil surrounding the menhirs is extremely heavy, being composed mainly of crystalline silicates or of calcareous silicates. It is to be inferred that the standing stones, firmly fixed in the ground, acted as a framework and support for the concrete and its outer casing.

The ground all around has been hardened by slight impregnation with colloidal silicates due to the crumbling of the mortar and concrete. In a way, the people one thinks of as builders of dolmens or cromlechs were, actually, builders of pyramids, temples and covered passages, all made of polished concrete and very likely sculptured.

Diodorus Siculus, speaking in all probability of Stonehenge, noted that he had seen a 'magnificent circular temple, adorned with rich offerings, at a spot which faced towards the country of the Celts'. And Scymnis of Chios made what seems to be an obvious reference to the Breton obelisk of Locmariaquer when he described the 'Northern Pillar standing at the far end of the land of the Celts, facing the unquiet Ocean'. He was clearly speaking of a real pillar of which the stone, which was at that time only the supporting framework, is visible today. The same may be said of the menhir of Oblicamp at Bavelincourt on the Somme; the Romans called it *obelisci campus*.

Everywhere, as has been established by physico-chemical analysis, the concrete and plaster, as they crumbled, seeped into the ground and hardened it.

This is not simply a more or less fanciful theory, but is the result of the examination of actual lumps of concrete fully three thousand years old, which have been miraculously preserved, sometimes between two blocks of marble, as in the Celtic settlement of Tourette-sur-Loup, or saved by a covering of stone as in the case of the pyramid at Couhard, where the concrete is gradually turning into a pile of rubble. In the same way, the Egyptian pyramids originally had an outer casing of which no trace now remains.

Tumuli, Pyramids and Barrows

Old-time authors, if they had not much to say about pyramids in Gaul, said nothing at all about obelisks or stone slabs, which seems to indicate that they saw nothing but tumuli or mounds of earth and pebbles, to which they paid no attention.

Definitely, says the Master of Angles, since menhirs and dolmens were originally concrete obelisks and pyramids, all our ideas about western civilisation need to be revised.

In particular it should be remembered that the great cromlechs were temples with concrete cupolas, just like the stupas of Afghanistan, some of which have by now disintegrated and are no more than heaps of rubble.

The tumulus is, in fact, a conical pyramid, containing an orientated grotto. In Egypt, the Saqqarah pyramid, the oldest of them all, has only the most indeterminate outlines, but all around are other, almost equally ancient pyramids, which are of exactly the same shape as the Celtic tumuli.

The pseudo-pyramid of Cholula, in Mexico, is either a barrow or a tumulus; and the same may be said of the pyramidal ground-work at Cuicuilco which has been excavated recently, and which, according to archaeologists, contains a core of earth (once concrete) kept in position by large stone supports. Except for the 'Cerro del Tepacalte', this is the oldest monument on the continent of America.

In Lydia (Asia Minor) the tomb of Algattes, the father of Croesus, is a pyramidal mound, with a stone base but otherwise built of earth. Also in Asia Minor, at Nemrut Dag, a tomb, said to be Nimrod's, is a veritable mountain of earth and stones. There are numerous pyramids in Peru; in ancient times there was one at Tiahuanaco built as a sloping platform; there were also some dolmens. Tradition says that these were designed by men of divine origin, who had fair skins, blue eyes and reddish hair, and who were the last descendants of the Viracochans.

Viracocha means sea-foam, implying that they come from the sea. Much more significant, however, is the similarity between the architectural styles of the Pelasgians, who erected *betyle*s (huge stones, regarded as being 'informed' by a god), and that of the Viracochans, the ancient Egyptians, the Mayas and the Celts, who built tumuli or pyramids.

In the old days, according to the traditions of Easter Island

84

as reported by Thor Heyerdahl in his book *Aku Aku*, a Vira-cochan king named Kon Tiki emigrated from Peru to Easter Island, accompanied by men known as Orejones, who had long-lobed ears and reddish hair, and who were the sculptors of the huge statues found on the island.

These emigrants introduced the *totora*, or sweet-water reed from Lake Titicaca, to the island; also the sweet potato, which is there known by the same name as that used by the American Indians—*kumara*.

At Rapaiti, in Polynesia, Thor Heyerdahl counted a dozen pyramid-palaces on the mountain tops.

The Brown Book

The greatest best-seller of all time is *The Bible*, which has been published in hundreds of millions of copies. On the other hand, books with the smallest sales are those which tell the story of our own lands and our own ancestors.

We do not know who were the first rulers in Europe, who were the first kings of Gaul and Britain; yet descendants of the people of those times can often recite the genealogies of men who lived in desert places which they have never seen and are never likely to see: Jacob was the son of Isaac, the son of Abraham, the son of Shem and so on until they come to the 'first created man', one Adam, the son of God and a handful of dust as some say, or according to others the offspring of a primitive Adam and Lilith. . . .

Contrary to biblical history, that of the western Celts is marvellously clear and full of magic, sweet-scented with the breath of seas uncharted and the flowers of Paradise.

All this may be found in *The Brown Book*, or Leabhar na h-Uidhri, which owes its name to the fact that it is bound in dark brown doeskin. It is the oldest of the great Gaelic manuscripts, and was transcribed by Moelmuire about the year 1100.

It tells the adventures of Condla, surnamed Ruadh ('the Red') or the Beautiful, son of Cond cet-chathac ('of the hundred battles'), king of Ireland from A.D. 123 to 153.

One day Condla Ruadh stood with his father on the top of Mount Usnach in Meath. He saw coming towards him a lady, clothed in strange garb, and he greeted her. 'I come,' said she, 'from the Land of the Living, where neither death nor evil nor strife are known, where we feast continually, and where every virtue is practised. We dwell in a great hill, whence our name *Aes Sidhe*' (People of the Hills).

Condla was the only person who saw the Lady, and his father asked to whom he was speaking.

'I am speaking,' he replied, 'to a young, lovely and noble Lady, who fears neither death nor old age.'

'I love Condla Ruadh,' the voice continued, 'and I ask him to follow me to the Land of Delights *(Mag Meld)*, where lives King Boadag (the Victorious); he will become its everlasting ruler, free from grief and evil, from the moment he takes the sceptre.

'Come with me, Condla Ruadh, the Beautiful, the Ruddy-Cheeked. If you accompany me you will lose nothing of your youth and your beauty until the last Judgment Day.'

The words were heard by all, although they were unable to see who spoke them.

Cond cet-chathac asked his Druid Coran to use his skill, and by magic and powerful spells to put an end to the bewitchment; and so the beautiful Lady could no longer make herself heard, and became invisible even to Condla, to whom she threw an apple as she vanished.

The young prince, disdaining all other food and drink, ate only of the apple, which never grew less. But he was plunged deep in melancholy.

A long month passed before he went again to the hill with his father. The same vision appeared and said to him: 'The Immortals invite you, Condla, to leave this country, where men's lives are brief and death is their fate. You are invited to rule over the people of Tethra (the Ocean), for they have watched you daily among your chosen companions.'

86

As soon as Cond cet-chathac heard her voice, he called on his Druid to silence her, but she was still able to continue: 'Oh Monarch, the Great Refuge of the Righteous and all his strange and unnumbered subjects do not love the arts of druidism and have them in scant respect. When his law holds sway, the spells of Druids will be brought to nought, together with the lies of the Evil One.'

Cond, full of surprise that his son said not a word, asked him why the voice of the Unknown made such an impression on him.

'I am grievously troubled,' replied Condla. 'I love my own people above everything, but I am afflicted beyond measure because of the Lady.'

She spoke again, persuasively: 'Beautiful youth,' she said, 'I will save you from all your griefs if you will come with me; we will sail in my pearl currach (*boat*) to find the Hill of Boadag. There is another world which is well worth the seeking. Although it is far distant from here, and the sun is already setting, we can reach it before nightfall. Everyone who comes with me is happy there.'

Hardly had she finished speaking when Condla leapt into the pearl currach and was lost to sight.

Condla was never seen again, and only the gods can say what befell him.

Such is the legend of the Land of Youth, the origin of which is to be found in tales told by the Indians of northern and central America about the wonderful Fountain of Bimini and about a river in Florida, both of which have the property of restoring youth to all who bathe in their waters.

The Land of the Hills may well be in Mexico, where barrows and tumuli are numbered in tens of thousands. The name *Aes Sidhe* recalls the Ase people of the hills of greater Ireland, a Gaelic colony which Icelandic sagas site in the north of Vinland, that is to say, in the peninsula south of the estuary of the Saint Lawrence River.

As far as most people are concerned, the ancient Mayas were a red-skinned race, who seem to have no kinship with Europeans. Yet, in taking a wider view of the subject, one is struck by the fact that White men and Red men have one thing in common, which is Atlantis; and this is true too of some African peoples, who share dolmens with the Celts. So one is driven to the conclusion that all these peoples must originally have been of the same race, and that the history of the ancient Mexicans is directly connected with that of the Celts, may even precede it, and explain its oldest parts.

Before describing the Mayan traditions, however, it will be convenient to keep everything in the right chronological and geographical order by making an excursion into the mythology of the North American Indians—that is to say into the land nearest to the Island of Thule, the cradle of the white race and of the Hyperboreans.

It is not proposed to give a definitive solution to the immense problem of the civilisations of the white races, but to try to throw some light on the confused tangle of threads linking the Aryans of Iran and Hyperborea with their relatives in Egypt, Greece, Mexico and Northern Amerindia.

At the same time, one must admit that, though Christopher Columbus was the first official discoverer of the New World, he did no more than follow a path parallel to that taken thousands of years earlier by Celtic and Hyperborean migrants.

The Canadian Algonquins, and more especially those of the Wapanachki tribes (which means 'eastern and white'), lived in Greater Ireland and the Hvitramannaland, that is the White Men's country of the Scandinavian sagas.

According to Algonquin tradition, it was not actually their ancestors who came from the east, but those who brought civilisation to them.

In stories told by Wapanachkis, who are also known as Abenakis, the Lord of men and animals was Glusgahbé (? Gilgamesh), the god of the Golden Age.

According to some, Glusgahbé was born in the eastern part of the Abenaki country; others say that he came in 'a great stone canoe, covered with trees (? masts)'. Nowadays ships are built of concrete; why should not Glusgahbé also have used one made of slabs of reinforced concrete?

He travelled about a great deal and, like Hercules, left traces of his passage everywhere—gigantic causeways, deep lakes, shattered rocks. He taught men the art of making weapons and the uses and virtues of herbs; and then one day he went off in his ship and disappeared—not for ever, but until his people should have need of him.

One sees how nearly this tradition is related to the stories of Quetzalcoatl-Kukulcan, of Gilgamesh, of Hercules.

Manabush, the hero-initiator of a number of other Algonquin tribes, performed identical labours and in the same way disappeared in the 'direction of the rising sun, crossing the great Ocean towards a rocky land, which was his home.'

Father Allouez, a Jesuit, wrote in 1667: 'The Illinioüek, the Outagami and other savages from the southern parts, believe that there is a great and good Spirit, Lord of all the others, who created heaven and earth, and who lives in the east in the direction of the land of the French.'

Chaouanons and Shawnees (Central tribes) claim that their ancestors came from the east, across the Ocean, by walking on the water.

The White Lady of the Leni-Lenapes

The Leni-Lenapes had a similar tradition. Though reduced in number to ninety-four individuals in 1890, and transferred from Delaware to Kansas and thence to Texas, they still kept a vivid memory of their transatlantic origin. One of them told the following story to a Swedish engineer named Lindstroem:

Long and long ago, a woman of your race came to visit us and, after drinking water from a creek, she found that she was with child. She gave birth to a son, who became so wise

89

and so skilled that there was never anyone to compare with him either in the arts or in oratory; he compelled the admiration of all. He also worked many signs and wonders.

One day he left us and was caught up into heaven, promising to return; but no one ever saw him again.

Other Leni-Lenapes said further that this miraculous individual had taught them hunting and manufactures. He had come from afar; and he left them, not because he died or went to some other place, but by ascending to the heavens.

He wore a long beard, and the ancestors of these Indians believed that their benefactor would return to them from the east—so much so that when they saw white men many generations later they looked on them as divine and did reverence to them.

These traditions go back beyond the dawn of history, since they also give an account of the Flood, which was attributed to the action of a mighty serpent who raised the waters above the mountain tops and destroyed almost the whole of the human race. The Gulf Stream, issuing from submarine volcanic springs in the Gulf of Mexico might, they thought, have something to do with this fearful reptile; so perhaps the great Flood was a flood of hot water!

Those who escaped went to Thule, to the island of their primeval ancestors, and begged that their lands might be restored to them.

Eugène Beauvois, the historian, said in one of his books that Gaelic migrants called Papas populated Iceland, then Mexico and Central America. Not that Beauvois is alone in holding this belief; it is also supported by other specialists in Amerindian history, by indians themselves and by recorded tradition.

From this it is clear that, without any possible doubt, the Mayans who in times past inhabited the north of America were descended from the Great White Ancestors who came from Hyperborea and Thule.

Mexican ancient history is told in their archives, most of which are recorded in ideograms or hieroglyphics that have not yet been deciphered—not even with the (illusory!) help of electronics. A Russian attempt, in particular, which was going to be absolutely decisive, turned out to be a complete flop.

The Popol Vuh

The most important of the records, the Popol Vuh or Book of Wisdom, which tells of antediluvian events, was transcribed into Latin in the sixteenth century by a 'learned Quiché', who was probably a Spaniard and a Catholic.

A remarkable French translation was made by the Abbé Brasseur de Bourbourg; some extracts, with notes, were published in France in 1954.

It is a well-known fact that the planet Venus dominated the Mayan religion, and had probably done so ever since that planet appeared in our skies some five thousand years ago.

Most of the pyramids are dedicated to it; Quetzalcoatl and Kukulcan, the two paramount gods in the Mayan pantheon, are personifications of that radiant planet; symbols of Venus are found on every page of every Mayan manuscript.

Curiously enough, with the exception of the Abbé Brasseur de Bourbourg, all writers on the subject—no doubt obeying some 'black-out' order—suppress the part played by Venus in the Mayan civilisation, sometimes even succeeding in the remarkable feat of never so much as mentioning the name of the planet.

By a curious coincidence, the same prohibition seems to have been enforced about any mention of 'the Star' which heretical Hebrews had a factious, but probably hereditary, tendency to worship together with the Bull (wrongly translated as the Golden Calf).

And it transpires that this 'Star' is Venus, and that the Bull, symbol of the 'angelic' procreators, also symbolises the Venusian Initiators among Mayas, Phoenicians, Assyro-Babylonians and Incas.

In short, everything confirms the idea that for the last 3,000 years there has been a conspiracy to conceal a truth that endangered our established institutions—a truth to which the key would be the planet Venus.

The Popol Vuh is a collection of maxims that were current in Tula (Mexico), and which have often been translated with apparently the express purpose of changing the original sense.

The Mexicans Came From Europe

Eugène Beauvois says that the hieroglyphics of the Popol Vuh make it quite plain that the ancestors of the Mexicans had previously dwelt eastwards beyond the sea, where they knew both black men and white men living 'without houses'—presumably nomads, therefore.

The ancestors left their country to seek the gods at Tulan-Zuiva, according to an early Spanish translation; but they had a wearisome journey before they got there. One of the gods referred to was named Yolcuat-Quizalcuat. (Quetzalcoatl).

'Sahagun says that the first wind comes from the east, where the earthly Paradise is to be found.' This is a highly significant statement.

Was it from their ancestors or from their European initiators that the Mayans had the custom of burying their honoured dead in tumuli built of earth and pebbles which the Ancients called 'hills'? Was the Land of the Hills, in Irish tradition, situated on Atlantis, in Hyperborea, in North America or in Mexico?

There was always a secret chamber within a Mexican tumulus, as there was in those in Europe.

The Mayas and Quichés emigrated in large numbers during the Fourth Epoch, as described in the Popol Vuh, and settled at Tula (or Tulan) 'which is near Mexico, as they call it now', says the transcription. When they left again, they said: 'We are going back to the land of our fathers, the land where the sun rises.'

The Mayas and Quichés could not have meant Africa by this description, because it lies in the same latitude as Yucatan; it evidently refers to Europe, which is situated in the same latitude as their old home in North America.

An Eagle perched in a Tree

It is, of course, well known that old traditions, passed on from generation to generation, say that the Mexican peoples came from the north. The general accuracy of these traditions has been confirmed by discoveries made of ancient buildings in the middle of arid Californian plains and on the Mississippi prairies and, even more convincingly, by the comparative study of great numbers of Amerindian dialects.

Ten thousand years ago the Mexicans, on the advice of their priests, left those North American lands, a part of which is known as Death Valley to this day.

What was the cataclysm that drove them away?

Whatever it was, tradition says that their wanderings would go on until they found an eagle perched high in a tree and eating a serpent. This place was in fact found when they came to what is now Mexico.

When the Great Ancestors left Europe, they did not go direct to America, but touched at Tulan (the Hyperborean island of Thule), where there was confusion of languages, as there was at Babel.

Their company broke up, some returning to the east [Europe]; and Tohil said to the Quichés and their allies: 'Your home is not here, let us go to our true destination'.

The narrator admits that he does not know how they crossed the sea, whether on 'floating stones' (which might possibly have meant icefloes) or by walking over the sand, the waters being divided....

There is a good deal of uncertainty in Mexican manuscripts over the name and site of Thule or Tula or Tulan. The Hyperboreans lived in Thule before the Flood. Their descendants returned to where they thought it had been, five thousand years after the Flood was over; but it can hardly have been possible for anything recognisable to have survived.

Some Mayas return to Europe

The Popul Vuh states:

> They were at Hakavitz when the four leaders of their peregrination disappeared mysteriously. Although they were very aged and had been travelling over great distances for a very long time, they were in good health when they bade farewell to their children, saying that their mission was now accomplished and they were returning to their home.
>
> They advised their successors to visit the country from which they had come, and left with them as a memento a package wrapped like a *quimilli* such as the Nahuas carry.
>
> Many years later, three of their sons set off eastwards across the ocean, to be invested with the insignia of royalty by Naxcit, Grand Master of the Orient, and supreme Judge. From Tulan they took with them the art of 'painting history'.

Another Quiché document, kept in the archives of Totonicapan, also sites Tulan in the east beyond the sea.

This document tells how, when the Quichés left Tulan, Naxcit, their grandfather, whom they worshipped as a god, gave them a mysterious packet, called *Giron-Gagal*, containing a magic stone—probably the same obsidian tablet now preserved in the church at Tecpan in Guatemala.

So that stone, after having served as a talisman and being consulted as an oracle, now forms part of the table of the high altar in a Christian church.

Initiators From The East

When the Quichés left Tulan their fathers said: 'Your place is not here; it lies beyond the sea, and there you will find your mountains and your plains. You will be watched over by Belch (*Bel, Belinus?*) and by Toh (*Thoth, Thor?*)'.

In 1581, after an investigation that Philip II of Spain had ordered to be carried out in all parts of Yucatan, the native inhabitants declared that the first Lord of Mutul, named Zak Mutul (that is, White Man), had come from the east, without saying exactly from which country, but that he was Indian, which made one of the Spanish chroniclers, Father Diego de Landa, think that the Mayas might be Jewish by descent.

The most celebrated of the Toltec Initiators was Quetzal-coatl, described as a white man who had come across the sea from the east.

Another investigator, Domingo Mañoz Camargo, tells how, when a grave, said to contain the body of Quetzalcoatl's father, was opened, a lock of fair hair was found among the remains, proving that the Elders spoke truly when they referred to their ancestors as white men with fair hair.

According to the Eskimos of Greenland, the Immortals live neither on the land nor in the waters, but in a 'subterranean Paradise, where it is warm and there is plenty of food'.

As far as the Iroquois are concerned, the god who brought civilisation to them was Tarenyawoga, who came down from heaven in a magic boat. On the other hand, Glusgahbé, initiator of the Abenakis and Micmacs, lived on an island in the ocean far away to the east.

The Celtic Megaliths at La Venta

This, then, is a reconstruction of the early pages of the history of Celts and Mayas, peoples of the same stock and the same origin. Other valuable indications will further corroborate the fact that the two civilisations are identical.

Seen through handbooks on archaeology and travel brochures, Mexico is a land of pyramid-temples, but no mention is ever made of the existence of tumuli and megaliths which, after all, are found all over the central provinces and the whole of Yucatan.

95

Another curious thing is that the origins of ogival and Gothic art are sought vainly throughout Europe. In Mexico, arches and flying buttresses have been typical of Mayan architecture for nearly a thousand years. At Kabah and Labna, city gates or triumphal arches may be seen which are the purest Gothic—showing that, whether European or Mayan, the Gothic arch does indeed belong to those two branches of the Celtic races, as though their memory-chromosomes had bequeathed the architectural secret to both.

Tumuli, are to be found in abundance, alongside the roads, all over jungles and archaeological sites, as common as mole-hills in our own fields.

All along the Avenue of the Dead at Teotihuacan there are at least some dozens, as many again at Chichen Itza, and even more at Palenque. There must be tens of thousands of them in the jungles of Yucatan and Guatemala, where it is hardly possible to walk a hundred yards without finding tree-covered mounds, a temple, a stone circle or other remains. Tumuli, innumerable mounds of earth and pebbles—Mexico must surely be the Land of the Hills spoken of in Celtic tradition!

At Uxmal, at the very foot of the Castillo (or Sorcerer's Pyramid), is a circle of phalli, roughly carved out of the rock, which reminds one irresistibly of Gaul and the site of Filitosa in Corsica. (See photographs.)

But it is in the gardens of La Venta at Villahermosa that the historic truth suddenly bursts upon one: Mexico is Celtic.

Menhirs are there, standing stones, a covered passage built of probably basaltic stone blocks, and long alignments of menhirs, like those at Carnac or in a village in Finisterre. (See photographs.)

Visitors stare in amazement at the relics of a civilisation, the existence of which they never so much as suspected.

Phallus circles, cromlechs, menhirs, tumuli, covered passages, megalithic enclosures—all these, six thousand miles from Europe. It seems impossible to believe one's eyes.

At the same time, one cannot but wonder why this Celtic

These two rockets, one two-tiered, the other three-tiered were
launched at Sibiu, Rumania, in 1529. They were
designed by Conrad Haas. Documentary proofs in Sibiu Museum.

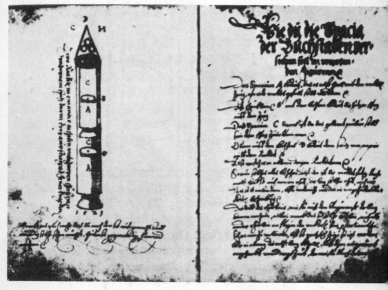

Published in the Rumanian Historical Revue, Vol. VI, No. 3, 1967; from
The Sibiu Manuscript.

Mysterious machine engraved on a stone block at Monte Alban, Mexico.

The Moebius Strip.

It has been said that the Mayas did not know the use of the wheel, yet wheels of stone or pottery, and even bobbins made of obsidian are found in abundance in Mexican Museums.
(Museum of Oaxaca.)

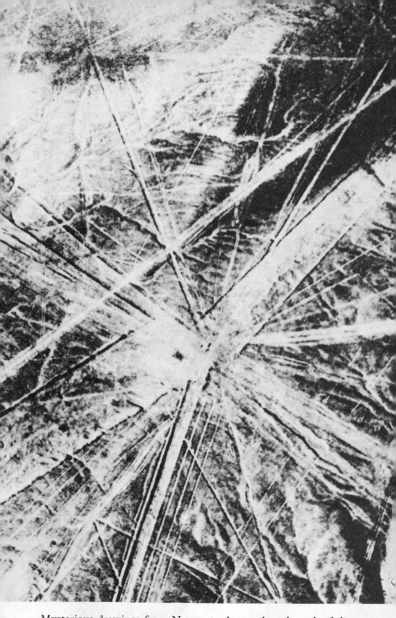

Mysterious drawings from Nazca: to the north and south of the town of Nazca, in Peru, huge drawings have been traced on the uninhabited mountains providing an enigma for archaeologists. Seen from the air they are reliefs of geometric precision.

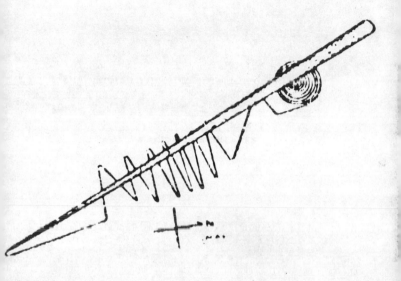

Message from people from outer space, found in Nazca. The drawing
looks very much like a fisherman's rod.

The finest French Dolmen, near St Saviol (Vienne). It is a monolith, and orientated north south.

The largest French Dolmen, at Bournand, near Loudun (Vienne). It is about 55 feet long, and the largest stone weighs nearly 160 tons.

civilisation has been passed over in complete silence in our history books.

Thule

The Popol Vuh, tradition, and these monuments all combine to prove that the First Fathers came originally from an island that is usually sited in the North Atlantic, about the latitude of the Arctic Circle.

Some historians have suggested that Thule might have been in Iceland or the Orkneys. The Americans have given the name Thule to one of their polar bases which lies off the east coast of Greenland; but this must be attributed rather to respect due to their forefathers than to any known connection with the capital city of the Hyperboreans.

Be that as it may, it is very certain that the island of Thule did once exist, and it is to be presumed that it vanished during the violent seismic disturbances that afflicted the world in the third millennium B.C.

The ancient Mayan Quichés used to go there, and they accepted it as the land of the Higher Ancestors; but it seems probable that for the most part they originated from the Celtic lands of Scandinavia, Great Britain, Germany and Gaul. The myths of the white gods Quetzalcoatl and Kukulcan are of much later date than the Thule stories, for they go back only about five thousand years, that is to say to the time when the appearance of the planet Venus coincided with the arrival on earth of Teachers who, there is good reason to believe, were extra-terrestrial.

No mention is made in the Popol Vuh of the planet, which confirms the argument and links it quite naturally and reasonably with the history of the peoples as outlined above—more especially as it concerns the Asianic peoples.

Were the Incas Celts?

Speculation is always rife about the Mayan tribes of Yucatan

97

and Guatemala, who faded out less than a thousand years ago, 'leaving no trace', according to earlier historians. Yet the mystery is extremely easy to elucidate.

The Mayans did not vanish as completely as has been stated. Thousands of them stayed in their own lands; but it is known that the Spanish invaders killed them off quite ruthlessly, from Mexico to Merida.

Moreover, a religious side has to be reckoned with, that partly explains the incessant wanderings of these ancient Celts who, in the course of eight thousand years, passed from Thule to North America, thence to Mexico and Yucatan and finally to South America.

The ancient Mayas, relying on the prophecies of their priests, believed that the world might come to an end every fifty-second year. Some tribes stayed in their own territories, content to raise monuments to their gods at the supposedly hazardous dates, to prove their faith and their gratitude for survival. Other tribes, however, moved on periodically in order to evade the danger, and their migrations took them ever farther south, to Colombia and Peru.

They left traces in Nicaragua where, in the Chontales area, fourteen truncated pyramids may be counted; and in San Agustin, Colombia, now being archaeologically investigated, which contains tumuli, small tombs, standing stones and even figures of divinities hidden under a dolmen which is itself concealed inside a tumulus.

The present writer believes the Peruvian pyramids and dolmens to be the work of the migrants. Even admitting that they intermarried with the indigenous population, there is nothing against the idea that the Incas were ultimately of Celtic stock.

At the time of the Spanish conquest, moreover, numbers of fair-haired and fair-complexioned people were seen in Peru; they were known as *idolos*, implying that they were descendants of the deified Great White Ancestors.

A more enlightened view is now being taken of *idolos* since Carlos Aliaga Silva, a police inspector, discovered in the San Martin district of northern Peru fortresses surrounded by ramparts, round towers and circular three-storeyed buildings, in some ways reminiscent of the mysterious city of Zimbabwe in Rhodesia.

Three distinct cities have been identified: La Joya, Atuen and Cochabamba, all believed by pre-historians to have been built by the legendary Chachapoyas, who settled in Peru before the Incas, perhaps in the time of the Aymaras. Moreover, the Chachapoyas were a white race, with blue eyes and fair hair, typically Aryan; one might even be tempted to say Hyperborean. In short, ethnologists discover Celts in Peru, but refuse to admit the fact, because they find it impossible to explain how they could have got there!

For a long time it was believed that there were two types of Aryans—one kind with fair skins, blue eyes and fair hair, such as Norsemen, Celts and Pelasgians; the other with bronze complexions like Latins, Peruvians and Hindus.

It may be that the first of these types more nearly resembles the original race; but it would be wrong, indeed criminal, to create a racial problem on the basis of such a distinction in this twentieth century. People of both types, as well as Arabs, Jews and Egyptians, are wholly Aryan—blood-brothers.

It is interesting to remember that the runner-up for Miss Universe 1968 was Miss Israel, a beautiful flaxen-haired girl, named Mirey Zamir, who was much more Hyperborean in type than most of the other competitors.

Blond types are often found among dark-skinned megalith-builders, as in Brittany, in Asia Minor, in Northern Africa, in Mexico and, as we have seen, in Peru.

Herodotus, who flourished in the fifth century B.C., says that the Libyans—Egyptians, Tunisians, Algerians, Moroccans— were white, which is evidence indeed. Scylax, a Greek navigator and geographer of the sixth century B.C., confirms this statement by saying that they were blond in his time.

These notes make it very clear that the intermingling of races is essential within the framework of evolution, and hence that 'racism' is to be condemned, wheresoever it appears.

Amerindians Have European Ancestors

It is an entirely mistaken idea to suppose, as some pre-historians and ethnologists have done, that the ancient inhabitants of America were descended from Mongolians, who in prehistoric times crossed the Behring Strait when the waters were frozen over.

There is nothing whatever to support such a theory. Nothing, except that some Mexicans have slightly oblique eyes, which proves nothing because there are plenty of instances of this idiosyncrasy all over the world; to speak only of France, it is found among Bretons, in Limoges and in Poitou.

One might with far greater plausibility say that the Chinese were descended from Amerindians, having made the journey in the opposite direction. In 1964 the Russians found, near Lake Uchkov in north-eastern Siberia, the skeletons of some Indians, beside whom were beads, necklaces and other ornaments of the kind called wampum. According to the Russian scientists, this had been an Indian settlement more than fifteen thousand years earlier. Similar discoveries have been made elsewhere in Siberia.

Apart from having definite proof that Amerindians are in part descended from northern Europeans, it would seem to be of interest to go further into the question of the incidence of slanting eyes.

All Humanity is One

It is not known what kinds and degrees of change took place on earth before the emergence of the first man.

Darwin believed that every species proceeded by natural evolution according to its genus. Some think that man is a special case, the result of a fortunate mutation; others that Adam was created by God, and exists only on our planet.

But there is another possibility that might be considered. Man could be the only one of his kind in the universe, semidivine, who populated the planets by travelling through intergalactic space from the beginning of time, in order that his spiritual evolution might be accomplished.

It is certainly allowable to suppose that earth-dwellers were on a number of occasions visited by extra-terrestrial Beings who were more fully developed than themselves.

The characteristics of people living on earth nowadays are very various, though never fundamentally different.

The Evidence of Pythagoras, Herodotus and Aristotle

From all that has been said, it would appear that the racial identity of Mexicans and European Celts has been firmly established.

There is no doubt that the hitherto accepted history of Mexico has been falsified, in fact invented, by those whose purpose it was to throw a veil of obscurity over our past.

The civilisation of the planet Earth was not born in Sumer as they would have us believe; it came from beyond the earth, and the Celts were its direct heirs.

This makes it clear why one may consider the Greeks to be the originators of all European civilisations.

Aristotle said that philosophy began with the Druids.

Herodotus, who had visited Greece, Egypt, Libya, Phoenicia, Babylon, Persia, Thrace and Scythia as far as the Danube, thought that 'the Druids had a knowledge of the heavens which was proof of the depth of their scientific thinking'.

Crowned at Olympia and anointed as the 'Father of History', Herodotus is one of the most universally famous geniuses of all time, just as Aristotle is known as the 'Prince of Philosophers', and is recognised even today as the personification of the scientific and philosophic spirit.

Their views served only to confirm that of the greatest Master of them all—Pythagoras—who, after seeking initiation in Egypt for twenty years, found it at last in Gaul. According to his chroniclers, Pythagoras was convinced that 'the Druids were the wisest men in the world'.

These statements are explicit and show clearly that Celtic

101

civilisation was pre-eminent in the East as in the West; more ancient, therefore, than the civilisations of Egypt, Greece and Assyro-Babylonia.

These men based their views principally upon the Druids' scientific achievements in astronomy and philosophy, upon their conception that matter is as eternal as spirit and upon their belief in one God, the sole creator of the visible world and of the Beyond.

It is hardly possible to cast doubt upon the judgment of Pythagoras, Herodotus and Aristotle for, throughout the millennia of history, there have never been greater and more universal geniuses than these three.

How does it happen, then, that most so-called historians never mention Celtic civilisation except to discredit and denigrate it?

How can one explain the fact that the Christian religion has bedevilled, throttled, the Celtic faith in the One God who is, after all, identical with the God of Moses and of Jesus?

Why were druidic monuments destroyed or christianised?

Why do our schools and universities teach the history, scinece and philosophy of all the ancient peoples, *except* that of our ancestors?

Why this scandalously biased approach, this conspiracy of silence?

Whom does the truth frighten?

The time has come at last when people are no longer terrorised by religious or political bugbears, and are insisting that they want to learn true History and not one based upon lies.

CHAPTER SEVEN

VANISHED CIVILISATIONS

'Thousands of millions of years ago civilisations comparable with our present one were flourishing all over the universe....'

Within the next fifty years a history of mankind will have some such opening sentence; but for the time being it is more respectable to believe that world civilisation began in Sumer about five thousand years ago.

Heretics, that is people who prefer to accept a more universal truth, believe that undoubtedly civilisations have existed at all times upon the planets, and for tens of thousands of years on our own planet Earth.

It is, of course, true that we have no definite proof of the existence of any other human beings in the universe (except the near certainty that Beings from beyond the earth did in past times visit us), but some of us feel convinced, on both rational and scientific grounds, that life is possible on most planets in the cosmos, and that man must have managed to make his appearance on some of them.

France = 30,000 Years

The oldest civilised country in the world might be France, where flint tools and cave dwellings are found dating back to at least 30,000 years before our era.

It seems, however, that these facts are not enough to vouch for a civilisation worthy of the name, that is to say one which understood the uses of metals and wood and how to build stone houses. As though a house or a temple, an iron tool or a wooden bowl, could be expected to last for thirty or forty thousand years!

But surely no reasonable person can believe that the artists who painted the Montignac-Lascaux caves knew nothing about wrought iron and the mason's craft?

Two separate laboratories have calculated that 25,000 years ago Africans in Malawi and Zambia worked haematite iron mines, with rich veins of copper. What did they do with these metals? We do not know; but the miners and the engineers who organised them must have had some idea!

In 1964, some 125 miles north-east of Moscow, on the Sungir site, Otto Bader, the pre-historian, discovered burial-places which, from the strata in which they were found, must have been at least thirty to forty thousand years old.

The bodies, having been lying in frozen ground, were still in good condition. Beside them were found 7,500 bone ornaments, and some kind of carved beads which had been sewn on to the garments. And the clothing, according to the discoverers, consisted of trousers, a pullover and leather shoes.

These prehistoric men, therefore, were not draped in indeterminate animal skins or bits of rag, but in actual properly-made two-piece suits. They were, therefore, the report insists, quite modern—which should make some people revise their superficial, old-fashioned ideas.

Glozel = 15,000 Years

Despite the efforts of those who refused to admit the truth, the present writer claims to have immediately recognised the absolute authenticity of the Glozel stratification.

Little is known about the Glozel civilisation, except that it must have existed before the Flood, the great cataclysm which blocked the caves at Lascaux and swallowed up the necropolis or religious centre at Glozel, all the inhabitants having died in the disaster. By good fortune, some thousands of relics have been dug up and kept in a private museum—shingle, flints, jars, incised tablets, bone carvings, etc., which bear witness to a very fairly advanced culture, for the script of Glozel is the oldest known, and is undoubtedly the immediate ancestor of Phoenician writing.

Since 1962, hundreds of people have visited the museum and have voiced delight and astonishment. Never a one has expressed disappointment. Even those who might have been expected to pooh-pooh the whole thing—experts such as Dr. Capitan, the Abbé Breuil, custodians of other museums—have all acknowledged the genuineness of the Glozel civilisation.

No Coffee Pots Carved on the Rocks!

The main grounds for opposition to the ideas advanced in this book have been of a religious nature: no mention is made of lost civilisations in The Bible, the Torah or the Gospels.

Secondly, earlier historians have felt that there are incompatibilities in having on the one hand an age of flints and caves, and on the other an age of temples, cities, metal industries and air-travel, not to say space-travel. As far as these objectors are concerned, men descended from apes 20,000 years ago, were clothed in animal skins, hunted and fished for food. If they had built cities, cars, aeroplanes, steam engines, some traces must have been found, even if only in rock carvings. No traces—no highly-developed civilisation! All the men of 20,000 years ago were animals, instinctive, unreasoning.

To be fair, some historians and archaeologists are perfectly sincere in their belief, which is indeed a tenable one. If only they could find the representation of a coffee pot, an aeroplane, a steam ship or even a chair, they would agree that prehistory needed re-thinking, revision and correction.

But no—not a vestige.

On the other hand, space-suits, propellers, rockets, are found almost one might say in abundance, on a technological level which exceeds the twentieth century level of science and life, for example on the frieze of the Gateway of the Sun at

Tiahuanaco, in the Temple at Palenque, on the slopes of Monte Alban. . . .

It is all rather confusing! It would surely be more logical to expect to find more primitive things on the ancient monuments and in the caves—say a bicycle instead of an ionised space-craft?

Actually, no.

In this year 1972 there is a civilisation which might be called atomic in Europe and North America; but at the same time a stone-age civilisation exists in New Guinea and some other parts of the world; and in Spain some carts still run on solid wooden wheels.

The aborigines of New Guinea still carve pictures on rocks and in caves, representing animals and hunting, or possibly the outline of a jet seen passing over the forest. They do not portray spoons or armchairs. And, as the fancy takes them, they very likely show the jet as a bird or a flying serpent.

The reason for this is that so-called uncivilised peoples pass nowadays without transition from the dug-out canoe to the jeep, from the conch to the transistor; and the same thing must have happened to antediluvians.

In any case, our civilisation is in the highest degree perishable. If we were to have a Flood, we may be sure that our electric toasters, our cars, our locomotives, our atomic centres and our space-rockets would be reduced to dust or mud in very much less than 5,000 years.

What would be left of our splendid twentieth century? Nothing—except possibly the flint tools of our ancestors, which our descendants in 10,000 years' time would dig up from what remained of our towns and villages.

They would come to the same conclusion as some of our present savants, that before this cataclysm men—that is, we—had only reached the flint age and lived in caves.

Which would be true, but only for about one in 10,000; the error arising from the fact that flint is the only indestructible material. The seas are still full of Phoenician, Greek and Roman galleys, which were made of wood while early steamers and the first ironclads have had their steel plating completely eaten away by the salt water.

Diving in Vigo Bay in 1960 to the wreck of the *Plata Flota*, which sank in 1702 the present writer fished up bits of pottery and pieces of timber in which cannon balls were embedded.

The ship's timbers were hard, compact, in a state of excellent preservation; the cannon balls, on the other hand, disintegrated at the slightest jolt.

It seems that, of artefacts, flints alone can survive a dead civilisation; and that anything made of this may be contemporary with atomic science—that is to say that co-existence is possible and normal between highly civilised men and people barely emerging from the animal stage.

Apart from the carvings at Tiahuanaco and in Mexico, the probability that there have been earlier, lost, civilisations is strengthened by plenty of other archaeological discoveries and by concordant traditions.

Every mythology has its stories of a Golden Age of advanced civilisation, and of the wars undertaken by its great men whom they called giants, or gods, or heroes.

Can one possibly imagine that all the peoples of all the continents separately invented this type of tradition?

Denis Saurat's Giants

It is difficult to believe that giants could ever have been the norm of earthly humans; but it is impossible to believe that traditions—which are unanimous on this point   could all have been fairy tales.

Remains of abnormally tall men have been found pretty well all over the world—in Java, in China, in the Transvaal. There is a necropolis in the Sahara where graves twenty foot long may be seen, in which, so they say, lie the remains of men nine or ten feet in height.

Denis Saurat, in his book *Atlantis and the Reign of Giants*, suggests an explanation for this strange phenomenon.

Some 300,000 years ago, he writes, the moon was no more

107

than six earth radii distant from our planet, and the gravitational pull of the moon was so strong that all round the earth the waters of the oceans formed a sort of envelope, which rose to a height of 10,000 feet in the Andes.

Hence atmospheric pressure on the earth was considerably less than it is now; and, as the height of an individual is proportional to the weight he can carry, a race of giants developed.

These giants, living in the Secondary period, civilised the people of the Tertiary. They were wise and kind, and they taught their human charges to build the sort of structures that are found at Tiahuanaco, Ba'albek, Egypt, Easter Island and Atlantis. . . .

This theory has its attractions, but one feels some reservations none the less, especially as regards the calculation of the date, for which no references are given.

That Tiahuanaco should have preceded the end of the Tertiary period by something between fifty and a hundred thousand years seems quite incredible.

Daniel Ruzo's Giants

Well before the Flood, says the Peruvian prehistorian Daniel Ruzo, there was a civilisation on earth the members of which —to our immense advantage—carved upon rocks representations of men and animals (some of which have long since died out), and also set up great altars in the mountains and the sacred forest groves.

This is how Daniel Ruzo explains his theory:

'In 1952 I found within quite a small area on the Marcahuasi plateau, north of Lima, a whole group of rocks engraved with human and animal figures. The rock mass was about 150 feet high and showed fourteen human heads of men of different races.

'There was, for instance a particularly striking "portrait head", which I later named "Head of an Inca"; there were snakes, sea lions, an elephant, a lion, an owl, a dog and so on,

108

as well as some animals unknown today.

'Some of the carvings, according to the angle of vision, had several faces, but you had to move into the right position to distinguish each of them.

'They were, apparently, three-dimensional figures, which would not give up their secrets unless they were viewed from a given point, and from this point only.

'Moreover, the play of light and shade did not produce the true image except on certain days of the year and at a particular time of day.

'Hundreds of discoveries and observations of this kind made in South America convinced me absolutely that these sculptures could not possibly be mere freaks of nature, but must be the purposive work of a people whose civilisation is as yet unknown. I called it the "*Masma* civilisation".

'All the works of this people had points in common— anthropomorphic and zoomorphic representations, executed within a restricted space, repetitions of the main themes, a combination of different designs on the same piece of rock, the complete effect visible only on a particular date.

'Between 1953 and 1958 I sent a number of reports to the Academies of Lima, Mexico and Paris about this.

'I observed the same effects in England at Stonehenge and at Avebury, where one of the finest druidic temples in Europe is to be seen. Careful examination of the enormous blocks of stone led me to believe that they had at one time been sculptured.

'One can only conclude that certain artists, whose origin is wrapped in mystery, but who were no doubt trained to a kind of four-dimensional form of art, had for thousands of years carried on their function as sculptors for the Masma civilisation.

'The Easter Island statues are of a similar antediluvian type —three-dimensional if considered as at the time when the stone was first quarried from the rock, but embodying the fourth dimension when it was finally put in position.

'These statues have no eyes in their sockets, but in the play

109

of sunlight and shade they can be perfectly clearly seen in the cavities at a certain time of year, which one may presume to be the date when the Easter Islanders celebrated the heroes represented by the monuments.'

(Might it be suggested that at these times the statues acquired magical healing powers if touched by sufferers?)

'The sometimes colossal size of the subjects carved in the Peruvian mountains, in Brazil, and on Easter Island, encourages one to believe that the sculptors themselves must have been members of a race of giants—of which, incidentally, express mention is made in sacred writings and tradition. But this is only a hypothesis.'

The 'Mater' of the Forest of Fontainebleau

Daniel Ruzo continues:

'In 1961 I carried out some fruitful researches in the Forest of Fontainebleau near Paris.

'Thanks to the collaboration of a talented artist, Mme. Edith Gérin, who had spent years in photographing rocks whose carvings could be descried only in a particular light, I became convinced that the Masma culture had spread to France.

'The tortoises in the rocks at Franchard, the elephant at Apremont, and above all the "Mater", are intensely moving works of a rare perfection, which no one could believe to be due simply to erosion and chance.

'The same may be said of the "Idols", gigantic heads discovered by André Millou and Guy Tarade in the hills above Vence in southern France.

'I found carvings of exactly the same kind in the Indies, in Indonesia and in Egypt.

'On the banks of the Nile, black basalt rocks which have managed to resist erosion and the passage of thousands of years of time, present some remarkable Masma sculptures, which the Egyptians seem never to have noticed.

'I found exactly the same kind of sculptures in the Carpathians.

'In conclusion, I am of opinion that in these places we have witness of a vast civilisation that spread over the whole earth in the days before the Flood, but which I was unable to analyse in greater detail.

'I am content to show photographs that prove the existence of the ancient sculptors, the extent of their spiritual develop ment, the evolution of their art and of their technique.

'They knew of animals which no longer exist and which one may presume to have lived before the appearance of man upon earth.

'They established communication between continents, whose fauna, racial characteristics and symbols they delineated.

'The Carpathian Mountains are in a part of the world which become the European centre of the oldest culture yet known.'

These quotations show the very remarkable discoveries made by Daniel Ruzo, which throw a new and most interesting light on the mystery of lost civilisations.

Certain geologists and experts in rock carvings, however, absolutely reject Daniel Ruzo's theory of the *Masma* civilisation.

This, they say, is a purely subjective interpretation of rounded bosses and the results of natural wear and tear. Undoubtedly the work of nature is astonishing, but you often get this kind of thing in places where there is a lot of sandstone. . . .

It is the sort of place where you find 'maidens', or 'monks', or 'mushrooms', or a 'giant's seat', and rocks carved into various queer shapes by the action of frost and sun and other natural forces, they say.

All the same, one feels that the odds are in favour of Daniel Ruzo's theory.

The Land of the Hills

In North America, and more especially in Ohio, mounds and enormous serpentines are found which were built of earth before the dawn of even prehistoric times.

These mounds can be seen by the hundred in the American

countryside, and there is no doubt that in olden days they existed in their thousands, before farmers destroyed them to level the land—which might make one wonder if the real Land of the Hills of our Celtic ancestors was perhaps not in Mexico but in North America, at least in the very earliest times.

Later on perhaps the Land of the Hills may have been in Mexico, when the first earthen tumuli were raised.

Whatever the truth may be, the number of artificial mounds in the U.S.A. is legion.

At Chillicothe, Ohio, there are twenty-four of them, conical in shape; the Mound of Columbus on the bank of the river Scio in Oregon, is one of the finest in America; round it is a circle of rough stones and pillars. Other mounds are to be found at Hillsboro, Bainbridge, Lebanon and elsewhere, but it is at Lotus Grove, on Brush Creek, that the longest and most magnificent earthen serpentines are to be seen; these are found only in the U.S.A.

The one at Lotus Grove is said to have been built by the Adena Indians, who lived at some undetermined prehistoric date. It is made of stone and a yellowish clay and its convolutions stretch for nearly fifteen hundred feet. Its open jaws hold a huge egg-shaped mass of earth.

Dream Days

Near Lyndavale, in the heart of the Australian desert, the sandy plain is broken by three rocky masses aligned in an east/west direction over a distance of about eighty miles. They are monoliths, differing greatly both in appearance and structure.

The first, Mount Conner, is of quartzite, and looks like the keep of a mediaeval castle. The second is a rounded granite hummock, known as Ayers Rock, and is considered by Australians to be one of the marvels of the mineral world. The third, of sandstone and granite, forms a circlet of minarets, domes and pillars, which the aborigines name the Many-Headed Mountain.

112

These monoliths lie in an absolutely straight line, so that an observer standing in line with the first or last cannot see the other two.

Geologists insist that the three hills are of natural origin, and that their caves, their strange shapes, the heads, the minarets and the domes are nothing but freaks of erosion. Ayers Rock looks like a whale; on its sides is a string of kangaroos and the very clear outline of a human head ... all this being the result of Nature's artistry!

It is a pity that Daniel Ruzo never visited the Australian desert, for he might well have adopted the opinion of the aborigines who do not believe that these prodigies are due to wind and rain.

The writer, René Libeau, suggests that in the long-distant past, which he poetically names 'Dream Days', the ancestors of the Arientas and the Luritchas, creatures who were half man and half animal, carved the rocks by magic.

Clefts on the tops are marks left by great carpet snakes, precipices are the work of lizards; and marsupial rats hollowed out the caves. As for the grey patches on the sides, they were made by the camp-fires of salamander-women.

Legend also speaks of a war to the death between the Men-of-the-seed-of-Mulga (a thorn bush) and the carpet snakes.

When the Chief of the vanquished snakes was on the point of death, all the other snakes wound themselves round his body, too grief-stricken to survive him, and committed suicide, chanting the Death Song.

CHAPTER EIGHT

ATLANTIS

The submerged continent of Atlantis is best known from Plato's story, which is corroborated by numbers of other Greek and Latin authors, such as Homer, Hesiod, Euripides, Strabo, Diodorus Siculus, Pliny, Tertullian, etc., who either repeat old traditions or add important details.

The most plausible story is that this continent was situated in the Atlantic; but it has also been sited in a number of other places. For a long time the very existence of Atlantis was doubted, but one may say that nowadays few would challenge its authenticity.

It is not proposed to give details about the origins of the story, which in any case are well known, but only to recall the main outlines, to introduce new features and to examine some of the most recent historical and archaeological discoveries.

The Story according to Critias

Two fragments of the *Timaeus* and *Critias* in Plato's *Dialogues* introduced Atlantis to the world.

Critias was an Athenian statesman and philosopher, living about the year 450 B.C., a contemporary and a relative of Plato. His account was as follows:

'Hear, O Socrates, a story that, though strange, is absolutely true according to Solon, the wisest of the Seven Sages. . . .

'Solon told that, when he visited the Egyptians, he was accorded great honour. He discussed ancient history with the most learned of their priests, and discovered that neither he himself nor any other Greek knew anything about the matter. . . .

'One of the priests, who was a very old man, said: Solon, you Greeks . . . how young you are; for you have no knowledge based on ancient tradition nor proved by the touchstone of time. . . .

'Of our two cities—Saïs and Athens—yours is the older by a thousand years . . . Since this land was civilised 8,000 years have passed, so say our sacred records. . . .

'I am therefore about to tell you briefly something of the laws and the splendid deeds of your ancestors of 9,000 years ago . . . We shall consider the full details on another occasion, when we have the leisure, by examining the actual texts. . . .

'Our books tell the story of how your city once destroyed a ruthless Power, which overwhelmed the whole of Europe and all Asia by attacking them from far out in the ocean.

'At that time, it was possible to cross the sea. There was an island beyond the gateway which, so you tell me, you call the Pillars of Hercules (*the Straits of Gibraltar*). This island was larger than Libya and Asia put together, and travellers could in those days pass from there to other islands, and thence, on the far side of that sea, to a continent (*America*).

'On the near side of the Straits of which we are speaking, it appears that there was only a single harbour, with a narrow mouth; but on the other there was the open sea and the land surrounding it, which one may rightly and in the true sense of the word term a continent.

'The rulers of that Atlantic island had created a great and splendid empire, which controlled the whole of the island, as well as numbers of other islands and parts of the continent. In addition, on our side, this island held Libya as far as the Egyptian frontier, and Europe as far as Tyrrhenia (*Southern Italy*).

'Having massed its forces, this Power determined to make one mighty effort to conquer your territory and ours, and all the other countries on the near side of the Straits.

'It was then, O Solon, that your city dazzled all the world by its heroism and its vigour. . . .

115

'In the time which followed, however, there were fearful earthquakes and floods. In the space of a single terrible day and night the whole of your army was swallowed up in the earth, and the island of Atlantis itself vanished under the sea.

'That is why, to this day, the sea in those parts is hazardous and impossible to explore, by reason of the tremendous depths of mud and slime deposited by the island as it sank (*The Sargasso Sea*).

'You have heard briefly, O Socrates, the story told by the aged Critias (*the grandfather of the narrator*), which he had from Solon. . . .'

Atlantis swallowed up

The *Critias* follows the *Timaeus*.

Critias speaks, telling Timaeus and Socrates of the high degree of civilisation attained in Atlantis.

Atlantis was rich in metals, in fruits and animals unknown to the rest of the world. Its inhabitants were men of honour and acquired their wealth in harmony and virtue.

Unfortunately they succumbed to the inexorable law of decadence; the human elements of luxury and greed gained ascendancy over the divine element.

They made war to aggrandise themselves, and God punished them by destroying their land.

It is clear from this description that the story which Plato ascribes to Critias is the absolute truth, and the author insists that it should be treated as such.

In *The Republic* Plato inveighs vehemently against Hesiod and Homer as 'dangerous romancers' distorting historical truth. The documents from which the priest at Saïs had taken his information undoubtedly existed in Egypt.

The events narrated occurred nearly 12,000 years ago, and it is worth noting that the Flood is dated just 12,000 years ago by geologists who have studied the action of ice.

According to this account Atlantis was situated in the middle of the Atlantic Ocean, between America on the one side and Europe and North Africa on the other. Its capital was Poseidonis. It is calculated that its centre was somewhere near the Azores, which would explain the very uneven depths of the sea thereabouts.

The Atlanteans invaded Great Britain, Gaul, Spain, Italy and all the Mediterranean countries; no doubt also, though it is not mentioned in this account, the American coasts.

These are the very places in which the greatest number of Celtic megaliths are found—tumuli, pyramids, dolmens, menhirs—an important point.

Before the Flood, therefore, several great civilisations existed—foremost among them Atlantis, and second Greece. These civilisations were destroyed by the cataclysm, and it goes without saying that the continent of Atlantis did not sink without occasioning world-wide tidal disturbances that caused destruction and disaster in all nations. It seems curious, by the way, that the priest of Saïs made no mention of havoc caused in Egypt during the 'universal' deluge, though it could hardly have escaped damage.

The story matches the account in Genesis (Chapter VI), where God repented that He had made man and determined to destroy all living things by bringing 'a flood of waters upon the earth to destroy all flesh wherein is the breath of life'.

One important point only has been omitted, that which speaks of a race of giants.

Proofs of the Existence of Atlantis

There are many indications to confirm the existence of Atlantis. Some of the main ones are as follows:

Numbers of small islands round the Azores, constituting navigational hazards, as mentioned in the Timaeus.

The fissure known as the Atlantic Ridge which runs from Iceland to the Antarctic like a great scar.

Between the Ridge and the continents are the submarine

beds of the rivers Hudson, Loire, Seine, Rhine, etc.

In 1898 a cable-ship working in the Atlantic pulled up, from a depth of 10,000 feet, a piece of vitreous lava with the chemical composition of basalt; the fragment is now in a museum in Paris. But lava will undergo this chemical change only under normal atmospheric pressure, so the bed of the Atlantic, some 500 miles north of the Azores, must have been covered by a flow of lava while it was still above water.

Madame Maria Klionova, an expert in mineralogy and geology, doing a tour of duty on board the Russian laboratory-ship *Mikhaël Lomonossov*, discovered an uncharted mountain under the North Atlantic which she believes to be part of a continent existing 15,000 years ago.

Plato could not have guessed at the existence of the lava, nor of the Great Ridge, nor the exact date of the Flood (which was only determined in 1964), nor the Sargasso Sea, nor the American continent beyond Atlantis, nor the existence of the Gulf Stream when, in the *Critias*, he spoke of a spring of water that was simultaneously hot and cold.

He was also unaware that, according to Wegener's theory, continental drift would account for the destruction of the great island lying across the line of the Atlantic Ridge.

Petrels, small brown migratory birds, cross the Atlantic from Europe to America every September and October. When they reach a point about 600 miles south-west of Cape Verde, they circle round persistently, then set off again towards Brazil. Their memory-chromosomes tell them that once upon a time there was a landing-place here—Atlantis.

The *inlandsis* of America and Europe, consisting of cumulations of ice resting upon a continental base, suggest that they must once have been part of a general *inlandsis* covering the whole of a terrain now lying beneath the ocean. This seems to show conclusively that during the Ice Age a continent existed half-way across the Atlantic.

There are similarities between the miocene flora of Europe and the present-day flora of eastern America.

Finally, there are the reproductive habits of eels, the

females of which, being accustomed to inland waters, go to the Sargasso Sea in the spawning season, impelled by their memory-chromosomes.

Secret Archives

According to Anubis Schenouda, an Initiate, 'secret Coptic archives refer to solid earth existing where the waters of the North Atlantic are now'. These archives also recall that on three occasions the poles changed their position in the plane of the ecliptic.

'We Copts,' writes Anubis Schenouda, 'know that the poles and the plane of the ecliptic have coincided, as shown in the Denderah Zodiac, where the Lion is on the tail of the Serpent. We also know that three dynasties signify three orders of celestial Spirits—Giants, Titans and Cabiri.'

Constant Basir, referring to the *Melpomene* of Herodotus, mentions someone who, in 2350 B.C., visited both the mainland of Atlantis and a maritime Atlantis.

Basir speaks of an exodus of Atlanteans to Locmariaquer, but without giving the source of his information.

Aelian, in *Varia Historia* (Chapter XVIII, Book III), says that Theopompus gave an account of an interview between the King of Phrygia and Silenus, in the course of which the latter referred to an enormous continent, larger than Asia, Europe and Libya put together, which lay on the far side of the Atlantic.

This story is repeated in greater detail by H. d'Arbois de Jubainville in his book *The First Inhabitants of Europe*.

He writes that, according to Theopompus, who lived in the fourth century B.C., the story of Atlantis was part of the information given by Silenus to King Midas of Phrygia, whose prisoner he was. 'Europe, Asia and Africa form an island surrounded by the Ocean as by a circle. There is only one single continent, and that lies elsewhere. It is of immense size; it breeds huge animals, and men who are twice as tall as we are.'

119

All traditions agree that the Atlanteans were giants. They may have come from some other planet, and were perhaps the men who built the cyclopean cities and sculpted the rock figures mentioned in Daniel Ruzo's description of the Masma civilisation.

'One day, it seems, these giants decided to come over to our part of the world and, ten million of them having crossed the ocean, they reached the country of the Hyperboreans.' (Which is to say those regions that were ruled over by Celts in the fourth century B.C. A Greek author contemporary with Theopompus calls the Gauls who had conquered Rome Hyperboreans.)

'The conquerors reconnoitred the country in which they had landed. They were told that the Hyperboreans were the most fortunate people in the world, but the invaders saw with scorn the wretched conditions in which these Hyperboreans lived, and disdained to go further.'

The teaching of the Druids, as reported by the Greek historian Timagenes, who lived in the first century B.C., agrees with that of Plato and Theopompus.

Another writer of about the same date refers to seven islands in the Atlantic near Europe (*the Canaries*), and adds that the inhabitants of these islands had preserved the memory of a very much larger island called Atlantis, which had for a long time ruled the other Atlantic islands.

'So,' says Arbois de Joubainville, 'there are four texts that report traditions drawn from different sources, all of which agree in describing the conquest of a part of the Old World by strangers from an unknown country, which is called "Atlantis" in two of the texts.'

According to Druidic tradition, the people who invaded Gaul came from very distant islands from which they had been forced to flee by the encroachment of the sea.

'At some times the earth seemed to rise up and at others to sink,' wrote the historian Posidonius in the first century B.C.; and he continued: 'One may admit that Plato's account of

120

Atlantis is no fiction. Indeed, there are more reasons to accept the story than to reject it.'

From Seneca to Paul Lecour

More receptive to the unusual, more open-minded than many a modern historian, Seneca, in his *Medea*, visualised the kind of 'end of the world' which the Atlanteans must have experienced. 'A time will come in future centuries when the sea will burst its bonds; new worlds will open before us; and, of the lands we know, Thule will no longer be the most distant.'

According to Baldwin's *Ancient America*, certain Central American documents state that the continent of America extended far into the Atlantic Ocean, but that that part of the country was destroyed by a series of appalling catastrophes, recurring at long intervals.

This is also what the Abbé Brasseur de Bourbourg found in the Troano manuscript, now kept in the Mayan section of the French National Library.

S. Bailly, French Astronomer Royal in 1779, working on some astronomical tables brought from the Indies by the Jesuits, sited Atlantis in Mongolia. Buffon, who was also interested in the question, thought it had been part of the mainland of America.

Thousands of people have written about Atlantis. Some, like A. Giraud, who founded 'The Atlantis Society of Tomorrow', located it in the Sahara, but it fell to Paul Le Cour, who first published the magazine *Atlantis*, to make the most telling point.

He agreed with Plato in siting the governmental centre of Atlantis in the Azores, and suggested that in the north it was joined to the Hyperborean continent by an isthmus.

The outlying parts of Africa, Europe and America were connected to Hyperborea, thus forming one enormous mass of land, united in the Arctic regions, where the New World met the Old World. This is the most generally accepted theory nowadays, and it seems very probable that submarine archae-

121

ology will in the end prove it to be right.

In a book (which is difficult to come by) called *Light Upon Atlantis*, its author, Dr. Emile Mir Chaouat, gives a curious account of the history of the human race beginning with Atlantis. The author does not state his sources, except by reference to family papers and oriental manuscripts.

Few writers would venture to quote his theories, which are often bewildering, not to say incredible; but it seems only fair not to reject something which cannot be *dis*proved if only because the history of man and of Atlantis is a matter of speculation and is often based upon nebulous clues.

In any case, Mir Chaouat's book is interesting and deserves attention for certain points about which the author may well have guessed correctly.

The Hebrews—Were They Bretons?

Every chapter of Mir Chaouat's book bristles with unexpected statements that are always friendly to the Hebrews—which seems civil of someone who is, presumably, an Arab.

Here are a few extracts from *Light Upon Atlantis*:

'*Homo Atlanticus*, or Cro-Magnon Man, is the biblical *chalti* or Celto-Hebrew.

'There is no such thing as an Aryan race, which is the invention of Gobineau, a poor historian and inclined to be arrogant. It is the Atlantean race to which Hebrew and Germanic peoples belong ... the sons of Mani, of Gagomir, of Poseidon, of Noah and David.... The Hebrew religion of the Torah emanates from Thor or Zeus or Cham, from the Jupiter of Romans and Greeks....

'The ancient texts of the Hebrews speak of a western land; they know that they came originally from the country of the Briths or the Kherubim (Atlantis)....

'The Atlantean stock never dies; its seed is always fertile. The Gaelic peoples (Bretons, Basques) are still the most advanced. The Bretons are the glory of France, they breed soldiers, sailors.... They are like the Corsicans in their sense of courage and loyalty....

'Napoleon was a Corsican, that is, of the Atlantean race.

'The Atlanteans came from the West. The name *Berith-Is* (the living Solar Fathers) is synonymous with Caledonia. Hence Caledonia is none other than Atlantis, the country of the Great Ancestors.

'In the olden days the Hebrews called themselves *Berith-ouns* or Bretons or sometimes Kherubim (worshippers of the goddess Kerra....)'

The author gives no references, but his unknown manuscripts may well exist, since every nation on earth claims to have had ancestors living in western Europe ('the east' to Amerindians). All except the Hebrews.

This seems to show that a great deal was intentionally omitted from the Judeo-Christian Bible. Take the pyramids, for instance, the existence of which is never mentioned, any more than other wonders of the Nile valley; not even the name of the Pharaoh of the Exodus, which could hardly have been unknown to the followers of Moses.

The Mystery of the Guanches

In the year 1406, Frenchmen, who were the first Europeans to land in the Canary archipelago, found a tall, fair-skinned people—the Guanches—who believed themselves to be the last survivors of the Flood.

The Spaniards, when they came later, were astonished to find the indigenous population, especially those in the Orotava Valley, fairer than the purest-blooded Castilians.

The Guanches were all massacred by the Europeans, and there are now no descendants whatever of this magnificent race, whose average height was over six feet.

Like the Celts, the Guanches, although gentle-mannered and hospitable, were fiercely independent, and preferred death to slavery.

Jean de Béthencourt, Chamberlain to King Charles VI of France, was 'amazed at their courage and their incorruptibility. His companions, having rounded up a number of women who had taken refuge in a cave at Fuerteventura, saw one of them kill her baby so that it should not fall into the hands of the invaders.'

In ancient times the hospitality of the Guanches to friendly travellers was renowned; they even felt it their duty to offer their own wives to visitors. One should perhaps add that on the island of Gomera all the women were held in common by the clan. According to tradition, these people claimed descent from King Uranus, the first ruler of Atlantis, who was believed to have reigned some 20,000 years earlier.

'Scratch an Egyptian, a Libyan, a Guanche or a Mayan, and you will find Atlantis,' writes P. Couteaud in his book about the Atlanteans. He adds that the Egyptians are the Atlanteans of the east, which agrees with the tradition that they came from a country far to westward.

The question is, were the Guanches refugees from Atlantis and so the most direct descendants of the inhabitants of Poseidonis? One is inclined to think so when comparing their rites and customs with those of hybrid Atlanteans—that is, Celts, Egyptians, Mexicans and Peruvians.

On the island of Fuerteventura there are megalithic monuments of the same type as those at Stonehenge and Carnac—cromlechs, menhirs, alignments.

On the island of Hierro there are cave-tombs where the Guanches laid their mummified dead beside altars that were either pyramidal or truncated cones, just like those in Mexico. A thousand mummies were found in a cave at Barranco de Herque, laid in niches, as in Peru. The mummies may be seen in the museum at Las Palmas, surrounded by all the things they would be likely to need in a future life.

Near Valverde, at a place called Los Letrero, is a slab of lava inscribed with some very curious hieroglyphics that have not yet been deciphered; the same mysterious script has been found in a ravine at Candia and on the island of Gomera.

Numidian inscriptions—Numidia was a country lying between ancient Carthage and Mauretania (Morocco)—seem to suggest that Africans also knew these other countries in olden days.

Barros, in his *History of the Portuguese in the West Indies*, refers to an equestrian statue said to have been discovered at Corvo, on the most northerly island in the Azores. The pedestal on which it stood was covered with inscriptions in unknown characters, believed to be Phoenician.

Did Jesus Visit the Guanches?

So much distortion has crept into the history of mankind, that it may not be altogether unprofitable to add to the file on Atlantis a few suggestions which, though they may appear far-fetched, might at some future date be found to rest on a more solid foundation than anyone would dare to suppose at present.

Maurice Guignard, author of the book *How I deciphered the Etruscan Language*, translated into French the sacred formulae chanted by Guanche, Lydian and Etruscan priestesses conducting what he terms proto-Christian rites—which, he says, means Druidic. He writes:

'For thousands of years the Guanches kept alive these sacraments, but certain heretics, the offspring of Lydian soldiers and Cushite women, seceded from the old religion, keeping only the doctrine of the One God. The orthodox, to counter the heretics, founded the Essene community in memory of their northern ancestors. (Essenes ═ is-sonir ═ sons of ice).

'Christ and his Mother were members of this sect. Christ was ordained priest in the Atlantean isles and, as an Essene priest, he could not have instituted the neo-Christian sacraments attributed to him. On the contrary, he would have restored the ancient Essene-Druidic sacraments.'

Maurice Guignard, in another book entitled *The Lydian 'A' Bible*, affirms that the Guanches had *innumerable* [sic] extracts from the early Bible graved on their tombstones. This primitive Bible was later falsified in translation, he thinks. In any case, apart from enigmatic inscriptions at Los Letrero, Candia and Gomera, it does not appear that any extracts, biblical or otherwise, have been found on Guanche monuments.

Again according to M. Guignard, Guanche or Kvan-Skessiks, was the cryptic language of Greek, Mayan, Inca, Egyptian and Etruscan priests in celebrating their mysteries and initiatory ceremonies. He states, moreover, that he has factual proofs that Jesus spent that part of his life in the Canaries which is referred to in the Gospels as being 'led up of the Spirit into the wilderness'.

No references are given by this author for his assertions; and, apart from anything else, the Dead Sea Scrolls prove, not that Jesus was an Essene, but rather the contrary.

F. Couteaud states that the Guanches worshipped the Virgin Mary, whom M. Guignard calls Thurma or Mikil, the Giant Virgin.

The most celebrated of the sanctuaries dedicated to Mikil by the Norsemen were the Mont Saint Michel and Chartres.

According to the ancients, Paradise lay in the West, variously sited near the Isles of the Blessed, at Thule, in the Garden of the Hesperides, the Isle of St. Brendan and the Island of Seven Cities.

What strange fantasies are concealed within these myths, in which one feels that there must be a germ of historical truth, though somehow lost?

And how can one fail to see the Canaries as the 'Island of Seven Cities', although it would more correctly be styled the 'Archipelago of the Seven Islands'—Tenerife, Fuerteventura, Gran Canaria (Las Palmas), Lanzarote, Palma, Gomero and Hierro?

CHAPTER NINE

OTHER SITES FOR ATLANTIS

As the 'myth' of Atlantis has gradually become history in the course of this century, so a whole literature has grown up on the subject, exciting even to people one thought of as perfectly matter-of-fact.

Archaeologists and historians are vying with romantic writers, each trying to bring Atlantis within his national orbit. As a result, the lost continent has been sited in almost every part of the world.

One pre-historian named de Baer considers that the twelve tribes of Israel lived on Atlantis, which he locates in Palestine; and he thinks that Sodom and Gomorrah were destroyed in the Flood.

Atlantis in the Caspian and in Heligoland

About the year 1960 a tidal wave some ten miles south of Baku, on the shores of the Caspian Sea, exposed the remains of a city which Professor Berezin of the University of Kazan had no hesitation in identifying as Poseidonis.

Jürgen Spanuth, a Lutheran Pastor, had no doubt at all that the submerged continent was in the North Sea just off Heligoland, where a diver named Beelte had discovered some enormous ramparts built of red and white stone blocks about twenty-seven feet down.

'It is Basileia, the capital of Atlantis!' exclaimed the Pastor. (Actually, there were several places in ancient Gaul named Basilia, but Basileia is unknown. In any case, the capital of

127

Atlantis was Poseidonis.) He quotes Plato to support his theory, but relies mainly on Homer's Odyssey.

It is true that, in the Odyssey, Ulysses lands on the island of Ogygia, which tradition sites in the Azores, since he travelled for eighteen days east-north-east, navigating by the constellations Taurus and Pleiades. This Spanuth affirms, would have been the exact time and direction necessary for him to get to Heligoland in those days.

The reasoning is comparatively sound, but it contains one fundamental error—the date.

Geologists agree that violent earthquakes caused a conflagration which destroyed part of the world, and at some time during the fifteenth century B.C., colossal tidal waves changed much of the geography of the earth.

Certain northern peoples, driven from their home lands by these catastrophes, migrated southwards.

Ovid writes in the *Metamorphoses*: 'The clouds were dissipated in steam by the conflagration; the mountains were consumed by fire, and great crevices opened.... Men and countries were reduced to a heap of ashes.'

On a stele in the temple of Medinet-Habu in ancient Egyptian Thebes, hieroglyphics tell the story of 'strangers from the north who had seen the utter destruction of their land'.

These accounts refer to authentic occurrences, but they happened long after the universal Flood of 12,000 years ago, since they are dated about 1500 B.C.

Atlantis in the Mediterranean

Some misconception seems to have made a number of archaeologists believe that Atlantis was in the Aegean.

That is the theory of Professor Angelos Galanopoulos, of the Institute of Seismology in Athens, who in 1956 discovered the ruins of a Minoan city at the bottom of a shaft on the island of Thera, under a hundred feet of volcanic rubble.

Thera, or Santorin, the most southerly of the Cyclades, is crescent-shaped nowadays; but some thousands of years ago it was known as *Strongyle* (the Round) or *Callisto* (the Beautiful).

In one apocalyptic night, figuratively speaking, its 2,000-foot high mountain exploded like a hundred megaton bomb. All the mountains round about burst into flames, and the epicentre of the earthquake threw up an enormous jet of water, half a mile high, which overwhelmed Crete and laid waste the Nile Delta.

Of the Thera of those days nothing remained but a rocky crescent and, facing it on the west, two islets and sandbanks that appear at times and disappear as quickly. Geological upheavals are by no means at an end in that part of the world.

These events took place in the year 237 B.C. according to Pliny; according to Strabo in 94 B.C. But modern experts put the date back to the fifteenth century B.C.

It was at that time that the Minoan civilisation of Crete vanished with the same suddenness as the civilisations of Lascaux and Glozel.

As in the case of the universal Flood, the only Cretan survivors were those who happened to be well away on the high seas at the time of the catastrophe or who lived up in the mountains. The refugees went to Argolis where, thanks to their cultural contribution, the Mycenean civilisation soon developed.

Professor Galanopoulos, by taking a zero off the figure, dates the end of Atlantis 900 years before Solon instead of 9,000, which would bring it to the Minoan age. He identifies Poseidonis with Knossos, the capital city of King Minos, and has found remains of dykes and wharfs in the sea off Santorin that might have been the three-fold line of defence built by the rulers of Atlantis.

Nevertheless, these facts and coincidences are inadmissible as evidence. The flood of the year 1500 B.C. cannot be equated with the universal Flood of the year 10,000 B.C.

The one point of interest in this theory is that it brings out the curious analogy that exists between the triple entrenchments of Atlantis and the Cretan labyrinth, built to house the

Minotaur by the demi-god Daedalus at the command of King Minos.

The Mystery of the Labyrinth

The likeness between the ground-plan of Poseidonis and that of labyrinths in general brings to light some surprising facts.

The effect of the Flood was to turn the concentric circles of the Atlantean city into boundary lines of the largest necropolis in the world.

The nations of the earth were so stunned by the extent of the catastrophe, that the Country of the West, where tens of millions of Atlanteans, all dying at the same moment, slept their last sleep, became for ever and in all parts of the world the Kingdom of the Dead.

The Kingdom of the Dead is the Ancestral Land and it is Atlantis. This is true to so great an extent that the Green Paradise of the Egyptians, as well as the Paradise and the Ancestors' Country of the yellow races, are in the West—not in Africa nor in Europe, in the direction in which the sun seems to set, but in the Atlantic Ocean, between Thule and the Azores.

Another curious fact is that, like the circles at Poseidonis, the ancient labyrinths—the oldest known being Egyptian—all enclose vast cemeteries, cities of the dead.

Still another point, which will be understood by anyone interested in secret societies, is that the first initiation ceremonies into the Egyptian Mysteries were carried out in a labyrinth. Which, put in plain language, means that the opening of eyes, knowledge, birth, begin with tradition and death.

Herodotus visited one of these labyrinths in the fifth century B.C., and Pliny about the year A.D. 50 speaks of it in these terms:

Even today one may see in the Nome of Heracleopolis in Egypt a labyrinth, the oldest of them all, which was built, it is said, between six and seven thousand years ago by either

130

King Petesuecus or Tithoës.

But Herodotus says that it was the work of the twelve kings of whom Psammetichus was the last. Opinions differ about the reason why it was built.

Demoteles says it was the palace of Motherudes; Lyceas makes it the palace of King Moeris; a good many people believe it was a monument dedicated to the sun, and that is the most generally accepted view.

This enormous conglomeration of buildings consists of a number of temples communicating with one another or superimposed upon one another. The passages between them form an inextricable maze.

Tired of walking, the visitor reaches a crossroads and finds rooms built over a slope, porticoes from which he has to climb down ninety steps. Below are porphyry columns, images of gods, figures of kings, monstrous effigies.

Some of the temples are so arranged that, as soon as the doors are opened, a fearful clap of thunder is heard inside.

Nowadays the facts are known about the great Egyptian labyrinth. It was an immense quadrilateral palace, some 650 feet by 500 feet in area, of which remains have been found under the village of Hawara, east of Lake Moeris. It contained twelve large apartments, and three thousand other rooms, 1,500 of which were underground and were used as burial places for kings and sacred crocodiles.

Archaeologists have identified it as being at the same time a city of the dead and the pyramid of Amenemhat III, of the thirteenth dynasty.

This labyrinth was, therefore, the resting place of dead Egyptians, just as Poseidonis became the city of dead Atlanteans.

The Myth of Pasiphae

According to the legend, Pasiphae was Queen of Crete and the daughter of Hyperborean Apollo. Venus, being angry that

131

Apollo, the Sun, had thrown light upon the love between herself and Mars, inspired in the Queen a monstrous love for a white bull which Neptune sent up from the sea.

The ingenious Daedalus made a brazen cow in which Pasiphae concealed herself, to beguile the bull. From their union the Minotaur was born, a monster, half man and half bull, whom Minos—understandably shocked—caused to be shut up in the labyrinth.

Athens, at that time under the domination of Crete, was obliged to send seven boys and seven girls each year, as provender for the Minotaur. How Theseus slew the Minotaur with the help of Ariadne, the daughter of Minos, is well known.

The Romans, who revelled in eroticism, reconstructed the amours of Pasiphae in the Circus, to amuse Caesar. Young women were thrust into the arena with rutting bulls, and Martial bears witness that copulation certainly took place.

These two accounts show how completely a forgotten piece of history can be debased and misunderstood.

The Romans recognised only the perverted, unpleasant side; the Greeks accepted the perversion. In reality one may suppose that it was a perfectly normal love that brought the beautiful Pasiphae into the arms of an Initiator.

At that time, some four to five thousand years ago, Initiators from outer space brought the higher knowledge to the Near East. They were deified under the name of Baal, of Marduk, of Thoth, and symbolised by a bull in Phoenicia, a winged bull in Assyria and the bull Apis in Egypt.

But they were men, and it was surely to a man that Pasiphae gave herself.

This makes it understandable that the labyrinth became the tomb of the Minotaur, the descendant of a divine Being, one of the tutelary geniuses of Crete.

Daedalus himself, a highly gifted architect and possibly an Initiator, was imprisoned there by Minos, but he escaped, according to the legend, by making feather wings for himself.

Although archaeologists may have discovered labyrinthine

structures in Minoa, they never found the Minotaur's; and Homer, who did not find it either, thought that it was simply another cave.

There is, it so happens, near ancient Knossos, at the foot of Mount Ida, a cave with some very complicated passages, which could well have been the maze in which Theseus got involved.

So the myth contains not only an Initiator from outer space but also a cave of initiation.

In 1702 the botanist Tournefort described the cave-labyrinth of Knossos in the following terms:

Having wandered through a maze of underground passages, the explorers reached a long wide aisle, some 1,200 paces long, which ended in a sort of Council Chamber of great magnificence. . . . The floor is level, with few uneven places. The walls are absolutely vertical and made of stone, which prevented our going further . . . but there are so many passages in all directions that one would undoubtedly get lost if proper precautions were not taken. . . .

This seems to explain the mystery of the Egyptian labyrinths, which were copied from the ground-plan of Poseidonis and similar buildings, or grottoes that, when their original purpose had been forgotten, became caves of initiation.

The Labyrinth and Pyramids of Clusium

On the Isle of Lemnos, where mythology sites Vulcan's forge (a fire-breathing mountain), there was a celebrated labyrinth containing one hundred and fifty pillars which turned on pivots.

The ancient Greeks regarded as labyrinths any caves that had numerous passages.

The labyrinths laid out on the floors of the cathedrals at Chartres, Reims and many other French and English churches, are not, as is often thought, symbols of the agonising

133

path trodden by Jesus on the way to the crucifixion, but a figure to show the complex ways leading to initiation and the last secrets of the holy of holies.

The labyrinth at Clusium, the ancient Etruscan city now called Chiusi, is the tomb of the Etruscan King Porsena.

The Etruscans were Celts, descended from Atlanteans, and Pliny quotes Marcus Varro's description of the monument:

He says Porsena was buried beneath the city of Clusium, where he had caused a square mausoleum to be built.

Each side was 300 feet long and 53 feet high. The base contained an inextricable maze; anyone going into it without a guiding thread would never find his way out.

Above this square were five pyramids, one at each corner and one in the middle, each of them 75 feet wide at the base, 150 feet high, and conical; on top of each was a leaden ball with a canopy above, from which hung little balls on chains; when they swayed in the wind, they gave out a continuous sound such as used to be heard at Dodona.

Above the leaden ball were four more pyramids, each 100 feet high; and above these last pyramids, upon a covering platform, were another five pyramids.

Clearly, these conical pyramids were stone tumuli, and the whole edifice obviously had a magical purpose.

A labyrinth placed beneath magic pyramids, shows the characteristic architectural system ascribed to the Atlanteans, which was bequeathed by them to Egyptians, Celts and Mexicans.

It is by a combination of all these separate indications, debased though they may have become in practice, that it is possible to catch a glimpse of the great historical truth that leads back to Atlantis.

Dodona, it might be mentioned, was the only known Pelasgian sanctuary; it was celebrated as an oracle of Jupiter.

The Atlantis of Christos Mavrothalassitis

Christos Mavrothalassitis, who had at one time been a diver, thinks he has discovered Atlantis.

Like Professor Galanopoulos, he sites its eastern part in the Mediterranean, but the larger, continental part in the Atlantic. His evidence is not without value, for it relies almost exclusively upon things he discovered during his life as a deep-sea diver.

He is preparing a book on the subject, a few quotations from which may be interesting:

'... "Doctor," said my father to one of the divers (who had, in fact, been medically trained) "historians do their job, and we do ours. I asked you to dive on to that fortified place, which has been under water for thousands of years, in the hope that you might find some proofs, because you've read the classics.

' "The place is built in the very middle of the Banco Greco, three degrees north-east of the frontier between Libya and Tunisia, and thirty miles (Habib Soussi says 35 miles) off the coast."

' "But I don't know anything about it, Captain," protested the "doctor".

' "That city," my father continued, "was found before our day by my father-in-law and by other Greek sailors—Scaris, the Parasquevas, the Dandacos, the Zathas and Vlakhakis.

' "I was only eighteen when I first saw it. I was with Parasquevas. They brought up a gold statue from there a hundred years ago."

' "We were with you, Captain," said two of the other divers. One of them was Mailes Theodore, and the other an Arab called Habib Soussi.

'That city was built on a rocky plateau which used to be an island. Seeing how deep the sea is all round it, I'm inclined to think that it might be an artificial island. Quite near there is a submerged hill which looks as if it had been worked on by man; and there's a geyser still active below the surface. It lies eighteen fathoms deep, but the hot water comes right up to the

135

top. All around, the sea is twenty-four fathoms deep; another geyser spouts a little further south.

'The most extraordinary part of it all is that the hot water was distributed in the town by those old-time people through a system of canals and pipes that can still be seen.

'There are four hills on that sandbank, and you find water-works on two of them. . . .'

Speaking of the earthquake on Santorin, Christos says that it occurred at the very time when the Greeks were planning to invade King Minos' realm.

The cities of Saranda and Mira were swallowed up.

'My father,' said Christos, 'saw the pillars of the theatres and temples, and some divers actually saw statues still in position on the columns. But all that had nothing to do with Atlantis; that went down when the earth collided with the planet Ares-Baal, which was the planet Mars.

'Two clairvoyants, Ayed and old Souffi, confirmed this. Our earth blew up in various places, and Ares hurled sand and fire on it. . . .

'I wasn't allowed to talk about it till I was eighteen, but later I discovered an Atlantean tomb with the help of Souffia's grand-daughter. It contained the body of a soothsayer from the city of Maou, which was the capital of Atlantis, and this man had with him the proofs of his art; I've got them.

'That Atlantean seer had with him some symbolic objects— an opal, six sapphires, that showed he was sixty years old, and some stone and metal tablets telling about great men who were to be born in the future, like Homer, Pherecides, Archimedes, Alexander the Great, Napoleon and so on. . . .

'His name was Pheuresseus. A rose was carved in the centre of his gravestone.

'Four sculptures showed: his army rank; things he had pro-phesied; his royal (North American) descent; and the mysteri-ous plant that imparts power.

'I know the name of that plant, but I must not tell it, nor where it is to be found.

'In the tomb there were also twelve pieces of information

about Atlantis, and the description of a mountain crammed with treasure; the figure of a cat is carved on it. Between the cat's paws is the entrance to the cave where the treasure lies … but it's something to do with documents. …

'When that cave is discovered, a new life-cycle will begin. But I've never managed to find out where the mountain is. Someone may know!'

It is difficult to sort out from Christos' yarns which parts are really his own archaeological discoveries and which are due to old Souffia's visions.

Besides, Christos has never told all he knows; at any rate, what he does tell will not be a matter wholly indifferent to occultists!

Atlantis in Mongolia

Jean Sylvain Bailly, French Astronomer Royal, Member of the Académie des Sciences, and Mayor of Paris in 1779, wrote a history of ancient Astronomy, which was published in 1781. One-third of the book was devoted to the East Indies, and described the scientific discoveries of a Northern people who no longer existed on the earth.

Basing his work upon the 'Tables of Tirvalour' and documents brought from the Indies by missionaries, Bailly concluded that there must have been a very highly developed antediluvian civilisation which has been 'obliterated as a result of natural and political upheavals'.

In checking the Indian astronomical tables, Bailly found that they contained mistakes, if one took them to have been worked out in India. On the other hand, if the author had been sited somewhere near the 49° latitude north, they appeared to be correct.

He inferred from this that the Brahmans, in whose charge they had been, must have inherited them from a people living in the Gobi Desert, whom he called Atlantean.

Bailly was mistaken on this point; not that he was unaware of Plato's writings, but because he attributed scientific work to

137

the Atlanteans which more probably emanated from another, and possibly hostile, civilisation, that of the Land of Mu, traditionally situated in the Far East and the Pacific.

The Land of Mu and Gondwana

Ten or twenty thousand years ago, places that are now desert were zones of rich, often luxuriant vegetation, as has been shown by archaeologists, zoologists and botanists.

Future deserts, it is thought, will occur in European countries which are, little by little, and inevitably, losing their arable land through erosion and intensive 'mineralisation'.

It is only reasonable to expect that great geological disturbances are likely to occur again, as they did in the past.

Tradition tells us that, before the Flood, there was an enormous continent in the Pacific, stretching from Polynesia to the Indian Ocean, and including the Gobi Desert, Malaysia and parts of India and China. This continent was known as the Land of Mu, and was, according to Pacific legends, the 'original earth'.

In Tahiti, the cradle of the human race is said to have been the continent *Fenua Nui*, which Ru, the god of wind, broke up into a multitude of islands with a puff of his mighty breath.

Easter Island was part of *Fenua Nui*, and remains of huge buildings have been found at Ponape, in the Caroline Islands, and on the atoll of Tonga Tabu, where gigantic stones, weighing up to twenty tons, are to be seen, supported on pillars.

Professor Robert Dietz, geologist and oceanographer at the Environmental Science Service Administration in Washington, has made a geographical reconstruction of the ancient continent of Gondwana, which extended over parts of Africa, South America, the Antarctic, Australia and India. He dates it about 150 million years ago.

The existence of these continents is not definitely denied by geologists, but their geographical configuration is to all intents and purposes unknown, and even tradition tells us little about them.

Some day the ocean bed will become dry land, for everything that is hidden shall be revealed, but of ancient Atlantis not a vestige will remain. Of the golden city gates, brazen cupolas, bronze statues, stone monuments and human relics of this once proud people, nothing will be left but heaps of sand and humus.

Men of the next cycle will speculate about an ancient submerged civilisation that they will perhaps centre in the sea around Mont Blanc; and it may be that, thanks to the laws of natural reincarnation, a splendid city named Poseidonis will come into being, with a triple ring of moats, in the deep valleys between Bermuda and the Azores.

Everything beings again, only the names of the gods are eternal, and sometimes those of their cities, and the clay to which everything returns to be remodelled in the image of the original archetype.

CHAPTER TEN

HYPERBOREA AND EGYPT

Antediluvian history means the history of Atlantis. After the Flood it becomes that of Hyperboreans, Celts and Egyptians.

No memory of the Hyperboreans remained after their disappearance, except that they were a sort of élite among white races, and that they lived at Thule, in the polar regions. They certainly vanished soon after the Flood, but, though they left a profound imprint of their mental and spiritual achievements on the civilisations of northern Europe, not a single material relic of them has ever been found, which leads one to think that they must have been a caste rather than a nation.

The ancient Greeks knew that they were Celtic in origin. It was in them that the Hyperboreans survived, even though for the last three thousand years they have been confused with Gauls and Brythons.

Hyperborea

Apart from a book on the Hyperboreans written by Hecate of Abdera, a Greek mythographer who flourished about the year 350 B.C., most of what we know of the Great Ancestors comes from Diodorus Siculus.

'Hecate,' he writes, 'and some others assert that in the Ocean beyond the land of the Celts (*northern Gaul*) there is an island at least as large as Sicily.

'This island, which lies far to the north, is inhabited by the Hyperboreans, so called because they live beyond the north wind. The soil of this island is so good and so fertile that it yields two harvests every year. . . .

'This where Latona was born, which explains why the islanders are particularly dedicated to the worship of (*her son*) Apollo. . . . They are all, one may say, priests of Apollo. . . .

'The Hyperboreans speak a language of their own. They are, and always have been, very friendly disposed to Greeks, and especially to Athenians and Delians.

'It is even said that a number of Greeks have visited the Hyperboreans, taking splendid gifts with Greek inscriptions; and that in return Abaris of Hyperborea once made his way to Greece, to revive the ancient friendship.

'It is also said that, seen from this island, the moon seems extraordinarily near the earth, so that the configurations of its surface are plainly visible.

'Apollo is believed to visit the island once every nineteen years.

'At the end of this period the stars in their courses have returned to the same relative position as they were at the beginning. This nineteen-year period is called the Great Year by the Greeks.

'During the time of his descent upon earth, the god may be seen every night, from the Spring equinox until the rising of the Pleiades, dancing to the accompaniment of his cithara, as though to show his appreciation of the people's worship.

'Government of the island and the guardianship of the temple are in the hands of its kings, who are named Boreades, and who are the descendants of Boreas.'

The fact that Apollo was born of a Hyperborean mother, and that he held a preponderant position in Hellenic mythology, would of itself witness to the northern and Celtic origin of the early Greek Pelasgians.

Was Apollo an Extra-terrestrial Being?

The end of Diodorus Siculus' text might lead one to suppose that Apollo was merely a solar symbol.

True, like all the gods of antiquity he was represented by

141

one of the heavenly bodies—the sun in this case—because it was the custom to show respect for a superior Being by likening him to a star. Apollo was not a myth, but probably one of the heroes, an Initiator from the North.

Among northern peoples and Scythians he was known as Abaris the Hyperborean, and he had the power of travelling about the cosmos on a flying arrow, like King Bran of the People of the Hills, who went from his country to the 'Land Beyond' with the speed of a jet. Like Manannan mac Llyr, the Irish wonder-worker, he navigated in space and regions of mystery, like Asshur, the Assyrian god, who was mounted on a winged bull; or Nin-Girsu the winged deity of Akkad and Sumer; Horus, the Egyptian, the Phoenician Astarte, Orejona, the Mother of the Incas, Quetzalcoatl, the winged serpent of Mexico—they all travelled through space, and were probably all extra-terrestrial Initiators. There was also the Hindu Rama, who piloted his 'spherical vimanas and travelled through the air by the power of mercury, which generated a strong propellent wind. . . .'

None of these gods or heroes was an astral myth any more than was Apollo. In all mythologies and according to accounts given by ancient historians, they really moved about the skies in flying machines, which were generally depicted by Celts, Mayas, Incas, Assyrians or Egyptians like modern aeroplanes, flying saucers or space-rockets.

Apollo's arrow reminds one of a jet 'plane; Orejona is said to have used an airship 'more dazzling than the sun', which may have been propelled by the sort of ionised solar engine shown on the Gateway of the Sun; Quetzalcoatl knew the space-rocket engraved on the plaque at Palenque; Astarte had her mysterious flying serpent with its screw propeller; Asshur's winged disc and the 'eye of Horus' soaring in the sky seem to have been actual flying saucers, and are much the same as the space-ships used by Other-World men from Bâavi, described by the 'mysterious Mn.Y.' (See Chapter 22.)

In addition to Abaris, tradition gives the names of two other Hyperboreans—the virgins Argea and Opis—who introduced the cult of Latona, Apollo and Diana to Delos.

On this point, J. Ponge-Helmer, a historian and scientific technician, recalls in one of his very interesting works the passionate desire of the Seleucid Kings of Persia to reintroduce the worship of the Hyperborean Virgin Laodice, and the Nazis' aspiration ot re establish runic and solar myths.

Thule, the gateway to ... ?

Tradition names the capital of Hyperborea as Thule, which in olden days was the extreme northern limit of the known world; whence its name *Ultima Thule*.

A sailor from Marseilles named Pytheas once undertook to go as far as possible north of Europe. He got beyond the British Isles, and discovered another island 'which at the summer solstice had day but no night, and at the winter solstice night but no day!' His contemporaries, even learned men, shouted with laughter—as if such a place could possibly exist!

Anyway, Pytheas came from Marseilles. And not even Athenians could beat a Marseillais when it came to travellers' tales!

Other sailors and historians also had something to say about Thule, and it was successively sited in Iceland, the Shetlands, the Orkneys, Finland and Greenland, with the result that to-day no one would know where to look for it, if Hyperborean traditions—abominably misrepresented by Hitler in 1938—did not give the necessary information.

Thule lay at the gateway to other worlds, the focus of earth-currents. It acted as a decompression chamber, allowing transit from one sphere of life to another, from one universe to another.

The Hyperborean capital therefore occupied a position which suggested a very interesting idea to Guy Tarade.

According to him, the North and South Poles were gates to the cosmos, in other words they were the two ports from which it was possible to leave the earth, the places where the Van Allen belts are inflected or modified, and where there are radio-active strata that can be highly dangerous to cosmonauts.

This was in fact what the Patriarch Enoch said when he went to the ends of the earth, to the place where 'the gates leading to heaven' were to be found, on his way to consult with the Early Fathers before the Flood. It is known that Enoch made interplanetary journeys, so that the Early Fathers, Initiators from Above, must have been cosmonauts.

These two gaps in the Van Allen belts, according to Guy Tarade, would be the points at which Initiators of those days arrived and departed. If these atomic belts were no longer there to protect us, the earth would be liable to a cosmic bombardment that might cause fearful upheavals. Fortunately, they are still in position, kept in place by the magnetic pull of the earth.

An alarm was raised at the Moscow Oceanic Congress in 1966 by the American physicists Heezen and Bruce. They had been studying what they called a fossilised compass found on the sea-bed, and from this they discovered that at some time the poles had been completely inverted, and that at present their magnetic strength was gradually diminishing. According to their calculations, it would not exist at all in two thousand years' time, and a prolonged series of natural catastrophes would endanger the normal evolution of mankind and other living species on earth.

It may be that it was for some similar reason that an extraterrestrial humanity had many ages ago been obliged to emigrate, and that they had decided to settle at the North Pole for fear of further disasters.

Moreover, if Hyperborean space-travellers had a knowledge of science superior to our own, as seems likely, they would have been in a position to inject into the nervous system of the globe—the earth-currents—a force which could in a certain measure have influenced human behaviour.

This is exactly what television is doing today—it is moulding the psychological attitude of viewers according to the standards of each nation.

So the Hyperboreans may be said to have been the real

144

Masters of the World by virtue of their geographical position.

An atomic war, described by both Hindus and Mayas, broke out between Hyperboreans and the eastern civilisers of the Land of Mu; the arena of battle was no doubt at the North Pole.

It is disturbing to realise that at the present day two great atomic powers, one situated partly on ancient Atlantis, and the other including much of the one-time Land of Mu, are contending for possession of the North Pole, where the largest city miraculously bears the name of Thule in this twentieth century.

The earth too has its memory-chromosomes, and what has been will recur, exactly as before.

Celts were Sea-farers

Archaeology and tradition show that the Hyperboreans and their direct descendants the Celts were certainly colonisers from very ancient times and that they dominated the whole world intellectually. The Celts, descendants of the Thule caste, were distinguished by their exceptional qualities as sea-farers.

They emigrated to North, South and Central America, infiltrated Polynesia and took possession of all the lands surrounding the Mediterranean basin. The Pelasgians, whose name implies that they came from northern seas, were the ancestors of the Greeks, the Phrygians and the Phoenicians, worshippers of Apollo, Baal-Bel and sacred stones; they raised megaliths in the shade of an oak tree or upon the slopes of Mount Ida (which is itself a typically northern name).

Torridans, Nuraghians, Sardi, Hyksos and other sea-faring peoples, wearing the ritual horned morrions, settled in Corsica, Sardinia and Egypt.

Phoenician ships sailed far beyond the Pillars of Hercules, and it is interesting to find that the outstandingly maritime peoples—Icelanders, Irish, Brythons (English), Norsemen, Bretons, Basques, Spaniards and Portuguese—are all of pure

Celtic descent, and live in countries where tumuli and menhirs abound.

Neither the black nor the yellow races seem to have had the temperament nor the desire to become sailors or pioneers. They were stay-at-homes, while Celts were migratory, driven by memory-chromosomes inherited from their space-travelling ancestors.

The purer-blooded the Celts were, the more they tended to be wanderers, 'sea-people'. So it was always the maritime nations who colonised the rest of the world. This is the reason why Egypt, one of the largest of empires, never succeeded in spreading its civilisation far afield, but on the contrary suffered one invasion after another, that of the Hyksos having the greatest consequences.

The Mighty Pharaohs were Kings only in Name

Egypt is traditionally the 'Land of the Red Men', because a cardinal purple is the colour of earthly royalty. God is blue, Satan is scarlet or green, though in the latter case his mantle is lined with purple, for indeed he rules over the human race.

Purely incidentally, it is interesting to note that while Egyptians are 'Red Men', West Africans are 'Blue Men'. 'Blue Blood' denotes noble birth among Touaregs and among Celts in Gaul and Iberia—one might imagine this to be a legacy from Atlanteans who lived at high altitudes or in other places rich in carbonic gas. In Tibet each of the four cardinal points has its own colour: that of the West is red.

Egyptians of high rank, descendants of 'divine' ancestors hybridised by Celts, benefited by this fortunate post-diluvian combination which enabled them to develop an extraordinarily brilliant civilisation.

The whole world profoundly admires the civilisation of Egypt. It is inscribed in history in letters of gold, its fame is unparalleled; and yet. . . .

And yet, truth to tell, legend and the blindness of Egyptologists dazzled by the gold and the glitter, have completely mis-

146

represented the facts.

The 'mighty' Pharaohs? They were no more than dummy kings, with less real power than the pettiest European land-owner. They were the only sovereigns on earth who never won a battle or so much as scared away a handful of marauders.

Did a nation or even a tribe invade Egypt? There was hardly a scuffle; the mighty Pharaoh and the mighty Egyptian army collapsed like marionettes.

Three-thousand-five-hundred-years ago the unorganised band of men and women who constituted Moses' people—the Hebrews, that is to say—stole sacred vessels and golden ornaments from the Egyptians and their temples and went out into the desert. They had no weapons, no armies, no elephants, no horses, hardly enough to eat.

Pharaoh's 'mighty' army followed at their heels; pursued them without being able to subdue them or even catch them up . . . on the contrary, it was the Egyptians who were destroyed, as the Bible tells, at the crossing of the Red Sea.

All very odd!

Staking Everything on a Future Life

Egypt was at all times an arid land, without natural resources, a country governed by almost powerless sovereigns who were called Kings up to the XVIth dynasty and subsequently Pharaohs.

Egypt is about a thousand miles long, but except round the Nile delta the belt of arable soil is barely more than a mile or two wide. No land, no water save that of the Nile, a noxious, an accursed river, in which for thousands of years the terrible germs of bilharziosis have bred, bringing death to millions upon millions of human beings. Egypt—a land of desert, of drought, of famine, of poverty. . . .

Nothing was ever built in the desert through which flows the narrow ribbon of the Nile. Nothing!

The desert has never 'blossomed' as some have said—though without any shadow of proof—unless possibly in prehistoric times. All known ruins, all the temples, are in the valley on the banks of the Nile, and nowhere else. Five or six miles away from the river, cultivation and civilisation come to an end, and always have done so.

In this desolate world, people and Pharaohs were subject to the same misery, the same privations. They had to be ingenious, like all desert dwellers, if they were to avoid dying of hunger, of thirst, of despair. The 'victorious wars' of these mighty Pharaohs? Pure invention!

There were no neighbours against whom they could want to fight, and they certainly had not the means to carry on a campaign.

History has, in fact, recorded only defeats; defeats inflicted by Persians, Macedonians, the Hyksos, Greeks, Romans, the English, the French, the Israelis. . . .

Being extremely wretched in their inhospitable country, the Egyptians centred all their hopes in a comforting religion which offered glittering prospects of happiness in an improbable after-life. So they sacrificed their earthly lives for the hope of a life after death, and spent their efforts in building—although they had not even houses to live in—building vast temples, gigantic pyramids and splendid tombs (mastabas), most of which still lie hidden in the Valley of the Kings, facing Luxor.

These tombs, they believed, would be their dwelling places when they had breathed their last. Then, after 3,000 years of Purgatory, if their mummies were proof against decomposition, they might reach the Green Paradise, which represented something they would never find on earth, something almost unimaginable—green fields where grass was growing and, who knows, perhaps even flowers. . . .

It was a vision of the wonderful place of which their Celtic and Atlantean forefathers had dreamt after they left the Green Land of the West where they had lived before the Flood.

One signal piece of good fortune that befell the Egyptians was to have been among the first in the post-diluvian world to have known Initiators 'from heaven', who organised the Egyptian miracle 10,000 years ago, while other nations of the earth were struggling painfully back to knowledge and civilisation.

Golden Keys to the Truth

The Egyptians forgot the meaning of their symbols and of their religion after the end of the Old Kingdom, that is to say after the Kings of Abydos died out. Zoser was probably the last to have any understanding of the ancient wisdom, and no doubt he owed what he knew to his architect Imhotep.

Memphis having disappeared, the only memorial of those far-off days is the temple of Abydos that, despite restorations and reconstruction, remains not merely the oldest temple in the world but the only place where some attempt can be made to read, or to conjecture, the primeval history of Egypt.

Egyptologists as well as tourists go into ecstasies over the reliefs at Karnak, at Luxor, at Denderah which, except for their artistic merits, have no historic interest and tell nothing of value about the history of ancient Egypt.

Rameses II and other more recent Pharaohs have immortalised their alleged exploits with the utmost magnificence, but the events and the protagonists represented have no greater importance than those figuring in the columns of minor newssheets today.

The great mistake people make in the study of *ancient* Egypt is to allow themselves to be dazzled by the later gods— Set, Isis and Osiris. Their story is only a witness to the failure of priests and people to recognise the truth, a sign of degeneration like some of the superstitious modern legends in the Christian religion. If Isis, Osiris and Set are eliminated, the History of Egypt will be found to be cleared of a great deal of waste matter.

The true History has four master keys:

1. Aten, the god of the earliest Egyptians (Red Men, blond and bearded).

2. Mnevis, the bull sacred to Aten, whose name is the Greek transliteration of the Egyptian Merou-our.

3. The flying serpent, or ram-headed ship (incorrectly styled the solar barque).

4. The flying ram, or Initiator, who may have been Aten (later called Amon).

Thoth, the great Sage, issued a decree commanding all future Kings to provide first and foremost and in preference to any other form of worship the offerings destined for the 'Living Ram', lest the most fearful calamities should come to pass.

There are also four minor indicators: Hathor (Venus), Horus, Thoth (the Messenger of Heaven and creator of the Eightfold City of the Gods) and Ptah, the second Initiator.

Starting from these eight premises, the primeval history of Egypt can be reconstructed coherently up to the end of the Old Kingdom, to accord with both archaeology and esotericism.

Mnevis is the sacred bull, the Creator. Merou is the sacred mountain of Hindu mythology, the original home of the first Aryans. Mount Merou is believed to lie either between the Aral Sea and the Caspian, or else on the high Iranian plateau. It is said to be pyramidal in shape, the eastern face being white, the western blue, the southern yellow and the northern red, the sacred colour.

By way of comparison: the loftiest pyramid in the world, nearly a thousand feet high, lies about forty miles from Sian, in the province of Shensi in China, and is said by archaeologists to be between 7,000 and 14,000 years old. According to the Chinese system, its colours are black to the north, green to the east, red to the south, and white to the west. The central point is yellow.

In the sanctuary at Heliopolis, which was dedicated to Aten and to Mnevis, the god was symbolised by a menhir-phallus, representing the creation of matter, the 'first stone to emerge' when the earth rose above the waters. Later the symbolism was changed to make the stone represent that upon which the sun shone for the first time—which already runs some risk of false interpretation. It was at Heliopolis that the worship of the obelisk was instituted.

In the association of Aten, Mnevis-Merou the Creator, the

pyramid where the earth first appeared above the waters, and the obelisk-phallus, the broad outlines are shown of the history of the post-diluvian world, a history as Aryan in Egypt as it was in the Caucasus and in the Indies.

Primeval History Falsified by False Gods

The earliest history of Greece, like that of Egypt, was essentially altered by the introduction of later gods, such as Zeus, Athene, Hermes, Ares and Aphrodite who in fact were ill-understood personifications of the initiators and heroes of the early epoch.

Flying sheep and oxen, avatars, the amorous adventures of Zeus and the exploits of Hercules, were not false in their esoteric meaning, but they rapidly degenerated into a mythology suitable only for the ignorant.

In their original purity, Apollo, the Cabiri, and still more anciently Hel among the Greeks and Phoenicians, Aten, Amon, the ram and the serpent among the Egyptians, were very different from the figures which ultimately prevailed.

Ra, the sun, is usually believed to have been the supreme deity in Egypt; in reality, Aten is an infinitely higher concept of the Creator of the universe.

Yet it was not a god or demiurge who encouraged the evolution of civilisation in the world, nor the false gods who grew out of its illusions, but the deified heroes, that is to say the Initiators.

The Mystery of the Uraeus

The gossipy bas-reliefs at Luxor and Karnak may be likened to the pathetically foolish ornaments that clutter up Christian churches.

A church has its major symbols in which those who understand may read the essentials of the religion: the cross which surmounts the whole edifice, the crucifix, the Holy Trinity, the tabernacle and so on. But—the side chapels, with statues of

151

minor saints, most of which are no more than friendly little reminders of good men and women, are completely foreign to the true essence of religion.

The esoterist avoids getting involved in the labyrinths in which the simple like to find oblivion, but he values at their true worth figures such as that of the Virgin Mother, genetrix of humanity, symbolised in the mystic almond and the cave of initiation.

Some Egyptologists are as bad as tourists in the importance they attribute to things that have no higher significance, in their delight in words and symbols and images that are purely exoteric, such as Isis, Osiris, the double crown of Egypt, the weighing of souls, cat-headed Bast, the lunar disc, the solar barque ... and so they flounder in a sea of wearisome fables which for ever veil the dazzling truth.

Yet this truth lies open before their eyes, more clearly than any of the anecdotes on the bas-reliefs: it is to be seen, first, on the lintel or pediment of the temple, a winged disc with a uraeus on either side and then, beneath the lintel, in the frescoes representing Horus the Falcon and his winged subjects. Finally, there are the uprights supporting the pediment which generally have snakes thirty or forty feet long carved on them.

These are the main outlines of the history of the temple and of Egypt, possibly of the history of the world, traced on the lintel and its supports together with the mystery of flying serpents, of Initiators who came from heaven.

The Mystery of the 'Solar' Barques

Abydos is the oldest Egyptian temple, indeed one may say it is the only really ancient one since it dates back 10,000 years, whereas Luxor, Karnak, Medinet Habou and others go back only 4–5,000 years.

In the archaic part of Abydos the bas reliefs and frescoes depict a multitude of snakes and of ram-headed ships which defy explanation by historians.

At Karnak a vessel with two rams' heads is engraved in the

stone; a magnificent, enigmatic reproduction adorns the entrance hall of the Hilton Hotel in Cairo.

The barque, incorrectly styled 'solar'—though the adjective was in fact correct in later times—is a modification of the serpent figure, as is shown clearly in numbers of manuscripts in the Cairo museum, the serpent being itself a variant of an engine found in this guise all over the world.

The ram's head symbolises the Initiators who married the early Queens of Egypt and introduced knowledge of the arts and sciences.

It was because in their veins ran the blood of 'divine Beings' that sovereigns might only marry into royal families who shared a similar 'extra-terrestrial' ancestry.

From the days of the Middle Kingdom onwards, the Kings of Egypt often took wives from the Near East, mainly from Phoenicia, where the second wave of extra-terrestrials had introduced the worship of Baal, Astarte and the Venusian Creators.

The Calendar of Sothis (Sirius)

The Egyptians being, as were the Celts, of an earlier civilisation than the Phoenicians, never instituted the worship of Venus except in conjunction with that of the older gods. According to Herodotus, there was a chapel with an altar in the Temple of Proteus at Memphis dedicated to *Venus, the Unknown Goddess.*

The Initiate Anubis Schenouda, known as the Master of Heliopolis, says that the pyramid at Saqqarah was dedicated to Sakhra, whose name in Egyptian meant 'the stone, the comet, the planet Venus'.

The morning star was also worshipped as the Lady, the Queen of Heaven, but she never had priority over the local gods and goddesses, for it appears that when the so-called Venusian Initiators lived on earth they taught their lore only to Mayas, Incas and Asianic (Middle Eastern) peoples. On the other hand, the star Sirius was particularly venerated by the Egyptians.

The first month of the year began ritually with the appearance of the star Sothis or Sirius, later known as the Star of Isis to conform with the new cult.

'The most accurate calendar made in Egypt,' wrote Madame Marcelle Weissen-Szumlanska in a French journal in 1957, 'dates from the year 4245 B.C.; it is based on the heliacal rising of Sirius, that is to say the time when this star appears above the horizon.'

The date is confirmed by Professor Etienne Drioton: 'In these circumstances, the most probable date would be between 4245 and 4242, in the middle of the neolithic period.'

These verifications show that 6,200 years ago Egyptian knowledge of astronomy was by no means contemptible.

Soto Halle, the historian, gives the date of the temple at Memphis as 7000 B.C., which would take the Egyptian civilisation back 9,000 years at least.

Atlantis and Egypt

One stone in the Lion Gate at Mycene bears this inscription: 'The Egyptians are descended from Thoth, an Egyptian priest in Atlantis.'

Binotros, a Pharaoh of the second dynasty, sent an expedition to the Atlantic coast, according to Fr. Pierre Perroud in a book published in Switzerland, 'to look for Atlantis, whence 3,350 years earlier the ancestors of the Egyptians had come, bringing the wisdom of their native land with them'. They found no trace of the continent of Atlantis, for the excellent reason, as Fr. Perroud points out, that it was at the bottom of the sea.

'Linguists, ethnologists, anthropologists, historians,' writes Madame Weissen-Szumlanska, 'spend their time looking eastwards for the origins of civilisation, despite every indication to the contrary from the Homeric epoch and other reliable archaic texts, such as those of Herodotus and Strabo.' Madame Weissen-Szumlanska is one of the few Egyptologists who, together with Mariette-bey, Gaston Maspero, Etienne Drioton and Vandier, have examined the Egyptian problem logically and without bias.

In their book on Egypt, Drioton and Vandier say: 'Teacher came from the West in small groups and reigned in Egypt for many centuries. Then they proceeded eastwards.'

These teachers were priests of Horus, the Hawk of Heaven, and were, according to Dr. Drioton, semi-divine, with undoubtedly 'higher powers than any men could have, even though they happened to be kings'. They ruled for thousands of years before the days of the kings listed on the Palermo Stone, and before any of the 'human' kings, of whom Mena was the first.

According to the *Sacerdotal Chronicles*, there were four royal periods, the most recent dating from 4200 B.C. From these data, Madame Weissen-Szumlanska deduces that civilisation on the Nile goes back between ten and twelve thousand years, which is agreed by other experts to be about right. One of these experts, a geologist, also says that the American atomic submarine *Nautilus*, on its voyage under the North Pole, passed along a great canyon carved out by an Atlantic current in ancient days.

While exploring southern Morocco, Madame Weissen-Szumlanska found traces between Cap Draa and Reggane of the *Path of the Great Nomads*, a continuation of the *Imperial Road* shown on Herodotus' map. This road, which is believed also to have been identified in Tunisia between Djerba and Lake Tritonis, may have been the route used by Atlanteans before the Flood when trading with Egypt.

The Land of Punt

According to Egyptian tradition, the Land of Punt was not a geographically defined country, but simply an area where travellers went for incense, myrrh, electrum (a natural alloy of gold and silver) and valuable timber. Nowadays it is generally thought to lie in Rhodesia, at Zimbabwe.

Others site the Land of Punt in an enormous island full of incalculable riches, from which came the original Initiators, the priests of Horus.

Egyptians themselves looked upon Punt as the holy land in which the human race originated.

In his *Stories of Ancient Egypt*, Maspero tells of an obvious connection between the mysterious island on which the action of his book takes place, and Atlantis or St. Brendan. No one ever lands on that island except as the result of a shipwreck, which is what happened to the hero of this book, the captain of an Egyptian vessel, who was warmly welcomed by the island's ruler, the Serpent King.

When the Egyptian departed, laden with splendid gifts, the island disolved into the waves and vanished from the visible universe, though it remained the more clearly in the memory of the shipwrecked mariner. The island, Maspero thought, was the anteroom to initiation in Egypt, and the Serpent King was king of the Land of Punt.

Brasseur de Bourbourg found an inscription on a piece of antelope skin in the ruins of a temple in Guatemala, which tells the story of an island that split open in a burst of flame. An enormous serpent coming through the ocean from the east swallowed up the giant inhabitants of the island, together with their vast treasure, and the massive golden gates of their palaces.

'The cataclysm spared the Serpent King, who disappeared into an underground tunnel leading to his other realm.' This Serpent King is, according to Madame Weissen-Szumlanska, the King of Tollan-Tlapallan—'the two are as like as brothers'.

This shows a common denominator between Punt and Mexico, which again suggests Atlantis.

The Shemsu-Hor, Servants of Horus, bore on their cheeks 'the deep scar of the men of Punt—the scar of the Chiefs of the human race'.

Torquemada said that Quetzalcoatl too had a scar on his cheek.

156

CHAPTER ELEVEN

BARBARIAN CIVILISATIONS

After the Flood the population of the earth, sparse though it was, began to reconstitute embryonic civilisations with whatever means were at its disposal.

Some tribes—no doubt those best suited biologically—migrated, and so came in contact with other races, which helped their development. Above all, they had the good fortune to receive instruction from certain 'Strangers', who taught them the fundamentals of knowledge that had been forgotten or perhaps never known.

Other tribes lived in geographically out-of-the-way spots, and vegetated there for a very long time before rediscovering how to make tools and other useful things or the more ad vanced knowledge that would bring them out of a state of barbarism.

Can one attribute any kind of 'civilisation' to these peoples? Certainly—if they managed to build some sort of dwellings, to develop a form of religion, to make pottery.

This obviously happened in the case of some prehistoric tribes, remains of whose settlements and artefacts have been found by archaeologists.

The Cradle of the Aryas

Oudh, a province and city near Lucknow in the Indian subcontinent, is the ancient Ayodhya where, according to the Ramayana and the Mahabharata, the Aryas settled in 2,163,101 B.C. It is hardly necessary to point out that this date does not mean anything by our reckoning; though if advanced to, say, 10,000 B.C. it would make sense to us. But legend is legend, and no doubt the two million and odd years have a meaning which escapes us.

At the same time, there is no reason why one should not suppose that two million years ago the city of Oudh was inhabited by people who returned there after each cataclysm to take up life again.

Atlantis was submerged 12,000 years ago. In a few centuries or thousands of years, when the oceans once again become continents, no doubt the far-off descendants of the Atlanteans —impelled by their memory-chromosomes—will settle somewhere in the neighbourhood of the Azores.

If an initiatory tradition were to survive (and one may expect it to do so) it would be incredible, though true, if the Masters said that the first king of that continent had been enthroned at a date very much more than twenty thousand years earlier. It may be that it is in this sense that the Aryan dating corresponds to actual fact.

The first king of Ayodhya was Ikshwahu, a name which is oddly reminiscent of the word *iks*, meaning Venus in the Mayan language.

Unfortunately tradition seems to have left gaps in the early genealogy of its kings. Between Ikshwahu and Rama sixty-two kings are named, but only thirty-three after Rama, who flourished in the year 867,101. Again, one may venture to revise the date to about 2000 B.C. according to our calendar.

By a simple calculation, based upon statements attributed to Rama, it would appear that if the figures were divided by about 220 according to our arithmetical system, this would bring the date to 9841 B.C.—very nearly to the year 10,000 B.C. which has been suggested as the approximate date when the Aryas settled at Oudh.

This would make Aryan civilisation in India about contemporary with that of Celts and Mayas.

'With my own eyes I saw a paved road and walls built of cyclopean stone blocks. . . . It was 25 feet down and about two hundred yards off Puerto Acosta in Lake Titicaca, in Bolivia.' So said a young Argentine diplomat in 1967.

Before him, Professor Malinowsky had 'discovered' a whole city at the bottom of the lake. Legend was rife in Peru and Bolivia about submerged cities (in the plural), and about treasures from the Temple of the Sun alleged to have been thrown into the Lake by Incas on the eve of the occupation of the islands by the Spaniards. Disenchantment followed.

In 1968 Commander Cousteau explored Lake Titicaca on board one of his little diving 'saucers'. Despite every endeavour—he went down to a depth of 1,000 feet—the Commander could find no trace of any submerged city.

Certainly, some villages which had been built on the edge of the lake are now under water not far from the shore, and a road or possibly a wharf can be seen in the lake; but there ends the pseudo-civilisation of Lake Titicaca.

On the other hand, Commander Cousteau managed to catch trout weighing over eighty pounds there, and he found a new species of toad, as well as some huge water plants.

As was to be expected, some of the many people who try to discredit any u.f.o. phenomena said that the dives had been made chiefly to find 'bases for flying saucers', which was, of course, nonsense.

More important was the discovery off the Peruvian shore, about 6,000 feet down, of a number of sculptured stone columns, some of them actually standing upright. The columns were photographed fifty miles from Callao by technicians of the oceanographic ship 'Anton Brünn'.

It was impossible to say whether the columns were relics of some vanished civilisation or whether they had been part of the cargo of an old Spanish ship. The same kind of unanswerable question has been, and is likely to be, put in plenty of other places all over the world.

In 1968 a Dutch expedition on a 'dig' at Deir Alla in the Jordan Valley came upon a piece of pottery with some unknown writing on it. On the same site a plaster slab at least four thousand years old was discovered, with a picture on it representing a religious rite, proving that a hitherto unknown civilisation had preceded that of the Hebrews, and of the Canaanites before them, in what is now Israeli territory.

And here is another mystery, this time from India: a skeleton was found, also about 4,000 years old, the radio-activity of which was fifty times greater than that of the surrounding soil; as though, in fact, the dead man had been killed by an atomic explosion.

It is well known that there are ruins in Southern Rhodesia, and in particular some towers with no openings except at the top, the whole site forming an architectural ellipse, in which all the sides, instead of being angular, as is usual elsewhere, are rounded. That place is Zimbabwe, and until quite recently it was believed to represent the most ancient civilisation of the black races.

Then a witch doctor, Wuzamazulu Credo Mutwa, of mixed Bushman and Bantu blood, decided that he should tell what he knew of the culture and history of black men.

Breaking his vow of secrecy, he wrote a book called *Indaba My Children*, which was published in Johannesburg.

After an introduction, the book goes on to tell the story of a people who were originally *red*, and who knew all about radio-activity, robots and space-travel. An evil earthly despot sent them on an expedition to another planet to take prisoner the Mother of all created things, Ninavanhu-Ma.

As a result, the whole of this people and its continent were utterly destroyed, all except one woman of the pure blood and one man of a low caste. These two boarded an 'artificial fish' at the mouth of the Congo.

The woman became the mother of pygmies and bushmen.

Then she and 'Odu, her travelling companion of the old race', populated the Cameroons, where it should even now be possible to find traces of the language of neolithic man.

When Africa began to be repopulated, the Phoenicians came and established a colony on the shores of Lake Makari-Kari in Botswana. They mined gold there which they exported besides a great many slaves. Their city was destroyed in a revolt.

The Phoenicians were known as Ma-iti. All over Africa witch doctors are believed still to keep hidden away helmets, swords and other gear captured from the invaders.

Later, other strangers came and sailed up the Zambesi in ships. They carried the stones from the ruins of the Phoenician city up the river in drag-nets as far as what is now Zimbabwe and built a fortress there; its real name is Zima-mbje.

On the subject of the mysterious foggaras in Morocco (Mauretania), Michel Poirier, a Canadian, writes:

'The foggaras of Adrar show that oases have at times been created by the genius of man. They consist of a network of wide subterranean passages dug sometimes as much as 250 feet below the surface of the desert, and passing through miles of country to collect water from reservoirs in the sub-soil formed by the very rare rains that fall in the Sahara—on an average once in ten years.

'The tunnels are ventilated at intervals of about a hundred yards by shafts called *soggias*. They are still looked after by people trained to the job; but nobody knows who first built them.

'The foggaras are indeed a titanic work, carried out with utterly inadequate tools; they deserve every bit as much as the pyramids to be numbered among the great works of antiquity.

'Even today, with all the mechanical means we have at our disposal, the creation of such a system of tunnels under the desert would present engineers with greater problems than would the building of a similar system in one of our big cities. . . .'

161

We have surely heard the last of the old myth that the dawn of civilisation first broke over Sumer. From now on Sumer, with only 5,000 years of antiquity, will always be reckoned among civilisations that came later than those of Egypt, Mexico, Peru, Gaul and Central Europe.

An archaeologist wrote not long since: 'Nine thousand years ago women at Hacilar and Chatal Hüjük wore jewellery and painted their lips; children played marbles in the streets, and men, like their probable descendants, the Turks of today, played knucklebones.' (*Science and Life*, June 1964.)

Chatal Hüjük and Hacilar lie on the high plateaux of Anatolia, about 180 miles from Ankara.

At Nea Nicomedia, in Macedonia, two archaeologists, Graham Clark and Robert J. Rodden, uncovered six houses built of clay supported by wooden posts, and in them some pottery containing the charred remains of wheat, barley and lentils.

This civilisation is entirely different from that of the neolithic sites at Karanovo and Azmak in Bulgaria, or those in central Greece.

In the Kara-Koum desert, in the south of Soviet Turkmenistan, on the Iranian frontier, in the Poket Dag Mountains, civilisations have been shown to exist, the most ancient going back 8,000 years. Cities in Kara-Koum dating from the third millennium B.C. were laid out in streets and squares, with residential quarters and artisans' quarters, and religious edifices. And in the second millennium B.C. step-pyramids would have been seen there.

Soviet archaeologists, who are certainly the most active—as well as presenting the greatest threat to those who cling to a belief in Sumer as the earliest civilisation—found an astronomical observatory in Armenia, dating from 3000 B.C.

This observatory has been carefully studied by Miss E. S. Parsamian of the University of Burakan. It consists of three platforms, one of which is triangular, and has an apex orientated north/south pointing in the exact direction at which the star Sirius would have risen in the year 2800 B.C.

Armenian astronomers have therefore concluded that their ancestors worshipped this star just as the Egyptians did.

Lepenski-Vir

Lepenski-Vir lies on the bank of the Danube near the Iron Gate in Jugoslavia, though the site possibly extends also to the other side of the river, in Rumania. In November 1968, Jean Vidal said that Lepenski-Vir, which is 7,000 years old, and Chatal Hüjük 9,000, 'will make scholars revise their ideas very radically'.

They will indeed!

Dragan Srejovic, a Yugoslav archaeologist, discovered three cities on this site, containing 108 houses in trapezoid form, some underground shelters, huts made of wood and dried mud, a valuable collection of microliths, of pottery, ceramics, all kinds of household utensils with fingerprint ornamentation, and—most important of all—engraved stones, some altars and a plaque with writing on it.

Certain of the sculptures, writes Jean Vidal, have been mistakenly referred to as 'abstracts', because they do not correspond with our ideas of the representative; but these 'abstract' designs are clearly a form of writing which we have not yet been able to decipher.

All these considerations, Jean Vidal continues, 'confirm the theory that History cannot be said to begin with the cuneiform inscriptions at Sumer, simply because its characters are more legible than earlier glyphs or symbols which have not been translated or deciphered'.

It is interesting to find that the sacred swastika symbol is found at Lepenski-Vir, which shows that the inhabitants were Celts.

The Celts of San Agustin

In Colombia, to the south-west of the State of Huila, at about 150 miles from Neiva, lies the San Agustin National Archaeological Park where a race of men, who disappeared as mysteriously as the Mayas, and were sculptors of considerable talent, erected some curious monuments. It is thought that these people were a branch of the Celts who, after passing through Mexico, Guatemala and Yucatan, continued their travels southward.

At San Agustin there are stone eagles, each holding a snake in its beak, which shows, as in Mexico, that their religion directed migrating Celts to spend fifty-two years in certain definite places, or else thirteen times fifty-two years, that is, 676. (It will be remembered that Mayas believed the danger-cycle for the recurrence of cataclysms to be fifty-two years. In various manuscripts and codices it is shown that the number thirteen, that is the number of months in a year, also had a sacred meaning.)

As in Yucatan, the physical type of some of the statues found in tumuli and dolmens is definitely European, and bears no resemblance to that of present-day Mexicans.

In one of the tumuli was found the figure of a crouching man, larger than life, and looking exactly like a modern Breton peasant, even to the traditional hat!

The site contains numerous standing stones and also, it is believed, megalithic stone circles and dolmens hidden among the tumuli in the forests. The date of this settlement is not known, but it must be at least as old as that of Chatal Hüjük.

In the Paracas region of Peru, some two hundred miles south of Lima, a flute has been found which, though it must be 8,000 years old, has been perfectly preserved in the dry soil.

In a cave at Fort Rock in Oregon, U.S.A., under volcanic debris from Mount Newberg, were found several pairs of sandals made of plaited cords, the age of which is calculated to be 'within 350 years of 9,053'.

By way of comparison: archaeologists, using the rather doubtful carbon-14 method, fixed the age of the Lascaux caves at 15,516 years, and that of the Mohenjo Daro civilisation in the lower Indus region at 5,500 years.

It is impossible to take an overall view of the history of mankind if no date can be assigned to the major stages of civilisation. Historical experts have given dates for certain events, but
not always accurately.

First, because they never take the Flood into account,
though admitting that it occurred.

Second, by neglecting the advent into our solar system of
the planet Venus, although this is vouched for by every people
on earth.

Third, by refusing to credit the coming of extra-terrestrial
Initiators.

Fourth, by accepting Judeo-Christian myths, the consequence of which has been to plunge into oblivion the real core
of civilisation which was developed by Celts (to use a collective term), and to create the myth of the Sumerian priority.

The present book is an attempt to discover what really happened and what has been suppressed.

Hence the myth that 'primordial' civilisation originated in
Sumer is utterly denied, its inaccuracy being obvious to any
honest thinker; it never played any important part in world
history but developed in obscurity, while Egypt, Mexico,
Peru and even Gaul throve brilliantly for thousands of years.

To give a wider public the opportunity to know the true
facts, this book contains an outline of the undistorted history
of man, based upon the systematic study of historically established data; to which other evidence has been added, disin-
terred from mythologics and secret or proscribed history.

THE OLDEST CIVILISATIONS IN THE WORLD

Les Eyzies	Caves (bones and flints)	20–30,000 years
Lussac-les-Chateaux	Grotto at La Marche (engravings on stone)	12–20,000 years
Glozel	First known writing	About 15,000 years
Montignac-Lascaux	Caves at Lascaux (Paintings). Cave civilisation contemporary with the much more advanced civilisation of Atlantis	12–15,000 years
Atlantis	Capital city Poseidonis. (Now at the bottom of the sea around the Azores)	12–24,000 years
Celtic Civilisation	(tumuli, megaliths)	11,000 years
Carnac	(Menhirs, dolmens, also more recent megaliths)	9–10,000 years
Chatal-Hüjük, Lepenski-Vir, Poket-Dag and others		8–10,000 years
Fort Rock, Oregon	(Plaited cord sandals)	9–10,000 years
Egyptian	Pre-dynastic, period of gods	10,000 years
	Semi-divine Kings in Abydos	8,000 years
	Mena (Thinite period) (I & II dynasties) (The Palermo Stone bears a V dynasty inscription, the oldest document in the world)	5,200–6,000 years

About 2200 B.C. |
Mayan	Teotihuacan, Cuicuilco (Huastecs, Olmecs, Totonacs; little is known about these people, but they are believed to be from the Gulf)	5–10,000 years
Incan	(Peru, Bolivia, Colombia, Tiahuanaco)	9–10,000 years
Dhun Aonghus Fort	(One of the 3 Isles of Aran) (Series of concentric stone walls; Celtic)	5,500–8,000 years
Oudh	(Anciently Ayodhya, the first Aryan settlement)	About 8,000 years

DEEPER MYSTERIES

CHAPTER TWELVE

THE MYSTERY OF THE PYRAMIDS

Certainly tons of books have been written about the pyramids without getting much nearer to any solution of the mystery. It seems probable that, like the tumuli, they were an architecturally stylised form of very ancient prehistoric monuments; but the questions is, when were they built and for what purpose?

It is not proposed to study the question of their date in this book, but to concentrate particularly upon the reason for their erection and—for the first time, it is believed—to reveal, by reference to the most secret sources, the scientific and cosmic laws on which the construction was based.

An Atlantean Form

It is no mere coincidence that Gauls, Brythons, Central European peoples, Egyptians, Mayas and Incas all adopted the tumulus or pyramid for their funerary structures.

The processes of civilisation, including the development of science and the arts, of industry and the various forms of social life, are ordered in the subconscious by hereditary impulses, that is to say by the action of memory-chromosomes.

The reason why we have 'invented' the steam engine, the turbine and atomic propellants is because our far-off ancestors bequeathed to us the impulse towards mechanical formulae and a special talent for developing them in the sense of the original momentum.

Celts built houses because it was their destiny to choose that form of construction. On a higher, more spiritual plane, they built pyramids, because in a previous civilisation monuments of that type had been erected.

Traditionally and intuitively, people have always pictured Atlantean monuments as pyramidal. On this supposition, the pyramid may be seen as a heritage from Atlantis, and its original conception—whether terrestrial or extra-terrestrial—must have been evolved at an epoch infinitely distant.

The fact that this kind of structure involves very high technical skill, might indicate that it derives from a form of architecture and science beyond our earthly progress.

Which again could lead to the notion of a universal lifeform in which all realms of nature obey imperative evolutionary dicta specific for each race and each genus. This in its turn inspires the thought that on all planets of the same kind men will build houses and make pottery in more or less similar ways; that swallows will build their nests in one way and peacocks in another; that oak trees will spread their branches and cypresses will be tapering; that daisies will shut their eyes at night and laburnum blossom will be pendulous.

Study of the pyramids and their mysteries has shown that the scientific knowledge governing their shape and their construction could have descended only from the Higher Ancestors in Atlantis, or from even farther back in time.

That is also the opinion of the Master of Angles.

Earth's Vital Forces

Earth and water above the biosphere hold enormous reserves of the life forces. These forces radiate negatively against the positive forces from above, and reunion takes place in an ideal zone where water in the form of ionised plasma is affected neither positively nor negatively by polarisation.

Some thousands of years ago it was at this level that the earth received 'the kiss of heaven', which was symbolised by the fertilisation of a virgin—very often the king's daughter— by a priest or a hero, at some high place such as the top of a

169

truncated Mexican pyramid or a Sumerian ziggurat. A child born of this mystic union was believed to incorporate the highest human qualities with certain others of a divine nature.

Differing in inspiration and architecture, the pyramids of Egypt and the pyramidal tumuli of ancient Mexico and Celtic lands had diverse purposes.

The Mexicans hoped to ensure peace between God and Man; the Egyptians planned to preserve their bodies for the length of time they would have to spend in purgatory—estimated at 3,000 years—before being reincarnated in the Green Paradise or in another world.

Technically the procedure may be explained as follows: at the base of the pyramid, as near as possible to the level of subterranean water, the vital waves permeating the earth's crust must be concentrated. These (negative) waves flow gradually towards the top of the pyramid, accelerating as the conductor—that is, each face of the pyramid—becomes more tapering. Finally, the electric fluid passes out at the apex. Thus the cavities inside the pyramid (niches, chambers or mastabas) are drained of their electricity, as happens in a Faraday cell; and so a sort of biological vacuum is obtained.

This phenomenon has never been studied academically, but its results are well known. For instance, mould does not develop in enclosed caves—as was seen at Montignac-Lascaux before 1942—instead, things are, as it were, mummified; seeds do not germinate, as was demonstrated on the famous occasion when some grains of wheat found in one of the Egyptian pyramids was sown in the ground and proved to be fertile 4,000 years after being buried with the Pharaoh. In short, all life is arrested in a biological vacuum, is in a neutral state, as though life and time were in suspension.

Farmers are well aware that, for similar reasons, seeds enclosed in a pot, beets in a silo, potatoes stored in a cellar, ham wrapped in a 'shroud' and hung in a flue, will keep a great deal better than in the open air.

In 1905, the leader of a French expedition to Bolivia found some funerary provisions in a cave, including a piece of mummified beef, and thought it might be a good idea to try cooking it. The aroma of the resultant stew was so appetising that the members of the expedition tasted it and declared it to be delicious!

The Celts realised the possibilities of a vacuum, and used to preserve fish by burying it in a jar, or sometimes in a double jar, producing double centrifugation.

The Saqqarah Pyramid

The most brilliant of architects and physicians in Egypt was Imhotep, who reconstructed the very ancient Saqqarah Pyramid, and was a Healer celebrated throughout the countries of the Mediterranean basin nearly 5,000 years ago.

From time immemorial, going back to the building of Memphis, the site of Saqqarah, fifteen or sixteen miles south of Cairo, was known as the 'plain of happy burial', just as was later the Valley of Kings near Thebes of the Hundred Gates.

Between Memphis and the pyramid, which dates from about the third dynasty, was, also from very early days, the Serapeum where lay, hermetically sealed, the mummified remains of the Apis bulls, symbols of the first initiators and genitors, who repopulated Egypt after the Flood.

Neither archaeologists nor Egyptologists seem to have troubled to find out why certain parts of the soil of Egypt, especially at Saqqarah, enjoyed a great reputation both among the populace and the priestly hierarchy, for miraculous powers of healing, of mummification and preparation for eternal life.

The Pharaoh Zoser I had his tomb built in the Saqqarah pyramid, and it is thought that Imhotep entirely replanned it, so as to ensure that it had all the necessary potency; it was found that two later pyramids were erected to enclose the first, all three being built like Mexican tumuli, though without the external stairway and without a temple to crown the summit.

Underground is a maze of passages, well below the superstructure of the royal mastaba that covers the vertical shaft at the foot of which lies the king's sarcophagus. The whole structure has the power to mummify. The bodies of the Pharaoh's family also rest there.

A pyramid is, in fact, a condenser, and its forces are diffused from the apex along its sides, to accumulate in the base which holds the cavity or tomb.

These forces are cosmic in origin, but they take effect subterraneously as a result of their refraction by isolating strata of the earth.

Imhotep probably encased the original small pyramid of Saqqarah in order that the burial chamber of King Zoser should be at a specific distance from the summit. If this hypothesis is correct, the ideal proportions for a pyramid, either to contain a mummy or for initiatory purposes, would be: base 22 m, slopes 21 m, height 14 m.

This would ensure that the cavity was affected by neutralising waves, corresponding with what the Master of Angles calls the biological vacuum.

The Royal Burial Chamber in the Pyramid of Cheops

In the pyramid of Cheops, the king's burial chamber lies about one-third of the way up the monument.

An entrance to the pyramid has been made in the north face, a dozen or so yards from the ground, then there is a long tunnel, more like an irregular cave, quite impossible to describe in detail. At the end of this, the visitor as if he were at the bottom of a pot-hole from which he has to climb out via some steps, a ladder and a steep bank. No one subject to claustrophobia or to palpitations should attempt the climb. For it is a real climb! It may be thought of like one of the steeper escalators in the London Underground, or rather of the shaft of the escalator without the stairs, but just as long and just as steep!

The incline is paved with slabs of iron, with wooden batons at regular intervals to steady the climber's feet. The partitions are of plain stone, smooth and square-cut. At the top of the incline, which is known as the Great Gallery, lies the burial chamber of the king, which is something like 30 feet long, 15 feet wide and 16 feet high. Two vents, ingeniously contrived in the masonry, communicate with the outer air, without allowing daylight to penetrate along their labyrinthine courses. Finally, to the right of the entrance, is the empty coffin made of polished red granite, 6 feet 6 inches long, about 27 inches wide and 33 inches deep.

Tradition gives the cubic contents of the burial chamber as equal to those of the Brazen Sea of Solomon's temple, a foolish story on the same level as predictions made by measurements of the interior of the pyramid.

The Sea of Brass—*yam moustak* in Hebrew—was, so says the Bible, a large round basin made of molten brass, ten cubits in diameter (*about 15 feet*) five cubits deep and having a circumference of 30 cubits. 'It was an handbreadth thick, and the brim was wrought ... with flowers of lilies'. It stood upon twelve oxen, also made of brass.

The priests performed their ritual ablutions in this vessel. It was broken up by the Chaldeans at the time of the destruction of the temple and the metal was carried away to Babylon.

The measurements of the Sea of Brass may have been exaggerated, but no real comparison can be made between its volume and that of the tomb, which must have been at least double the size.

The King's burial chamber is a cavity eminently suitable for the purpose of natural mummification, but it is also a place for meditation, where psychic powers could be greatly intensified.

Egyptian initiates, it is said, knew how to practise a sort of mental disintegration of matter, which they called separating the soul from the body.

In the *Harris Magic Papyrus* (discovered and brought to Paris in 1789) it is written that 'the adept must remain in the "casket" of the pyramid for three days and three nights irradiated by the higher forces, before he can hope to dissever soul and body.'

Usurpers of the Tombs

It has never been known whether the pyramid of Cheops contained a body at any time. It probably did, even if illicitly.

Actually, those who broke into the pyramids were not always bent on pillage; sometimes they were believers who, in the hope of attaining the Green Paradise promised by the priests, appropriated the place of a sovereign in order to benefit by the wonderful properties of the 'chamber of immortality'. They felt sure that if their families or their servants buried them in a pyramid, their bodies would unfailingly pass through the three thousand years of purgatory and enable them to wake up to another life. If during this time of waiting a mummy disintegrated, its owner would be reincarnated in the body of an animal.

It is interesting to find that some of the mummies of kings or Pharaohs that have been found intact recently had well and truly passed the 3,000 year mark.

By the functioning of some mysterious defensive system, no radiographer nor clairvoyant has ever succeeded in locating a tomb hidden in the side of a mountain, even in the Valley of Kings.

The Curse of the Dead

This has nothing to do with the famous 'curse of Pharaoh' said to have fallen upon the discoverers of Tutankhamen's tomb, especially since Howard Carter, the leader of the expedition, enjoyed a long life. At the same time, it is worth drawing attention to a curious coincidence connected with an archaeological investigation at Chichen Itza in Mexico.

In April 1968 a 'dig' was in progress, and a crane was used with the help of an air-lift, to extract from the mud at the bottom of a shaft large quantities of carved stones; some divers took part in the work.

The finds were considerable—five tigers, three snakes and an idol, all made of stone; the skulls of 250 sacrificial victims,

174

some knobs of rubber, ceramics, hundreds of potsherds, children's sandals made of gold, two sculptured benches and much else.

One of those taking part was a deep-sea diver named Jean-Albert Foëx, who later described the affair in a magazine:

'The anger of the god Chac (a Mayan deity) was roused, and all the fury of the elements was let loose upon the expedition, bringing cyclones, frightful forest fires. . . .'

Even worse was the news received from another member of the party on his way home:

'In the months following the suspension of the work at Chichen Itza Christian, the pilot to the expedition, died suddenly, and so did Alberto Gabilondo, whom we called the Gipsy, chief of the Mexican divers, Dr. Eusebio Davalo Hurtado, Director of the Mexican National Institute of History and Anthropology, and Kirk Johnson who financed the expedition.

Four dead in four months. . . .'

The Neutralising Djed

The Egyptian *djed* is a pillar made of a single piece of stone or wood, the purpose of which is lost in the darkness of prehistory.

It seems probable that the totems of American and African peoples, linked with the idea of generation and of ancestors, have some connection with the *djed* whose cult was celebrated more particularly at Memphis, in honour of Ptah the Initiator. To initiates, the *djed* is the symbol of the spinal column through which passes what the Hindus call *prana*, that is to say man's vital fluid. It represents *kundalini*, the conductor of the cosmic force which condenses and conveys upwards the earth forces, and also certain harmful waves which the *djed* is believed to neutralise.

Imhotep is thought to have discovered the secret of the vacuum in combining the pyramidal form with an internal crypt and negative green rays.

175

A *djed* was placed in the vacuum chamber at Saqqarah, so that its power should be allied with that of the pyramid; and it was in this place, the antechamber to eternity for the dead man, that initiates were able to find the right atmosphere for peace, healing and rest from the tyranny of the body.

These ideas are very closely akin to those of the most ancient Hindu science, according to which the Brahman must learn to enter into a state of grace by identifying himself with the AUM, the eternal soul which is immanent in everything and which is the ultimate cause of things.

Is not the Truth of the Great Vehicle in India today the notion of a perfect vacuum, even the Buddha and God being ultimately reduced to a state of non-being?

It is the concept of the perfectly wise man.

The Forbusch Effect

Returning to the principle enunciated by the Master of Angles, it is found that our earth functions exactly like the cavity of a pyramid, only to a lesser degree. This emerges from an analysis of cosmic bombardments made by physicists, the most noticeable effect of which is to accelerate biological evolution.

The sun exhales something called the 'solar wind' which flows across its planetary system; but the earth forms a magnetic cavity which causes the flow to deviate, so that we receive practically none of it. The solar wind is subject to cycles of activity, and its magnetic field is affected by the fluctuations.

Cosmic radiation reacts to this combination of phenomena, and its intensity in our planetary system is in inverse ratio to the intensity of the magnetic field of matter. The magnetic field of the earth's surface is not constant, and its distribution is unequal. Moreover, there are certain mineralogical strata in the earth's crust in which the magnetic current is opposite to that on the surface. This is the case in parts of England, Brittany and South Africa.

All this comes under the heading of the Forbusch Effect, so

Serpents engraved on the wall of the tumulus crypt at Gav'rinis, in Brittany. Above them are concentric circles which signify the creation of the world in the druidic concept.

A fallen Menhir outside the tumulus at New Grange (Ireland),
engraved with spirals symbolising the creation of the world in the
Celtic cosmogenesis.

The great 'pyramid' of Teotihuacan known as the Pyramid of the Sun. Actually, it was never dedicated to the sun, but merely acted as a pedestal for the temple that was originally built on the top. A splendid stairway led to the summit.

Monte Alban, Mexico. There are no real pyramids in Mexico; the Mexican architectural system was limited to the so-called platform style, as may be seen from this photograph.

The pseudo-pyramid of Cholula, Mexico, is in fact simply a great tumulus, on which a Christian church has been built. 'Progressive' Mexicans are threatening to destroy this sacrilegious church which "insults their religion and their civilisation".

On this and the following 3 pages: Celtic Monuments.

A covered passage.

A megalithic circle.

A menhir.

A circle of phalli.

Neither. There are thousands of these so-called pyramids in Mexico.
At Chitzen-Itza, at La Venta (Villahermosa), at Kabah in Yucatan.
Ancient Mayas were Celts.

called from the name of its discoverer, the American astronomer Scott Forbusch.

Cosmic rays (70 per cent protons, 20 per cent alpha particles and 10 per cent gamma photons, electrons, mesons, etc.) most of which come from the Milky Way, bombard our planet, their trajectory being affected by interstellar magnetic fields about which very little is known. Only the gamma particles travel in a straight line, with the speed of light. All these electrified particles have a prodigious force, something like 1,000 milliard electron-volts.

Thanks to its magnetic field, the earth is to some extent sheltered from the action of the solar winds, which are deflected by the magnetic cavity of the earth, in the same way that certain waves pass over the face of a pyramid without penetrating to the central cavity, that is to say the mastaba.

So it seems that, well before the days of Forbusch, initiates understood the effects of this phenomenon—even at the time of Imhotep, nearly 5,000 years ago.

Cosmic rays (independent of the solar wind), whether they come from the sun, the Milky Way or the bottom of the universe, reach our planet only with difficulty unless their nature is considerably modified as they pass through the atmosphere.

Earth, a Privileged Planet

It appears, then, that our earthly habitation exists in space like a sort of enclave under particularly favourable conditions, since most of the cosmic particles, which have tremendous modifying powers biologically, never touch it at all.

This fact is of such immense importance that one may say that it governs the evolution of the planet, of its species and of its civilisations.

It is known that certain cosmic rays, the gamma rays in particular, produce very rapid mutations. A foetus exposed to gamma rays in a laboratory may develop into a monster within a few days, or into some possibly greatly improved creature but differing from the normal species. Other members of the

177

natural kingdoms also change, but very, very much more slowly, their mutations extending over periods of thousands or millions of years.

Most fortunately, the immense majority of cosmic particles do not attain the speed of 200,000 kilometres per second which would enable them to penetrate the magnetic field of the earth or the Van Allen belts. Owing to this fact, our growth is retarded and our evolution slowed down, but instead our conscious life seems to be considerably prolonged.

If the magnetic field of the earth had been much weaker, as is the case with most of the other celestial bodies, everything would have developed quite differently. The Earth would probably be an almost dead planet like Mars or the Moon, there would no longer be any human beings and our cycle of humanity would have passed long since.

Should we have been anything better, anything worse, should we have come under the control of universal forces? It is hard to think of an answer to that question, but it is fair to assume that our slower evolution ensures that we have a real existence as human beings, and this surely is much better than the everlasting uncertainty of ascesis.

Isn't the present acceleration of history bad enough? It looks like becoming an increasingly mad rush into the future— but what a future! Yet the almost incredible privilege enjoyed by the earth in the solar system encourages one to think that perhaps man too may have an abnormal destiny.

The Sign of the Phoenix

'When a distinguished but elderly scientist thinks that something is possible, he is almost certainly right. But when he says that anything is impossible, he is very probably wrong.' That is the adage of the French Cryogenic Association whose optimistic aim it is to enable a part of twentieth-century humanity to reincarnate in several thousands of years' time, to live in the Golden Age that awaits our descendants.

The emblem of the Association is the phoenix, the legendary bird which is burnt when it dies, only to rise again from the ashes. Its life-span is considerable—Pliny says five hundred years, and Tacitus thinks it could be 1,641 years. Herodotus says that the reincarnation of the phoenix is typified by a young bird carrying its dead father, wrapped in myrrh, from the Land of Kush (southern Egypt, Ethiopia and Arabia) where it died, to the sanctuary at Heliopolis.

The ancients believed this fable, and according to them the first phoenix appeared in the reign of Sesostris in 2550 B.C., the second 654 years later, the next under Claudius, at the time when the island of Thera rose from the waves and there was a total eclipse of the moon.

More informed authors say that the phoenix dies in India and goes to Egypt to reincarnate, which seems to suggest a cycle running from the civilisation of the Aryan Hindus to the Egyptian descendants of the Atlanteans.

Initiate priests of the great epoch took the cycle to be 3,000 years, which corresponded with the duration of the 'external' death of bodies placed in pyramidal chambers to await resurrection.

The French Cryogenic Association uses refrigeration to preserve the bodies of people hoping to return to life after a given period of time. (The word cryogenic is derived from the Greek *kruos*, cold, and *gennein*, to engender.)

Hibernation at Minus 196° Centigrade

The process is already practised in America. Since the law forbids it to be used on a living individual, the Society implements the appropriate freezing process from the moment the heart of a sick or wounded person stops beating. The body is then put into an isolating sheath filled with liquid nitrogen at a temperature of $-196°C$. (This gas, called azote, has for some time been used for storing fruit.) Reactions and alterations in organic tissues, which take place in one millionth of a second at a temperature of $37°C.$, need a thousand million years at $-196°C$.

179

A highly complicated chemical procedure is necessary to congeal the brain without damaging it, and this is the most delicate part of the whole operation.

When the body is sufficiently frozen, it is placed in a casket of stainless steel, with double walls separated by a vacuum and super-isolated from infra-red rays. The internal measurements of the casket are about eight feet by two feet, and it contains fifty-five gallons of azote, about one-third of which is lost every month by evaporation.

As may be imagined, 'cryogenisation' is an expensive business—something like £8,000 for the actual process, plus about £2,000 for the permanent casket, and £100 a year for topping up the liquid.

A body treated in this way may remain in a fit state for resurrection for several centuries, until such time as science makes de-freezing and reanimation by massage of the heart possible.

The Association already has a 'dormitorium' near Bastia in Corsica, which will hold fifty caskets. It is built deep down below the surface of the ground, and so constructed as to resist earthquakes and atomic shocks.

Some hundreds of French people have by now joined the Association, if only as sympathisers; and in America there are thousands of members. The bodies of several Americans have been cryogenised, and buried in the cemetery at Phoenix, Arizona and in the Washington Memorial Park of New York.

Travelling in Time

The chances of resurrection on this system are at present nil; but it is hoped that before a century has passed science will have found a solution to the problem. Animal sperm cells kept at a low temperature have already been proved to remain fertile. It was even found possible to freeze the brain of a cat for seven months at a temperature of $-20°$, and the cat returned to normal life at the end of that time.

Obviously, the freezing process does not of itself put anyone at risk, since it is practised on someone who is already dead. Normally, a dead man has every chance of staying dead. Anyone who is cryogenised has some chance of being revived in a hundred years' time, and probably a greater chance at a later date.

In any case, it is very sure that when we reach the year A.D. 2000 cryobiology will be a very up-to-date science.

'By the year 2100,' says the Vice-President of the Association, 'everything we can imagine now will be achieved. After that date, we shall be able to do things that we cannot even imagine at present.'

Perhaps that is carrying optimism rather far. At any rate, if by a miracle the earth should escape the next great cataclysm —which seems to be almost inevitably in prospect—every sort of miracle will be possible, including travel in time, which in itself has all the advantages of all the other miracles put together.

To go into the future? A time-machine! To go back into the past, relive a great romance, an exciting adventure? A time-machine!

To die at eighty.... Why should one, if some day it is possible to be young again, if one can have the body and the knowledge of the third millennium A.D. while living in the days of Cleopatra or Joan of Arc?

Predictions for the Years 1970 to 2100

One day the earth will come to an end, Jean Rostrand prophesies: 'The human race will disappear, as dinosaurs and stegocephalia have gone. All life will cease and the earth, a dead asteroid, will revolve everlastingly in boundless space. Nothing will be left of any human or superhuman civilisations, discoveries, philosophies, ideals, religions.'

No doubt all that is true as regards terrestrial civilisation, but it is just possible that man may be able to emigrate to other planets and continue to work out his strange destiny there.

181

However that may be, the Cryogenic Association is publishing a list of predictions covering the next hundred and thirty years, with a view to sustaining its members' faith in science and the possibility of resurrection. The predictions have been set out in *Profile of the Future* by Arthur C. Clarke and six groups of international experts.

'The earth will have no more than five milliard inhabitants, because of birth control. A considerable proportion of their food will consist of synthetic proteins and of products resulting from intensive exploitation of the seas. Controlled atomic fission will provide all necessary power. The sea beds will be a source of fresh mineral wealth. Rockets with some form of nuclear propellant will explore space beyond our solar system. Mars will be colonised and the moon industrialised.

'All the organs except the brain will be replaceable by artificial substitutes, and all diseases will be completely eradicted.

'Chemical intervention will make it possible to correct hereditary defects at the embryo stage.

'An elementary form of life will be created artificially.

'Many kinds of activities, such as domestic or routine office work, will to a great extent be performed by robots. . . .

'Anyone will be able to communicate instantly with anyone else all over the world.

'Machines with a high I.Q. will carry out various mental tasks such as translation, and will take decisions.

'The pleasantest pastime will be to settle down to study. Vehicles will move on ballistic trajectories.

'There will be numerous individual helicopters thanks to the distribution of power by wireless means.

'Continental defence will be secured by anti-missile ground–air and air–air projectiles and by guided rays.'

To this programme, which will surely make people want to be alive in the year 2100, will be added further and equally remarkable discoveries.

'Inter-stellar flight at the speed of light by means of anti-gravity will make it possible to get in touch with extra-terrestrial beings. Man will be able to acquire a super-intelligence

182

either by swallowing pills or by putting himself under the direction of a teacher.

'Animals bred for intelligence will be set to perform everyday chores.

'Thought transference will be practised freely, old age will be overcome and human immortality achieved.'

The first great results will be seen in the year 2000, with a universal language and literature, newspapers printed at home, the elimination of hereditary disabilities, automatic motor ways.

A.D. 2010 chemical improvement of brain-power.

A.D. 2030 contact with extra-terrestrials, transmutation of matter.

A.D. 2050 anti-gravitation, education, without schooling, by injection of information into the brain.

A.D. 2100 extra-terrestrial encounters; immortality.

What Use should We be in the Year 2100?

This sanguine view of the future, which must nevertheless be taken seriously if only to hearten us, is not without its hazards.

At least four serious dangers seem to be involved in the speeding up of history and the evolution of civilisation:

1 The proliferation of species, which will demand appalling, but essential, holocausts within the next few years.

2 Racial wars, already simmering between the white and the yellow races, will take place.

3 The invasion of Europe and America by the yellow races, for many reasons believed to be unavoidable when the cycle of white civilisation approaches its end, probably in the course of the third millennium.

4 The development of a new form of existence in which the laws of necessity will compel us to eliminate everything concerned with the old system of love, anthropocentrism, egotistical middle-class sentimentality.

That is neither an aspiration nor a political manifesto, but

183

the future as seen by one who tries to take an unbiased view of history.

If all this were to come to pass, people resuscitated by cryobiology would, after they had gone beyond the stage of being regarded as interesting specimens, almost certainly be thought undesirable in the society of the future; the population would be too dense and would be disinclined to be cumbered with fossils of no positive interest, unable to work, with no monetary income or means of subsistence, and who, as likely as not, would have to be kept in an incubator or a hospital because conditions of life had become too difficult or dangerous for them.

In particular, it might well be that some of those cryogenised in the twentieth century could neither digest the food of our descendants in the centuries to come, nor get used to the social rhythm, nor, in all probability, bear the irradiation, the electrical conditioning of cities. Still less would they like the intellectual and psychical conditioning.

Even in these days, country people and those from backward places are often thrown off balance, really hurt, by contact with urban civilisation. Cryogenised people would be as much shattered and out of touch with the future world as would Greeks of the time of Alexander the Great be if they were to be resuscitated in our day.

What one hears of the mentality of the Red Guards in Peking, the probable ancestors of our invaders in the third millennium, leads one to suppose that they would be unlikely to saddle themselves for any length of time with 'capitalists' preserved in an ice-box. But what are such possibly illusory risks compared with the prospect of regaining one's life?

If these ideas are worth considering, the problem would resolve itself into putting to sleep scientists and other interesting people of our epoch, so that they might have a chance of being accepted by the men of the future.

184

The religious belief of the Pharaohs in a future life was in fact a debasement of the truth that their Higher Ancestors and the Kings of the early dynasties must have known: the procedure for the biological preservation of the human body by means of the pyramidal cavity, in the expectation that it would be resurrected by scientists in millennia to come.

According to initiates, the instructors of the people of those days still live in mysterious sanctuaries such as Mount Merou and Agartha, waiting to return to earth. So too the Gospels hint that Saint John did not die and Jesus, as we know, was personally resurrected.

In Egypt, the chamber of immortality lost all chance of functioning when the later and sacrilegious practice of embalming was introduced. From that time on, it became impossible to reanimate a body, which had been deprived of all its viscera—brain, heart, lungs, etc. Once again, ancient knowledge had been perverted to speculation and experiment.

The twentieth century, with its cryobiology, has, it may be thought, in a sense recovered a lost or forgotten truth, and scientists have, quite logically, taken the place of the initiates of olden days.

From this viewpoint, there seems to be no doubt that the suspension of life will, as always, be reserved for an *élite* and in particular for great men, chiefs, initiators.

The Paradise of Sleepers—since one must give it a name— would in that case have a good chance of being sited in some northern region, say in the Hyperborea of the ancients, at the Pole, where the inviolability of the sanctuaries would be easier to preserve.

Was the 'Land of the Fathers', one wonders, a chamber of immortality, a place where frozen bodies were kept securely? Why not, if one agrees that the Higher Ancestors were—which is very probable—as far evolved as ourselves, or more so, that they had developed great civilisations, and had invented a technical procedure for survival analogous to that which is coming into use now, towards the end of our century?

There is nothing new, you might say, even under the midnight sun!

If one may go a little further along this hypothetical path, it might be suggested that instructions should be carved on marble or flint in the Garden of Sleepers, such as may have been inscribed on the vanished casing of the Egyptian pyramids: 'To be resuscitated in the year 3500.... To be reanimated when interplanetary communication has been established between Earth and Venus....'

Resuscitation according to Genetics

Professor Elof Carlsson, an eminent scientist at the University of California, affirms that in the future it will be possible to reconstitute the personality of Pharaohs whose bodies were mummified 4,000 years ago. To obtain an exact replica, it would only be necessary to recover the genes of the original man from the dried tissues of his mummy.

Professor Carlsson is sure that the crystals of nuclear acid required to establish the dead man's genetic code could be reanimated.

Later, it should even be possible to make copies of the Pharaohs, and in the same way of great geniuses of the past—musicians, painters, sculptors and so on.

The method of operation would be as follows: 'To synthetise the nucleus of one of the mummy's cells, and implant it surgically in a fertile cell whose nucleus had been removed.... Starting with sixty-four identical cells, the whole process of multiplication could be carried on, allowing the new cells to continue development until they grew to be human children.'

Professor Ernest Karlsen is working on a similar process, beginning with a stock of genetic codes obtained by various methods that would make it possible to reconstruct an original memory which might be introduced into a new body and a new brain.

It should therefore be easy for biologists to transfer the per-

186

sonality of one individual into the brain of another; and no doubt such a miracle will one day be feasible.

Pyramids for the Year 3000

If our ancestors were betting on travel in time and death, in the expectation of being resuscitated in the twentieth century, they would seem to have lost their stakes.

We have never found either a Hyperborean cemetery or a dormitorium; the Immortals of Agartha and Mount Merou give no sign of life; so it seems that only the kings of Egypt may achieve a sort of resurrection, through their genetic codes. Are we therefore to expect tremendous revelations and the discovery of means of reviving dead bodies within the next few years?

It must be remembered that during the first half of this century physicians and surgeons were not yet capable of giving new life to a mummy. The premature discovery of the tomb of Tutankhamen, of Egyptian, Peruvian and Canary Island mummies, was a catastrophe which took all chance of resurrection from these time-travellers.

Biologists are better equipped nowadays, and soon they will be able to reanimate bodies that have been cryogenised or mummified. So we may well expect to see the establishment of dormitoria of a kind such as we cannot yet imagine.

In the cosmic vacuum the temperature is something like $-273°C.$, which may encourage cryobiologic technicians to envisage the creation of dormitoria in satellites.

Some day perhaps an orbital track at, say, 2,000 miles from the earth may be reserved for space capsules containing cryogenised bodies, which will float like angels round the globe until the time appointed for their resuscitation.

No doubt a great many new legends will be developed when the real story of the space capsules has been forgotten. And there will also be the risk of collision with meteorites and of unexpected atomic bombardments, not to mention thunderstorms.

A better idea would be to have shrines built on huge bases, their pointed superstructures rising high, shaped so as to resist weather and floods, and provided with the largest possible cavity rich in azote and neutral radiation.

To sum up, the mystery of the pyramids and of the resurrection of the body seems to suggest the cosmic cavity in which the earth floats, protected by its magnetic field and the operation of the Forbusch law.

This digression into the subject of cryobiology has brought us back once more to the cosmos and the question of resurrection; so that quite naturally and logically we have returned to the pyramids, who purpose is no longer mysterious, unfathomable or an object for foolish speculation, but clear as crystal. Everything overlaps, is connected and dovetailed, and the truth is that there is no longer any mystery about the pyramids: they were built to overcome death and decay and the effects of the 'end of the world', which seems more and more certain to come upon us during the third millennium.

CHAPTER THIRTEEN

THE MYSTERY OF PHANTASMS

Unfortunately, it is impossible to tell the whole truth in this book about a good many important matters. No author can say all he would wish to say, and a historian less than most.

As everyone knows, though perhaps without altogether believing it, the whole world is subject to imperatives, to ordinances, to censorship ... and, of course, to the rules of normal decent behaviour.

The truth could not be told under Hitler, under Stalin ... nor can it under any government which happens to be in power. For initiates the situation is the same: what has to remain secret cannot be told except under a threat of death, not only to the one who makes a revelation but also to the recipient of the revelation; certain things may only be told, or rather whispered, to the very few.

While awaiting the time when all will be made clear, the time of the Apocalypse (Revelation), initiates and neophytes may only learn the absolute essentials, and then under a disguise.

Buddhism, for example, preaches a doctrine which is the absolute reverse of what the Buddha himself said; and the Christianity of the twentieth century would be utterly disavowed by Jesus. The God in whom we are asked to believe is really the Devil, while Satan and Lucifer, under these or other names such as Prometheus, Baal, Horus, are indeed the tutelary geniuses of man. ... Need one say more?

So how can one tell to 'the few' the things that are important, the things that these few have the right to know? Any forbidden truths that can be told here, will be told in a certain fashion, and he who would know must first understand how to read between the lines.

Initiation cannot be given in writing, and never will be until the end of time.

Sigfrid Klein, the French physicist and a member of the Academy of Science in New York, said not long ago: 'Anyone can make an atomic bomb between now and tomorrow morning. But do you think any scientist would take the responsibility of telling him how to do it?'

The Initiate Must Speak

In our mad century, values have been turned upside down, and the staggering advances made by science have not succeeded in bringing peace to our souls.

In the old days, a patriarch, an ancestor, a sage, acquired initiation with the years, for all those words etymologically mean an Elder. Deterioration set in when the priest took the place of the patriarch and preached the religion of false gods.

With the decline of the priesthood, alchemists and scientists took over, and today the young and arrogant are reversing the direction of the traditional stream, by trying to throw out scientists, relegating God to the lumber room and patriarchs to an Old People's Home.

Nevertheless, it is the student who aspires to initiation and no doubt he has a right to do so in the kind of society that we have created, for he is the strongest, the most ebullient, the most ready to burn himself alive in the fires of the apocalypse.

Gwyon the Golden is watching the bubbling cauldron of the western witch, patiently waiting to receive a drop of the mixture that will make him free of the whole globe, give him the power to visit other worlds, to travel in time, to meet God face to face, as an equal. Until the conquest of heaven by giants begins afresh, and the war of the gods that men in ages to come will tell of as legends that are incredible, impossible....

It is thought that the great Teachers ended their cycle of

190

activity on earth nearly three thousand years ago.

Even in the days of Pythagoras and Plato, true knowledge (which had been perverted by priests in their Mysteries) lived on only among a very few initiates.

Scientific discoveries have, of course, made some of the secrets of the Great Ancestors obsolete, but the chief reason for the degeneration of the present age is due to the diabolic trend of our type of civilisation.

If any Guides still exist in the Invisible or in unknown sanctuaries, twentieth-century man has every reason to question their omnipotence.

And the initiate—what part does he play in all this? Of what use can his pathetically feeble efforts be in a struggle in which the combatants are not even aware of his existence? Should not his part be more than ever to make himself felt, to speak?

It is very certain that it is the imperative duty of the man who has knowledge to tell all that can be of use to his contemporaries.

It was for this reason that Pythagoras was in the sixth century B.C. initiated into the practices of the Asclepiads, so that he might learn about medicaments and the curative methods that degenerate Healer priests concealed under the veil of ritual.

Similarly, in 460 B.C. Hippocrates took the science of the human body out of the hands of priests and away from sanctuaries in order to make it a part of the heritage of all men.

The Hippocratic Oath has no connection with the mystery with which certain charlatans like to surround themselves. (*In recent years the oath has ceased to be administered in Britain.*)

The wording is as follows:

'I swear to consider as my father the only who initiated me into the science of medicine; as my sons, his sons and their fellow disciples; never to allow myself to be seduced by any bribe to deal in poison or abortion; to be above suspicion in the treatment of women; to keep absolute silence about any family's secrets; to make myself worthy of general esteem.'

191

If one may judge from this, medicine is the only science in which the word 'initiate' is mentioned, and in which the oath, the transmission of knowledge, the moral sense and the biological protection of the race are the rule.

There is no doubt that medicine is one of the main branches of initiation, if not the chief one.

An initiate is not, therefore, one who offers vague and nebulous assertions none of which can be proved, but a man who gives clear, reasonable, convincing, moral explanations of any mysteries he is obliged to divulge.

Cerebral Waves in Man

The cavity of a pyramid is an oasis for relaxation and for the recharging of the brain's electrical batteries.

Some Initiates used to go there to find an atmosphere that would help them to meditate, others spent time in crypts and caves, knowing how terribly the human spirit is battered in everyday life, and how necessary it is to eliminate the waste matter from the psyche by bathing in 'negative green rays'.

The human brain both emits waves and receives them.

It emits them by the power of thought, and receives them because it is an actual receiving station and can store up benign energies—or the reverse in the form of injurious waves.

Cerebral waves, shown on an encephalogram, have given some strange results. In one case it was found that a subject was able to switch on an electric lamp simply by concentrating his thoughts sufficiently—in other words, he emitted an electrical impulse.

A cerebral wave of this nature could, by a system of accumulators and amplifiers, control powerful machinery, give the impulse for launching a space-rocket or detonate an atomic bomb.

In a state of peace and quiet, the human, or *alpha*, wave has a frequency of from seven to fifteen Hertzian waves and a voltage of from five to fifty microvolts.

In a state of tension (meditation or thought), the *alpha* wave changes to a *beta* wave, loses power but vibrates at the rate of between 15 and 30 Hertz per second.

Communication with some other brain may then take place, since it acts as a voltmeter; it is thought that this explains what is usually called 'sympathy' between two people.

Can it be controlled so as to convey messages in the way that radio waves do? It has not been found possible to check this, but it seems probable that it can be done on the initiate level, whereby ideas and impressions may be exchanged.

Messages from Other Worlds

If simple electrodes are applied to the scalp, the subject of the experiment immediately receives a medley of sounds on a number of different wave-lengths. A man with a good head of hair and a beard is more receptive than one less well-furnished. In the old days an initiate never shaved his face nor cut his hair. Women are by nature more sensitive than men to electric waves, but also because their hair is generally longer. Since they have taken to cutting it short they have lost a part of their clairvoyant and prophetic powers.

It has been proved by experiment that during the day we receive a mass of emissions, good and bad, in our subconscious minds, and that these have a definite effect upon our nervous system.

This being the case, it is obvious that it is a vital necessity for us to escape for at least some hours of the day or night from the assault upon our tissues by all those more or less beneficial sound-waves.

The hermit who takes refuge in a cave—or in any sort of Faraday cell—to retire within himself, is only obeying an instinct of self-preservation.

Some people endowed with particularly developed brains, or who have simply been accidentally conditioned, may well receive radiophonic messages or even television pictures.

Perhaps this may be the explanation of Joan of Arc's 'voices'; she may have heard them not by self-induction (her own thoughts and imagination), but from the Mysterious Unknowns whom she called Saint Catherine or Saint Michael.

To an ever-increasing extent, astrophysicists as well as spiritualists are coming to believe that extra-terrestrial beings, or other unidentified individuals, are trying to make contact with us.

Electric signals can be perceived by radio-telescopes, but it is not impossible that the human brain—which is much more perfect and sensitive than any scientific apparatus—might be able to pick up waves and emissions as yet unidentifiable by technical experts.

A 'revelation', for example, could be a message *en clair*, spoken or televised, emanating from the mind of an Unknown Superior—or, of course, it might equally well come from a demonic entity, an Unknown Inferior.

Messages from other worlds, which should be treated with the utmost reserve, are, as far as we know at present, emitted on cerebral *beta* waves.

The Mystery of Spheres

Human electric waves are peculiar in that they are dependent upon intensity of thought.

In fact, one knows nothing about them except through recorded manifestations. It appears that these waves play some part—and also some practical jokes—which cannot be attributed to chemical reaction.

Converters (glass beads hermetically sealed) form a part of diodes (lamps etc. with two electrodes and therefore highly sensitive).

In electrical factories, the girl workers wear a slip, brassière, overall, gloves and a veil over their hair; and if one of them touches a converter during her menstrual period, it is discarded because it will have become useless. It is thought that some kind of electrical reaction causes a change in the glass beads. Normally, women in the factories take over a different job for four or five days during their 'periods'. In some factories red-haired girls are never allowed to work on cathodes.

The little glass balls which form the converter call attention to the mystery of spheres which, as is well known, are of great importance in magic and in physics—and in the universe.

The properties of spheres are analogous to those of pyramids insofar as no electric radiation takes place in their cavities, or in other words, electricity remains on the surface.

Physicists are not as much interested in these properties as are those who prefer the empirical method; and here is an observation made by experiment:

If you suffer from insomnia or if you just want to sleep more soundly at night ... if you want to be kept safe from ghosties and ghoulies, lang-leggity beasties, and things that go bump in the night, festoon your bed with rings of round beads. They will give you protection, a zone of relative neutrality in which you will be able to relax more completely.

The result would no doubt be the same or possibly even better if you were to sleep between two sacks of coal knobs or potatoes, in fact anything round.

The example is taken from on high and from afar, and it seems fair to ask what part do the planets play in their rounds as regulators and diffusers of beneficent waves in the life of the universe?

Phantoms do Exist

Hallucinogenic drugs, yoga and initiation all play a part in helping us to delve more deeply into the mysteries of our unknown egos; implicit in this are also fantastic possibilities of integration in non-visible universes.

Sometimes, however, it is a simple paranormal phenomenon that brings our 'real' wave-length into accord with that of the 'unreal' which occultists call the Other World or The Beyond.

Our unknown ego, which is not identical with the external physical ego, is in some sort our ghost, with a life of its own, which one imagines will survive after the death of the body.

Spiritualists say that the two entities mutually repulse one another, but that when the positive ego dies the negative ego can manifest without being impeded by its opposite.

It is this mysterious entity that is evoked in occult séances, with enquirers sitting at a round table, and obtaining more or less convincing results.

In this twentieth century, it is difficult to believe *a priori* in such manifestations.

But certain discoveries in electrophysiology and in biology may confirm spiritualist theories, since some unexpected phenomena have been discovered in cellular organisms, almost at atomic level, which seem to prove that, after they have disappeared physically, something persists, of which neither the nature nor the life-span is known. The phenomenon is not, they think, something left over from real life, but an unknown phantom existing in a universe different from our own.

Professor Bernard d'Espagnat of the Collège de France said recently that certain waves have the gift of ubiquity. Without rupture, without subdivision, but always remaining themselves, they may yet change their nature and exist simultaneously on several different planes.

They live in a universe, therefore, which the scientist registers, but which he does not understand and cannot explain.

Dr. A. J. Glazewski, an American scientist of Polish extraction, agrees with this opinion, and says that 'we have now been able to prove, by purely scientific analysis, the existence of an invisible and immaterial world. This result is the fruit of twenty-seven years of research into gravitational waves.'

Perhaps the investigations of mediums into this parallel universe will prove that there really is a door through which we may pass. . . .

The Ghost which Tula Followed

To sum up, then, one may say without being too venturesome that every organic body, and probably all bodies, have an equivalent in another world, with which they are linked in a kind of harmony.

A certain affinity, though not an exact synchronism exists between the material ego and its equivalent, to the extent that one may disappear and the other remain, at least for an appreciable time.

Of course the time question comes into the story, because each of the entities lives in a different though parallel universe, and their system of measuring time is likely to be different too.

On this principle, it is within the bounds of possibility that, even if our planet were to blow up, its double might continue to revolve round the sun's double.

We may therefore permit ourselves to believe in ghosts, even if it is difficult for us to understand their nature.

If appliances used in physical and biological observations have been able to make discoveries on the atomic level, it seems probable that the human brain, which is infinitely more receptive, should be able to perceive the phantom of someone who has gone from us.

Animals are particularly well able to do this, and have given many proofs.

The master (or should one say the human brother?) of Tula, a little Boxer bitch, died.

They had been in the habit of going to fish at a particular part of the local river, and it seems that the bond between the two friends had been more than usually close.

When the fishing season began, Tula, invited by some phantom invisible to everyone else, went straight to the spot where her master had during his life-time been used to arrange his fishing gear, then she went on towards the river, turning round every now and then to make sure she was being followed, loitering for a moment by some rocks, but always running back to walk beside the companion that only she could see.

She stopped at the places where no doubt the dead man had been accustomed to cast a line, and came back home punctually every evening, remaining there quietly and sadly, as though a beloved shade were no longer with her.

The same thing happened every time the weather was right

for fishing. Was it only the result of a conditioned reflex, of a habit she had enjoyed?

People who watched the little creature and everything that happened in her comings and goings, are sure that Tula was not alone, but was really accompanying a phantom able to take the initiative and having a certain amount of free will.

The Ghost of Eva J.

R.J. had spent all his life very happily married to a wife whom he adored. Then his wife died and his grief was intense.

But suddenly R.J. appeared to get over the shock and to rediscover his joy in life, to the great surprise of all his acquaintances. He explained the change of attitude to a very close friend.

'Eva is not dead,' he said. 'I know it sounds incredible, and nobody will believe me, but she has taken to coming back every evening to be with me; she manifests her presence quite indisputably. She is helping me to go on living and I know that when she dies for good, I shall die too.'

The man to whom this strange confidence was made, knew that R.J. was a particularly well-balanced person, had never had anything to do with spiritualism, nor believed in ghosts, nor in flying saucers, not even in God.

Little by little, as further details were given, he was able to reconstruct the strange scenes that took place in the haunted house. The husband laid the table for two and served his wife's favourite dishes. No food and drink disappeared, of course, but evidently the ghost managed to convey her satisfaction to her husband, and they arranged the menu for the next day. After the meal, the two of them sometimes watched television, or in winter they sat beside a wood fire.

R.J. realised that Eva's was not an absolutely material presence but, though incomplete, it was undeniably authentic. When he spoke, the ghost did not reply in a voice that could be heard by anyone else, but which was somehow audible to her husband. R.J. found it impossible to explain how it happened, but he was absolutely conscious, in full possession of his senses and in no way the victim of hallucination. The phantom was not a physical entity, but neither was it a shadow or a vision; or if it was a vision it had the consistency of some tenuous form of matter and was quite incontestably a manifestation, though different from reality.

One day R.J. said to his friend: 'Eva can't go on visiting me; she has lost the power. I think we shall have our last meeting this evening. So I'll say goodbye to you, my dear friend. I'd like to be buried beside her.... No, don't worry ... the only thing I'm afraid of is that I might lose Eva after I'm dead, because I'm not sure if I can join her.'

No one knows what happened between them that night; the ghost must have faded out of our three-dimensional world like the afterglow of a sunset.

Next morning R.J. was found dead.

In view of the fact that the story was highly confidential, obviously none of the details could be checked, but there is absolutely no reason to suspect that the facts were not reported as they actually occurred.

Phosphenes

Dr. Lefebure and M. René Morand have studied the phenomenon of the creation of mental images known as phosphenes.

The word phosphene is derived from the Greek words *phos*, light, and *phainein*, to appear. Phosphenes are sensations of light, illusions therefore, resulting from pressure on the eyes by closed eyelids or from the effect of damage to the eyes caused by looking at too brilliant a light, such as the sun, or a crystal ball, or the reflection on a sheet of water, or even a bright star. The effect is particularly noticeable if, after looking at the light, the eyes are opened in a dark or semi-dark room.

There seems to be some affinity between this phenomenon and visions, clairvoyance, the creative power of thought, telepathy, in fact with many unknown mysteries and possibly with UFOs. To this mystery is added that of hallucinogenic drugs and foods.

There are apparently good reasons for thinking that phosphenes are not solely the result of an organic mechanism, but may be a real chemical and organic reaction sparked off by thought. In that case, one would need to know if thought could create or accelerate the secretions of hallucinogenic substances or induce intense irrigation of the brain such as by an accretion of glucose in the nerve cells, which would activate them and awaken in our internal ego a parallel world in which we should be conscious only of luminous effects.

Shepherds, says René Morand, play a game with phosphenes to pass the time when they are alone with their flocks. They amuse themselves by staring at the sun for as long as possible and find it gives them a sort of mental 'movie show'. It is, in fact, a very dangerous form of entertainment, because the eyes can be seriously damaged, and it may even lead to blindness. It is even more dangerous on the mental plane, because the person making the experiment reaches a point where he can no longer distinguish between what is real and what has been called up from his own thought processes; he is likely to end by becoming either a charlatan, inventing imaginary visions, or a sick man, or a dangerous lunatic.

How to See Flying Saucers

Phosphenes following upon staring for too long at the sun or a bright light, remind one that shepherds are great discoverers of flying saucers, and that there are plenty of people who spend the night watching for the appearance of mysterious celestial aircraft.

Such enthusiastic observers, often with preconceived ideas, stare so hard at the stars in the hope of seeing unusual movements, that quite naturally phosphenes are caused in their interior vision and, in all good faith, they see wandering lights and unidentified objects; then, as time goes on, they reach the stage of seeing anything they want to—flying saucers, cigars, straight or snaky flight paths and finally large or small extra-terrestrial cosmonauts, green men, and machines landing in a cornfield or alongside a railway line.

This, of course, is not the whole explanation of flying saucers; foods inducing hallucination and mental derangement also play their part.

It is easy to understand why so many honest seekers find it hard to discriminate between false observations and true.

CHAPTER FOURTEEN

WORDS, APES AND DOLPHINS

Speech is more than an asset, it is a marvellous gift which creates in and around us an imaginary world, giving us the privilege of being demigods, singing reeds. The word, in its glory, is the creator of written language, of thought brought to life in colour, in sound and in architecture.

Yet it is not the only means by which man and civilisations have progressed. To say that, would be to denigrate our thoughts or other means of expression, and possibly our actions, even involuntary ones.

As old Aesop said—more or less—words are the best and the worst of our possessions. Certainly words bring thoughts alive, but only approximately, only relatively correctly. This is why Buddha called words *maya*, illusion.

Heredity transmitted by Words

'In the old days,' said Philippe L'Héritier, the geneticist, in a television broadcast, 'we used to think that evolution could be explained by natural selection, which of course is always true; but nowadays we add heredity.'

Family resemblances, the way we build houses or ships, but also our capacity for understanding mathematical concepts and philosophical systems, are legacies transmitted by our chromosomes; but they would remain only potentials if we had not language in which to express them. Which is to say that man, if he were dumb, could not evolve.

But what perhaps seems the most extraordinary fact to a

biologist is to know that linguistic and genetic structures are similar and act in the same way. Genetic information is inscribed in millions of elements all along the fibres that make up the chromosomes.

'The transmission operates,' says Professor Jacob, a biologist, 'by giving a kind of sense to a genetic message, as if it were spoken in words.'

Roman Jakobson, a linguist, observes: 'The whole is determined by the parts, as a sentence is by words in language.'

A single word means nothing by itself; to give the full meaning a whole sentence is needed.

In short, no unit can function alone, it must be combined with others to form an alphabet from which proceed the rules of composition. Then, as one goes higher up the scale, other and more essential organisms are created. Molecular heredity comes first, but tuition is a prime necessity: a nightingale needs a good master. If it is brought up in solitude it will sing, but less well than if it is in the company of other nightingales older than itself.

A human child, in the same situation, would not speak at all, says Professor Jakobson (though not everyone would agree with him on this point).

Nothing can be done without the use of language, which is, as it were, a creator in that it can explain things far away in time and space, can give general ideas which allow of scientific and artistic development.

Other societies, other civilisations, have different means of communication—symbols, drawings, writing, telepathy, the choice of particular social forms, of architecture, of expression; but they all assume the existence of a spoken language.

Whether through forgetfulness or distrust of mythology and religion, none of the authorities mentioned above has referred either to the biblical axiom: 'In the beginning was the Word', or to the profound Hindu philosophical concept of *maya*, that gave to words the nature of the primordial matter of which the universe was made ... but also of illusion that deceives the senses and leads us astray.

To convey information by the use of language is a part of verbal heredity, but it is not solely the prerogative of man. Young birds learn the customs and the language of their kind even while they are still in the egg.

By use of language, allied to sight, they learn to avoid snares, to give the alarm if an enemy is approaching, to find a cherry tree full of ripe fruit.

Animals have their dialects too. Members of the same species but living in different parts of the world do not speak the same language. An African parrot does not understand the language of an American parrot, but no doubt if an American bird were transferred to Africa and were accepted by members of the local breed, it would soon learn the dialect. Something of the same sort is probably true for migrant species.

The fact has been evidenced by making a record of the danger call of rooks which is broadcast on some aerodromes to scare off the birds, for fear of their getting in the way of the 'planes. The procedure is effective in the place where the record is made, and the rooks make themselves scarce. But if used elsewhere, the alarm call has no significance, and the rooks stay put.

It has been said that only human beings are capable of learning all languages; but this seems to be open to doubt. Verbal acquisitions by animals are only of a secondary order, but they prove that this form of heredity exists at all levels and that it is an important step in the climb towards evolution.

'It is interesting,' said Professor L'Héritier, 'to see what happens to a human child brought up without contact either with its parents or with other members of society. This is the case with what are known as "wolf-children".' He was repeating a belief current in India, where it seems that wolf-children are sometimes found.

'If these children return to human society, they can learn the language if they are under seven years old; after that age they lose the ability and can never become human. Yet one knows that they are born with full biological equipment for development.'

Apes are descended from Man

Parrots, starlings, crows and magpies easily learn to imitate the human voice; but, with the possible exception of parrots, they seldom have the intelligence to form a sentence that is not purely imitative.

Although apes have not nowadays got vocal cords like ours, there was a time when they used to speak, we are told by ancient writers. This statement cannot be absolutely disproved, because the principal sign of regression observed if man returns to a state of savagery is, except for an increase in hairiness, that there are considerable changes in his vocal register.

The ape was venerated in olden times by the Phoenicians and, according to the Egyptians, 'he could understand everything that was said as soon as he was brought from Ethiopia, and was much more amenable than a human pupil. . . .'

Engraved or painted on mastabas and on the walls of temples in the Valley of the Nile are pictures of baboons looking after children, or picking fruit off trees, as faithful servants of man. Apes also played an important part in the migration of souls, either by chasing them away or by fishing for them with a net. The ape was deified and incorporated with the myth of Thoth the Initiator.

The Egyptians were greatly impressed by apes, for obscure reasons connected with traditions of the earliest ages, and also by the fact that, as soon as they felt the approach of dawn, they called out as though to salute the appearance of the sun and clasped their hands in a gesture of ritual or prayer.

From 5–8,000 years ago, therefore, apes seem to have been much more rational than they are now; and if their intellectual faculties have receded considerably, one may suppose that in very, very ancient times they were perhaps analogous to those of humans. Apes must in that case have been able to speak, to pray, to work, until some catastrophic happening stultified them and drove them back to the animal stage.

This is exactly what the Mexican Popol Vuh says: 'Of the men of the third epoch none remain except the apes of the forest. It is said that apes are degenerate descendants of man.'

Hanuman, the Friend of Rama

So apes are our brothers who have come down in the world, according to the Popol Vuh. The Ramayana of the Hindus also says that they are our brothers, on a lower plane than ourselves yet capable of becoming gods.

It is a remarkable coincidence that two of the most ancient sacred books, as well as the *bas reliefs* of Egypt which may be even older, see the ape as a kind of human being and the helpful associate of man.

In the Ramayana, apes were created by the gods at the order of Brahma, to help Rama in his war against Ravana. They were brave and kindly, and they had the power to change themselves at will into anything they liked. Their king was Sougriva, but more celebrated was Hanuman, who became the very dear friend of Rama. Hanuman was mischievous, but good humoured, loyal and immensely brave, as one may read in the Sanskrit text. At a single bound he leapt over the straits dividing Ceylon from the mainland, carrying a mountain on which grew a plant needed to cure the god Lachman of a wound. Singlehanded, he took the city of Lanka, which was held by the traitor Ravana, and saved the lives of Rama and his brother.

Hanuman therefore receives his just meed of praise in the Ramayana, and has ever since been revered as a god; a chapel is dedicated to him in all temples sacred to Vishnu.

In memory of Hanuman, all apes are sacred in south-east India, and in Calcutta there is actually a temple where apes are kept at large and are fed by the offerings of the faithful.

Hanuman is also represented as a poet and musician. Legend says that he celebrated the great deeds of Rama in splendid verse carved on a rock.

Valmiki, believed to be the author of the Ramayana, read this epic, and thought it so sublime that he decided to destroy his own work. But the kindhearted ape threw the rocks on which he had inscribed his own verse into the sea; later, some fragments were recovered and arranged with a commentary by Damodara Misra, to become the poem entitled *Hanuman Nataka*.

The Yeti—is it Hanuman?

Aryan traditions inform us that in ancient times apes spoke a human language.

The *Mahabharata*—a Sanskrit epic believed to be older than the Ramayana—contains a curious anecdote.

Bhima, the half-brother of Hanuman, was one day looking for a magic plant up in the mountains, when he saw an old ape lying asleep across his path. Haughtily, he requested him to move out of the way, but the ape asked first to know with whom he was speaking. Bhima boasted of the glories of his family.

'But,' said the ape, 'how is it that anyone as illustrious as yourself is not the ruler of a kingdom instead of wandering about in the wilds?'

Bhima refused to answer the question, but repeated that he wanted to pass. The ape said he was ill, but that Bhima might climb over him.

'No,' replied Bhima, 'I will not do that, out of respect for my brother Hanuman who is an ape.'

Neither would he pass round the head, but after discussion he decided to go round by the tail, which he proceeded to do. But the tail grew longer, and longer, and longer, so much so that when he had walked several miles, he decided to remove the obstacle with his stick. It broke in two.

He now realised that he was dealing with someone out of the ordinary, retraced his path and asked respectfully: 'Who are you?'

'I am Hanuman,' said the ape with a mischievous smile, and then he told Bhima of the splendid feats performed by his family in the battles of the Ramayana. Bhima asked him to show the shape he had adopted when he leapt over into the city of Lanka. Hanuman rose, and began to grow and grow, until he was terrifyingly large, and Bhima fainted with fright. Hanuman restored him and, as he knew every corner of the mountains, he showed the young one where he could find the plant he was looking for.

Distinguished by his strength, his courage and his kindliness, the Chief of the Apes was also famous for his wisdom. 'No one could equal him in knowledge of the Scriptures,' says the Ramayana, 'and in the interpretation of them. In all knowledge and in the practice of austerities, he rivals even the teacher of the gods.'

When Rama, on the point of returning to Ayodhya, asked Hanuman what reward he could give him to show gratitude for his loyal service, the faithful ape asked only for grace to live as long as the world should sing the glories of Rama.

This favour was granted. Hanuman retired into the mountains, fasting and passing his days in meditating upon his great Master. It was there that he met Bhima.

In India it is believed that Hanuman still lives in some inaccessible mountain, and that he and perhaps his descendants are the creatures known as yetis.

The Mystery of Dolphins

Dolphins are, and always have been, popular all over the world. They have figured in legends, and people say that in the old days they spoke a human language.

Until quite recently this was, of course, taken to be just another fairy tale.

Privileges like those extended to apes were also conceded to dolphins by the ancients; which is to say that they occupied much the same place among men in those days as horses and dogs do among us. Dolphins were believed to be the most intelligent animals in creation, and a mysterious, sacred relationship existed between them and human beings.

Among early Christians they symbolised the peregrinations of the soul. It has been suggested that they owed this honour to their ability to jump high towards the heavens; but this does not seem very convincing, and the real reason is lost among traditions that have not come down to us.

On the physiological plane the dolphin is remarkable, indeed unique, among animals for the weight and volume of its brain and for the number and depth of the convolutions in that brain. Was it, like the ape, more rational at one time than it is now? This question has not been studied either by historians or zoologists, but tradition replies with an unqualified affirmative, and informs us also that it had a pronounced love of music and poetry, and enjoyed friendly relations with human beings —which is, actually, rather surprising in view of the fact that it lives in the sea.

If captured, it was said, a dolphin would burst into tears, but it was never known to attack man, seeming to have respect and liking for the human race. It enjoys following ships on the high seas—which sharks also do, though in their case it is done for the sake of eating any fish there may be around and anything that is jettisoned by the crew.

If this may be thought to apply also to dolphins, there is no doubt that something of sentiment, of play and of affection, comes into it. Actually, they do not usually follow ships, but precede or escort them, just like dogs going out for a walk, with no discernible material interest in the matter.

When they see dolphins, Mediterranean sailors still carry on the hereditary custom of whistling tunes to please them.

Legend tells numbers of stories of dolphins who have shown themselves to be good friends to man.

The Greek poet and musician Arion, who leapt into the sea to escape assassination, was saved by them.

Pliny tells a delightful story of a boy who was great friends with one of them, and who used to ride to school on its back.

209

Of course these are legends, but there might still be a slight basis of truth.

Dolphins talk with Men

Between a man who plays at being a fish and an animal who aspires to live with man, bonds of affection and confidence are sometimes established even in our day, to provide a link with the distant past.

On various occasions these kindly creatures have saved deep-sea divers in distress by bringing an extra oxygen capsule or by guiding them to the surface in a difficult spot.

Tuffy, a pet dolphin at the Point Mugu Naval Centre in California, works in the closest collaboration with American divers.

Delicate missions are entrusted to him, and Tuffy carries them out unfailingly, to the admiration of all.

To seal the pact between men and dolphins only one thing is wanting—to solve the language problem; Professors Bateau and Bastian are convinced that this will in fact be settled in the very near future.

The blunt-nosed dolphin, so they say, is able to imitate the human voice, although its own language consists of whistling, barking, clicking, in a succession of cadences not unlike those of humans. It is said that the language, that is to say conversation between dolphins, is on a much higher level than any that has been observed between other animals.

Professor Lilly has succeeded in teaching quite a little vocabulary to his pet dolphin Elvar, and says that the animal understands and speaks some twenty words of English.

Two dolphins, one of them in a pool at Seattle, Washington State, and the other at Vancouver, British Columbia, had a chat on the telephone lasting nearly half an hour. In their own language, of course!

On 17th October 1967, the Soviet newspaper *Selskaya Jizu* (Rural Life) reported that a trawler sailing off the Crimea was surrounded by dolphins who showed quite unmistakably by the way they were swimming and whistling that they wanted him

210

to go towards a particular buoy. When the spot was reached, the fishermen saw that the sea all round the buoy was abnormally disturbed. They lifted a floating net, and discovered that a baby dolphin had got itself tangled up in it. When the little creature had been freed, its friends and relations uttered sounds that seemed to be exclamations of joy, and then they followed the trawler up to the coast, as if to say thank you.

Being extremely affectionate, a dolphin is said to pine to death if its consort disappears, but at a 'wedding' it shows its satisfaction in just the same way as a human being. Christos Mavrothalassitis, the diver, claims to have been present at a dolphin wedding in the Mediterranean. The couple swam between two lines of dolphins who were, so he says, 'yelling their heads off' to show how pleased they were.

This most delightful and friendly animal has one hereditary enemy—the shark—which it does not hesitate to attack and which it always overpowers. A shark is a good swimmer, but its speed is far inferior to that of the enemy; moreover it has to roll onto its back to use its jaws, which are underneath the muzzle.

Dolphins know this and, confident in their tactical superiority, they attack in Indian file, hurling themselves at the shark's belly with terrific speed, and end by disembowelling it.

When Dolphins tell the History of Man

Never has a dolphin been known to attack a human being. On the contrary, it is as friendly as any dog, so much so that one feels strongly inclined to believe that there really was a mysterious alliance between them in a far-off Golden Age, when all earthly creatures were united in brotherly love.

This is what the initiate Grégori B ... also believes. He dates man's first appearance on earth in the second tertiary period, at the same time as tapirs, parrots, Barbary ducks and dolphins.

Humanity of the Great past had no ambition to govern the earth; it lived in harmony with all creatures, but made particular friends with some of them, among whom was the dolphin, perhaps the most intelligent of all.

When scientists have succeeded in deciphering the language of dolphins, says Grégori B ... they are very likely to discover some 'hitherto unpublished information' about man's past.

In fact, dolphins have kept the characteristic of the Golden Age, which is the *lack of envy and ambition* that ensures good relations between all earthly beings.

Nothing particularly noteworthy has therefore happened in their own history and, since they never mix with other animals, one is entitled to hope that they have in the ample convolutions of their brains preserved, as though in a magnetic memory, the remembrance of important events that happened some hundreds of thousands of years ago. In that case their memories would have reference to cataclysms, floods and the story of the relations between men and dolphins.

In the same way, serious study is being carried on into the possibility, if not of dialogues with parrots, at least of discovering in their language some words which might have been part of a universal language in ancient times.

Parrots can imitate the human voice perfectly, and if in olden days they lived in contact with men, some words or phrases are likely to have been stored up which, through the action of their chromosomes, might from time to time crop up in their soliloquys.

For example, if a particular parrot nowadays often sang 'God Save the Queen' or 'Pop goes the weasel', its descendants would inherit a tendency to find these songs easy to sing, and after a few generations this would turn into a hereditary characteristic.

Animal brains, like human brains, have an immense number of cells, not, perhaps, disposing them to broadcast anything, but possibly registering something. To bring these memories into the light of day would be an almost insoluble problem if men had not the great good fortune to be able to try the experiment with our super-intelligent friends, who also have the gift of words—the dolphins.

212

CHAPTER FIFTEEN

THE WATER OF LIFE

The biological functions of man, as also his intellectual and psychic faculties, are to some extent the outcome of his dietary habits. The part played by hallucinogenic substances in the awakening and stimulation of the convolutions of his brain suggest a possible reconstruction of what life was like in pre-historic days which, though necessarily hypothetical, may contain some elements of truth.

Hallucinogenic Couch-Grass

Post-diluvian earth-men—if one agrees that in the early stages they enjoyed no external 'providential' aid—must have begun their great adventure as human beings at a social level not far removed from that of animals. Food will have been lacking in the proteins needed for the development of muscular, nervous and bone tissues. Having no meat, they probably began by eating roots and fish, and then perhaps they tried wild berries, fruit, herbs and fungi. After some centuries they will have realised, helped by instinct, that certain things made them quicker in the up-take, perhaps gave them extra strength, and certainly made them work more steadily.

So a first set of 'initiates' will have been formed, to keep secret the existence of certain foods that helped them to make, say, better fish hooks or to produce better pottery.

What was the plant that gave them these benefits—was it a fungus, or grapes, or a wild cereal? Most probably it was couch-grass!

213

Couch-grass, a variety of wild wheat with a creeping root-stock, is known to be usable as the base for a tonic, and for a long time its root was an ingredient in bread-making, as it contains starch and certain sugars. There was even a suggestion during the nineteenth century that this plant might be grown instead of the sugar cane, because it contains no inconsiderable amount of compound hydrocarbons.

Nowadays, though looked upon by most people as a tiresome weed with only short-comings—dogs find it useful to cure their internal upsets.

If one may imagine couch-grass to have been the first wonder-working herb, one must also believe that the secret cannot have been kept for long, and that early man as a whole began to consume quantities of this primitive form of 'LSD', which encouraged progress by increasing his brain power. The next step must have been that couch-grass ceased to act hallucinogenically, just as penicillin loses its efficacy with use. So one 'initiatory draught' failed, or rather was worn out, and no doubt another took its place.

Initiatory stimulants must have been continually superseded because the human organism grew accustomed to them, and they gradually came to be used as ordinary foods and drinks.

Two thousand years ago, wine was a divine beverage, which opened the gates to the Elysian fields. Nowadays anyone may drink as much as he cares to pay for, without getting anywhere but into a state of inebriation. One might say that quality has been sacrificed to quantity.

Some day, no doubt, it will be possible to use opium to flavour stews; and already the terrible fall-out from atomic bombs has begun to be stored up without apparent harm in the bones of children born since 1946. One may well believe that many of our normal foodstuffs, such as corn, potatoes, sugar, mushrooms, tea, coffee and so on, were originally hallucinogenic drugs to which our biological flexibility has made us immune. The recondite always ends by becoming a matter-of-course.

An extreme optimist might ask himself whether atomic

bombs, petrol fumes, the appalling noise of urban life, wars, atrocities, alcohol, tobacco, are not major opportunities given to help humanity to win through to a final triumphant apotheosis. . . .

The Great Chinese Initiation

This again is only hypothetical, but it could be much more to the point than might at first appear.

In a very short time the yellow races will rule the world.

The victory at Poitiers in 732, when a great Moslem army was decisively routed by Charles Martel, was a victory for the West; the defeats at Dien Bien Phu and Khe Sanh in 1954 and 1968 heralded the advent of the supremacy of the yellow races. The almost inert mass of the Whites, heavily anaesthetised by television, cars, drink, cholesterol and the cheap Press, lost its last chance in Vietnam; it will not come-to until it is awakened by the explosion of Maoist communism.

The Great Panic will come later, when China finally reveals her contempt for Cartesian philosophy, capitalist mathematics and the degenerate authorities of Western Governments.

Mao Tse-tung said at the end of December 1968 when, to the intense astonishment of our super-strategists, he caused a small H-bomb to be exploded at high altitude on the same day that Apollo 8 returned from its trip round the moon: 'We are progressing rapidly in nuclear science, because we are not depending on the old western capitalist ideas.'

The Whites are mentally numbed by the television screen, intoxicated by alcohol and carbon dioxide, by noise and idiotic entertainments which stultify them, without giving anything worth-while in return. Quite the contrary.

The Chinese, too, are intoxicated, and irrevocably so, by the opium they have been smoking and absorbing for thousands of years past, which has modified the race biologically. They are in general small and slender; but they are strong, lithe, tenacious and highly intelligent. Far more so than either the white or the black races, simply *because* they were initiated on

215

opium. Opium, in fact, whether it acts as a poison or a tonic, greatly stimulates the unused convolutions of the brain.

In 4,000 years the Chinese have become so immune that they no longer feel the debilitating effects of it as a poison, but on the contrary, are able to take advantage of the tremendous mental boost that it gives them. At the end of the twentieth century the Chinese are the most highly initiate people on earth, and they naturally aspire to dominate the decadent old world of the Whites.

Mao Tse-tung is the initiator of the teeming masses of the yellow races, and he is working to hasten the downfall of the capitalist world by unloading on to the foreign market practically the whole of the opium and other anaesthetic drugs made in China.

'Money,' he said, 'will do to buy rubbish. Reason and knowledge are not to be had for pounds or dollars.' (*Thoughts of Chairman Mao*.)

And in secret conferences with his inner circle, he adds: 'The Golden Calf must destroy itself by its own corrosive venom and by its stupidity.'

These prophetic words may give us cold shivers; but, honestly, are we not forced to admire the logic and the wisdom of such a policy? To induce the Golden Calf of capitalism to poison itself with its own substance is a masterly project! If hallucinogenic drugs give special opportunities to the Chinese to bring into use new tracks in the convolutions of their brains, the knowledge has come to them by tradition.

This opinion is shared by some orientalists, such as Frida Wion, who writes: 'After the last war, the Americans paid in gold for all the Chinese alchemical documents and manuscripts they could find in the libraries of Europe and Asia. But most of the ancient Chinese books on science are not available to western translators. The libraries of Peking, Canton and Nankin are immense mines of information, by no means without relevance to the astonishing technical success of the Chinese in nuclear matters.'

Actually, when they made the miniature H-bomb, the Chinese took a mere five years to complete what had taken twenty-five years of work by the vast American industry, backed by the wealth of Fort Knox and by the 'black market' import of European brains.

The Power of Rain-water

Water has always been one of the mysteries most closely studied by alchemists.

Combined or mixed with various chemical substances, it has stimulated men to research aimed at discovering the 'water of life', eternal youth or a means of purification from sin.

Conclusive results have been scant, possibly because the seekers concentrated too much on their retorts and not enough on the observation of nature. Marcel Violet has not made that mistake:

'Every gardener knows,' he says, 'how much a really heavy storm of rain stimulates growth. It not only makes plants grow, but it seems to have a special power of fertilisation that one might think came from chemicals in the atmosphere, perhaps resulting from lightning and dissolved in the rain-water. ... But all efforts to reproduce the particular properties of rain-water by adding chemicals to ordinary tap water have failed; obviously the power is not due to chemicals.'

The water cannot be reconstituted artificially; to acquire its power it must, as Marcel Violet has proved by years of experiment, stand in shallow pools exposed to sunlight.

Animals make no mistake about it; they always prefer to drink water that lies in pools after a storm, because they know by instinct that it will do them good.

Plain Water is Deadly

Elsewhere it has been shown that plain water has an astonishing power as a solvent, and that on both the esoteric and the physical planes it signifies *death*. This idea has been questioned by some, but never by any expert in chemistry. Members of the Rose Croix know this secret, which is no doubt taught in their mysteries. Initiates are always ahead of scientists!

Marcel Violet did not know that rain-water had this property until he manufactured several pints of it in his laboratory.

'I put a couple of pints of the water into a crystalliser,' he says, 'and then I dropped a tadpole into it, alive and kicking. Almost immediately the creature stopped moving—it was dead. I aerated the same lot of water strongly, and dropped another tadpole into it. The same thing happened. So then I enclosed some of the water in a glass receiver, sealed the tube and put it out into the sunlight. This was during the summer. . . .'

A month later, Marcel Violet tried the same experiment again, using the water that had been standing out in the sun, and found that tadpoles throve in it . . . 'couldn't have been better'. The water of death had become the water of life by being put out into the sun. The proof seemed convincing. Ordinary water, exposed to the radiations in which the earth is bathed, becomes vital and life-giving.

'If it is heated to a temperature of more than 65°C. (148° Fahrenheit) or kept for any length of time in contact with metal, the radiations fade and it becomes lethal again. And yet, *it does not change chemically*.

'This seems to establish as a fact that the fundamental part played by water in biology is essentially its capacity to absorb and rediffuse certain radiations that are capable, among other things, of affecting directly any living organism.'

Numbers of experiments have now been carried out by the French Ministry of Agriculture and by doctors, and the general opinion is that 'this discovery is likely to have consequences that at present we can hardly foresee'.

The Water of Life

After several years of further research, Marcel Violet, in collaboration with Michel Rémy, tried to produce artificially

218

water that had the properties of irradiated rain-water.

By using an antenna, he captured various radiations of biological waves, and by means of dielectric filters made of beeswax, succeeded in producing water the effects of which in accelerating the germination of seeds were great enough to allow for measurement and registration.

Quite recently, thanks to the progress made in electronics, it has been found possible to show that 'the use of dielectric filters in beeswax profoundly modifies the graph of the oscillatory currents obtained by means of condensers, by covering the initial sinusoid with a vast number of secondary waves of very high frequency....'

On 17th July 1957 a report on the experiments was sent to the French Academy of Science by two men named Jatar and Sharma.

Upon several generations of guinea pigs which had been dosed with water modified by electro-vibration:

—no genetic mutation was produced;

—some of the animals lived to *double* the normal life span;

—several of them were given injections of dangerous viruses, from which they recovered completely. At the point of inoculation a small membranous cyst developed, which remained for some months until the virus, isolated in this way from the organism, had lost its virulence.

After a race horse, whose speed had dropped considerably, was given a course of treatment with the electrolised water, he recovered fully. Sportsmen and sick persons too have found the treatment beneficial.

Marcel Violet himself—he is now eighty-two—having had a heart condition diagnosed in 1942, recovered all his former powers of work by drinking one litre (about a pint and three quarters) of this 'sun-tanned' water every day. Four months after he began the treatment his electro-cardiogram was practically normal. He believes that the virtues of the water, analogous to those of torrential rain, reconstitute in living organisms the exceptionally favourable conditions that prevailed on earth when life first appeared there. It is a fascinating theory, which

219

prejudices one in its favour because it seems so logical, and opens up such wonderful possibilities.

No Evolution: no Initiation

Evolution is a fairy-tale for grown-ups, said Jean Rostand. The biologist Louis Bonnoure goes still further, and thinks that evolution has been confused with the myth of progress, and has become 'a principle which allows prophets to foretell the future, to promise the eventual perfecting of man and to postulate God Himself'.

The opinions of these two great scientists are deeply disturbing to spiritualists, to whom the notion of progress and discipline are a fundamental doctrine. And yet ... what if Rostand and Bonnoure were right?

The very principle of evolution, without being entirely rejected in scientific circles, is seriously at issue. Darwin's theory of evolution is based principally on natural selection, on the fight for life, on the law of the survival of the fittest and on the heritability of acquired characteristics. But quite a number of exceptions, such as the survival of the coelacanth, and the mutations of the fruit-fly (drosophila), throw doubt upon the theory.

On the other hand, even more numerous observations in all realms of nature decide in favour of Darwin, notably in the strange case of certain carnivorous plants which, in order to be more sure of life and to grow more rapidly make a direct attack upon the protein of their victims.

What would be particularly interesting on the spiritual level would be to know if species have evolved from matter believed to be inanimate to the organic complexities that are ceaselessly in progress, and if, in consequence, we men are evolving towards ever higher, more subtle, more spiritual planes. If it is not so, all esoteric doctrines must collapse like a house of cards, and theological doctrines, ideas about the soul and about the deity itself would make no sort of sense.

For neither God nor evolution are clear, self-evident propositions.

Man is in Regression

Regression is evident in a good many species. It is seen in the case of domestic animals, apart from dogs and cats; they are nervous, apathetic, bored, sullen, indistinguishable from one another; none of them has improved physically, and all are more subject to disease than wild animals. If ever they acquire transient characteristics, they always revert to their original type. Even a thoroughbred dog prefers to pair with a mongrel bitch.

This seems also be true for the human race, for whom ignorant theorisers claim descent either from apes or a mindless nullity. It is indisputably true that Neanderthal man had a quite appreciably larger cranium than that of modern man.

And we know very well that the Higher Ancestors, Hyperboreans, Atlanteans, Initiators and so on, were very much more highly evolved than we are. Here is a very peculiar thing: spiritualists, if they admit the existence of the Higher Ancestors, should also be prepared to agree that man may become retrogressive. Instead, they propound the dogma of spiritual evolution and preach a sanguine eschatology that biologists often repudiate.

Truth has so many aspects, most of which are hidden, that it is highly probable that it is to be found somewhere behind one's back, the binary system regression and evolution (0 and 1)—being in reality no more than the consequence of our intellectual failure to formulate other propositions.

Safety and humility therefore demand that we should stick to Leibnitz's wise and optimistic precept: 'Everything is for the best in the best of all possible worlds.'

Besides, evolution and regression have no meaning nor validity except at an arbitrarily chosen time and in a universe reduced to the dimension of our own minds.

All the same, one is entitled to ask a few questions.

Was there ever a time when bees did not know how to make honey? A time when man did not know how to think, to produce, to create? Except during the abnormal periods of great cataclysms, one feels sure that bees have always known how to make honey, that man always spoke, fashioned, invented, from the 'very beginning', because it was innate knowledge.

And in the same way we have the feeling born of a deep certainty in the unconscious ego, that all does not end with the physical death of the body.

Extra-terrestrial Man

That the earth is a privileged planet in the solar system is certain, but it would be absurd to think that it was the only one privileged in the whole cosmos.

It would not be reasonable to imagine that in the eternity that was before the five or ten little milliards of years during which our globe has existed, nothing of importance had happened in the universe, at any rate as regards the life of man. It is unthinkable that the universe had in milliards of space-time periods populated and repopulated the worlds, so that at long last the Earth might emerge and bring forth a creature swollen with pride and self-conceit: Man.

Man—the ultimate result of the travail of millions upon millions of galaxies, all to produce Us! Or even, for that matter, the greatest thinkers and philosophers of our historic era!

It seems more likely that man has been born many milliards of times somewhere in the cosmos, and not as a once-for-all phenomenon on earth.

There seems no reason why one should not suppose that each planet could produce the sort of humanity that was suitable for it, by the evolutionary process suggested by Darwin. Perhaps aboriginal man was born of an accidental, miraculous mutation?

The creation upon earth by evolution from a primordial atomic globule to a lower animal, and from that to man, appeals to some sort of rationality in us, but remains improbable

222

because, to this day, no one has managed to find a link between us and anything else.

An extra-terrestrial origin still seems the most logical proposition, in accord with the universal laws of evolution and hybridisation, and with the theory—that is attested by all traditions—of a humanity that has migrated from planet to planet.

The origin of man would then be infinitely distant, milliards of years away. But what do milliards of years mean? What does time mean in an infinite, limitless universe, governed by cycles of endings and beginnings—recurrence?

CHAPTER SIXTEEN

ANCIENT MYSTERIES

It is quite clear that originally all ancient Mysteries were concerned first to give thanks that humanity had not been wholly destroyed but had increased and multiplied after the Flood, and then also that scientific truths had been handed down from the Great Ancestors.

The best documentation on the subject is to be found in Egypt and Greece, where the Mysteries were under the special protection of the Mother Goddess and of the Cabiri.

The Egyptian God Asari

Lewis Spence, in his book *The Mysteries of Egypt* (published in 1930), says that the Mysteries expressed the wisdom and the occult science of antiquity so clearly and systematically that, if they had been preserved unchanged, they would have taught us everything.

Unfortunately, one has to realise that accounts of the rites which have come down to us have been so corrupted that it is extremely difficult to make any sense out of them.

In the Valley of the Nile, the Mysteries were sacred to Isis and Osiris, relatively late deities who, about the year 5000 B.C., supplanted the old gods Asari, Anzti, Khent, Amenti, etc.

The mysteries were celebrated mainly at Heliopolis, Memphis and Abydos, and as Abydos is the only one now in existence, and its foundation goes back nearly 10,000 years, it will be convenient to use the information that is given in this temple.

Tradition, as reported by Manetho, says that 'in the days

2,000 years ago one of the largest centres of Celtic civilization existed at Chateau-Larcher (Vienne). A crucifix has been raised on a dolmen, symbolising the victory of Christianity over the ancient religion.

Émile Fradin, holding one of the astonishing tablets from his museum at Glozel.

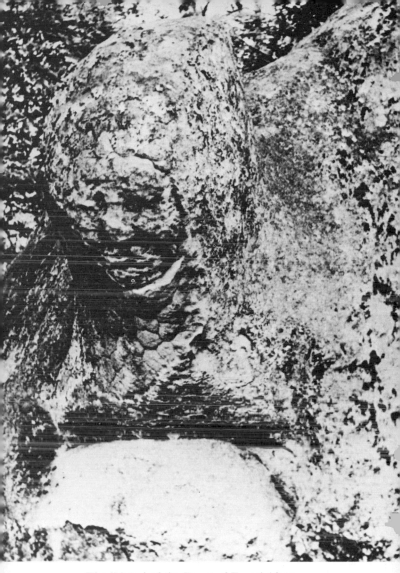

The 'Mater' of the Forest of Fontainbleau.

The sacred uraeus, the symbol of extra-terrestrial initiators, appears
on most of the pediments of Egyptian temples. (Temple of Denderah).

The mystery of the solar barques and serpents. As in other parts of the world, these so-called 'solar barques' represent aircraft used by Initiators; both the machine and the person are symbolised by a ram or a serpent, because Initiators came down from heaven on ships or flying serpents.

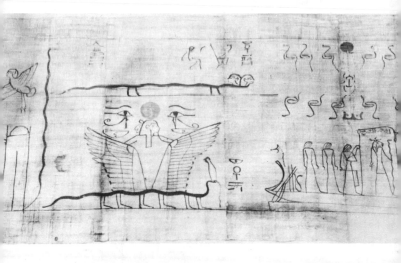

Extra-terrestrial drawing and writing, according to the correspondents of R. P. Reyna.

A specimen of Baal handwriting. Not yet deciphered.

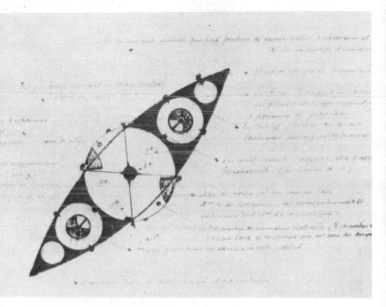

Section of a vaïdorge

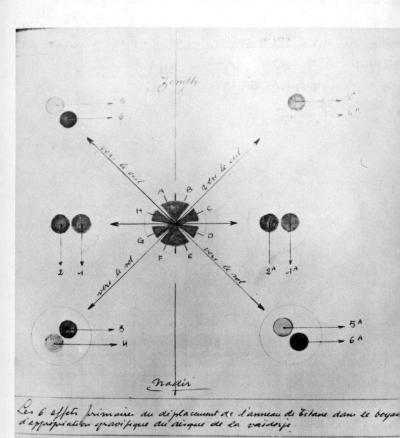

The six possible results of the movement of the titanium ring in the inner tube when the vaïdorge adapts to gravific speed.

before the Flood, Thoth or Hermes Trismegistus himself inscribed on stelcs, in hieroglyphics and in the sacred language, the essence of all knowledge. After the Flood, the second Thoth translated the inscriptions into the vulgar tongue.' This shows that initiation, in the early days, was meant for clerics, that is to say, for people who could read. Certain pieces of information only were reserved for 'the few', which suggests that those who were not considered worthy to receive the knowledge would not in any case have been able to understand its meaning.

Nearly 4,000 years ago I-Sher-Nofret, a high dignitary under King Sesostris III, went to Abydos to find out why the celebration of the mysteries was being badly neglected; it appeared that Egypt had hardly any initiates. He caused the orders of the King, that this state of affairs must be remedied, to be graved on a stele, referring to Sesostris as 'Son of Osiris, the First of the inhabitants of the West, sovereign lord of Abydos, great monarch of the Thinite nome'. ('Thinite' refers to its chief city, This.)

The name Osiris is a corruption of the name Asari or As-ar, who was an Aryan or Asianic god. Isis was always, as among Celts and Greeks, the Mother Goddess (Da, Koridwen, Cybele, Demeter), who has been worshipped as the Virgin Mary in Christian times.

Associated with the Celtic god, and with the Mother Goddess, with Dionysus and Bacchus, is the myth of the coffer, the central feature of all mysteries, containing the remains of Osiris in Egypt, cult-objects in Greece, and everywhere the phallus, the symbol of generation and resurrection. In Jewish and Christian mythology, the coffer became the Ark, then the Graal. It is a memorial of the Ark that saved humanity from total extinction in the Flood.

The Legend of Eleusis

The most ancient Greek mysteries seem to have been those celebrated at Eleusis, a village—nowadays called Lefsina—

north-west of Athens; they date back to pre-Mycenean days, as archaeological explorations of the site have shown. A Homeric hymn of the seventh century B.C. tells the legend of the foundation of the sanctuary.

Zeus and the Mother Goddess Demeter had a much beloved daughter named Core, who was one day carried off by Hades, the King of the Underworld.

Demeter was distracted with grief, and sought vainly for her child. One day, disguised as an old woman, she was admitted to the court of King Chelios and asked to be given a drink made of a mixture of barley, water and poppy seed (cyceon). This was done. By way of thanks she took into her care the Queen's newborn son and, in order to make him immortal, she anointed him with ambrosia in the morning and exposed him to the purifying flames of a sacred fire at night.

The Queen surprised her at the rite and was horrified; but the goddess revealed her identity: 'I am,' she said, 'the goddess Demeter, who regenerates man and gives life to all things. Build a temple here, and I myself shall teach the mysteries.' Then she disappeared, leaving behind a divine radiance and the marvellous scent of all the flowers of spring.

Zeus ultimately allowed his wife to see her daughter again for half the year, the other half being reserved for Hades who had meanwhile married Core. This was the earliest myth of Persephone.

Demeter, happy once more, revealed to Triptolemus, Diocles, Eumolpus and Cheleos, the rulers of Eleusis, the mysteries which were to be celebrated.

There are many versions of the story, some of them giving a more prominent place to Bacchus or Dionysus (Soma, the god of the Aryans, whose name was also used for their initiatory potion), which seems to bring the myth into relationship with the oldest Aryan cults in Gaul and India.

In another version, repeated by Clement of Alexandria, the mystery begins with Aphrodite (Venus) and the Corybantes or Cabiri. His description of the scene when Demeter asks for the drink completely distorts the meaning of the rite. He makes fun of what he considers to be just a dirty story:

'Baubo (the queen) received Demeter at her palace and offered her a draught of cyceon. But the goddess, overcome by grief, refused the cup and would not drink. Baubo, offended by the refusal, took off all her clothes and showed herself naked. This amused the goddess, and she decided to accept the drink after all.

'So there you have what the Athenians hide in their mysteries; it is not worth-while for them to deny it, because I have the description of the whole affair given by Orpheus.

'I will quote his very words in order to bring the witness of the mystagogue in person for this disgraceful tale: "Saying these words, she raised her tunic and showed that part of her body which is usually kept hidden; beside her was the baby Iacchus, who laughed and patted Baubo below the breast; seeing this, Deo was amused and accepted the ornamental cup into which the cyceon had been poured." Truly an edifying scene, and very proper for a goddess! . . .

'There is nothing more unspiritual than the mysteries . . . they are a law without validity, a vain imagination; and the mystery of Eleusis is a lie like the rest. Initiation connected with it is anything but true initiation.'

The Greeks did not believe in their Gods

Clement of Alexandria (A.D. 160) was, of course, a Christian Greek philosopher, and naturally biased; nevertheless one can only agree with his conclusion.

Undoubtedly the Egyptian mysteries 4,000 years ago and the Greek mysteries 2,000 years ago were no more than parodies of true initiation, and of knowledge which the sacerdotal caste had completely forgotten.

A sketch will be given later in the chapter of the Eleusinian rites, but there are good reasons for believing that the mystery of the coffer (which had by now become simply a basket), was that it contained a phallus made of wood or stone, and a vulva; the 'work' consisted in inserting the one into the other.

The sarcasm of Clement of Alexandria is understandable in a century in which Christianity was very new and was concerned only with purity and the spirit of sacrifice. In addition, it must be remembered that fundamentally the Greeks were anti-religious, their mythology consisting of smutty stories of incest, adultery, rape and other jollifications suitable for soldiers and Olympian gods.

In the legend of Eleusis, the story is introduced on a scabrous note: 'Jupiter copulated with Deo, his own mother, and then with Proserpine, his daughter. Having generated her, he deflowered Core.'

As regards the contents of the basket: 'a phallus!' says Clement with an indignant snort. Evidently, he did not know that his own Christian religion revered the rod of Aaron, the mystic almond, in the shape of the radiant vulva that surrounds pictures of the Virgin, and even the sacred prepuce of Jesus, in honour of which the largest Roman basilica in all Christendom was built at Charroux (Vienne).

The Greeks, who enjoyed eroticism, and were aesthetes and sceptics by nature, 'de-sanctified' their divinities by making up fables about them as though they knew that the gods had simply been angel-initiators in human form, who were virile, and sometimes unscrupulous, so that it would have been sacrilegious to put them on a level with truly celestial beings. . . .

Anyway, the Greek Olympus was on the earth and everything was arranged to draw the gods down to earth and to do away with the distance that separated them from men. With that attitude of mind, Greek initiation could not have had a religious character, at any rate in historic times.

The Secrets of Eleusis

The Eleusinian mysteries were basically the same as those consecrated to Apollo at Delos, and those dedicated to the Cabiri at Samothrace. In all of them the secrets transmitted were those of the Initiators who had come down from heaven: their identity, belief in another home far away upon a star, a know-

228

ledge of astronomy, of physics, of chemistry, of magic, of flying serpents, the Flood, the paramount law of the sanctity of human life and the necessity for secret transmission of hereditary wisdom. Such were the initiatory secrets in the Mysteries.

As among the Celts (and in the Book of Enoch) initiation at Eleusis was given by a woman: Demeter, with the rite of the magic draught of ambrosia or cyceon. The bards Eumolpus and Musaeus, who were the High Priests, primarily taught women.

The Eleusinian Mysteries are sometimes said to have come from the Phoenician mysteries of the Cabiri, which themselves were descended from Celtic mysteries dedicated to Taliesin, the son of Korrig or Gwyon and Koridwen.

In the rite, the 'coffer' had a double importance: first intrinsically, and then because it contained the secret of 'the objects'. Since the mysteries were instituted for the transmission of knowledge after the Flood, it seems probable that the coffer represented the Ark, the ship that saved some part of the human race.

In 1696, a reliquary was found near Rome, shaped like a cask or coffer. It was of very ancient Greek date and contained twenty pairs of animals, and more than thirty-five human figurines, all in the posture of people trying to escape from an inundation. The women were carried on the shoulders of the men. It is thought that this vessel was used at the festivals called hydrophoria which, according to Apollonius, as quoted by Suedas, were celebrated in memory of those who perished in the Flood.

Similar containers are believed to have been used in the Eleusinian mysteries.

These facts appear to be reasonable to our twentieth-century minds; but two or three thousand years ago, the creation of the world (omphalos), the refraction of light, the function of the pineal gland, were among mysteries known only to initiates and which it was not thought necessary to teach to the masses.

The Eleusinian rites were the more rigidly kept secret by the priests of the decadent period because they did not understand them themselves. They also felt it necessary to keep up some semblance of dignity by assuming an air of mystery and by giving everything a nebulous significance.

The Eleusinian mysteries which were celebrated every five years, were at the beginning carried out by priests, or *hiero-phants*, and by priestesses, or *thysiades*, crowned with myrtle and carrying a key, as a symbol of the mysteries.

They went on for a fortnight at least, nine of the days being particularly important:

1st day: Assembly of the neophytes.

2nd day: Known as *alaze mystoi*, purification by water.

3rd day: A day of fasting, when the nuptial couch of the divine virgin was spread. In the evening the fast was broken; cakes of millet, barley and poppy seed were eaten, and the sacred draught of cyceon was drunk.

4th day: Procession of the calathus (*coffer*).

5th day: Torchlight procession at night.

6th day: Departure for Athens on the way to Eleusis. Worship of Ceres, Iacchus and Dionysus.

7th day: Return to the temple, with ceremonies of the sacred fig tree, and gephyrism (that is, horseplay) on the bridge. The bridge was the one at Cephisa, over which the procession passed to showers of chaff and coarse jokes from the crowd. The reverend company gave as good as it got!

8th day: Consecrated to Aesculapius who had on the eighth day arrived in Athens from Epidaurus after the end of the ceremonies, but was initiated the same night, a custom which was perpetuated for any who found themselves in similar case.

9th day: Last day, called *plemochoe*, from the name of two jars filled with wine, and placed one to the west and the other to the east; they were later broken to the sound of magic words. The sense of this symbol is clear: 'Knowledge (the two jars) is brought from the west by Pelasgian Celts, and from the east by Indo-Europeans and Persians. The jars can be broken, knowledge having been transmitted to the initiates.'

The mysteries were celebrated in the Spring and Autumn, the times when seeds were sown, corresponding with the greater and lesser mysteries which were obligatory for all initiates.

There was also a higher degree, known as the *epoplię* or *autopsia* (from the Greek *autos*—oneself, and *opsis*—sight), that is to say, looking inwards, ecstasy, being in communication with God and acquiring supranormal powers. Initiation was given in the Temple of Demeter, which was built on the side of a hill beneath a fountain. Entry to the sanctuary was forbidden to the laity on pain of death.

The Fast involved mainly abstention from the flesh of domestic fowls, fish, beans, pomegranates and apples (the fruit of knowledge).

To help them over the fast-day, hierophants were allowed to drink the juice of the hemlock which, although it is a poison, has curative and stimulant properties if diluted. A young boy, who must be of pure Athenian descent, watched over the sacrificial fire.

In later times, men, women and children were initiated, only barbarians, murderers, sorcerers and Christians being excluded.

'Mysterious Rites' took place in the evenings at Eleusis: slow peregrinations through shadowy places, tests for resistance to fear and shock, horrifying sights, mysterious, unintelligible voices, then a sudden brightness for the admission of the neophytes, trickery, phantasms disappearing through trapdoors—in short, the whole mumbo-jumbo of conjurors and charlatans.

The most important moment—and probably the one nearest to the earliest truths—was the identification of the 'mysterious

231

objects' and the revelation of the sacred words.

Clement of Alexandria gives a brief summary of the pseudo-mysteries:

'This,' he says, 'is the Eleusinian prescription: I fasted, I drank cyceon, I took what was in the coffer and, having done the Work, I put it into the basket; then I picked up the basket and put it back into the coffer.'

Cyceon

Cyceon is not the simple drink that Demeter asked for: water, barley and poppy seed, although the mixture could be hallucinogenic. According to old documents, the principal ingredients were wild barley, milk, honey, oil or wine—but every author has his own recipe. Anyone drinking this was expected to have gained a knowledge of the past and to give satisfactory answers to the hierophant's questions.

As regards the 'mysterious objects' kept in the coffer, there is a list which certainly grew longer in proportion to the increase in superstition, the ignorance of the priests, and the corruption of the original secret: the six colours of the rainbow, the six 'plants of healing', a phallus, a vulva, an omphalos (an egg, representing the primordial germ of life), a serpent (the initiator), corn, honey, a pine cone (symbol of the pineal gland, the third eye), a clod of earth, some 'manna' and the *xoanon*, a black stone that had miraculously fallen from heaven in the reign of Cecrops, and with which the fate of Athens was bound up.

In addition there were effigies of gods and goddesses, 'idols roughly carved of wood', Tertullian called them; some were enwreathed by a serpent, in memory of the fruitful union of terrestrial women with flying Initiators.

The handling of these objects was supposed to transmit to believers the mysterious forces which animated them and to establish a kind of divine affiliation.

During the first half of the fifth century B.C., the Mysteries of Eleusis had degenerated so far that people had to pay for initiation. No money, no mysteries! A good, guaranteed initiation cost 30 drachmas, plus a pig, plus a 'little something' to the priests!

The Cabirian Mysteries

The mysteries of Samothrace, of Delos, of Mithra were descended from a primordial initiation, like those at Eleusis and elsewhere. It is believed that those of the Cabiri at Samothrace were more elevated spiritually and altogether of a higher type than other mysteries. The Island of Samothrace in the Aegean Sea is a kind of pyramid dominated by the cone of Mount Saoce.

The mysteries instituted by the Pelasgian Cabiri, who had 'come from the northern seas', assured privileges and protection to all travellers. The Cabiri or Kabiri (the name is derived from Kab, heaven) were traditionally space travellers, who had come in their ships (Arks) to act as instructors to men at the beginning of a cycle, that is to say after a cataclysm. Their sanctuaries were at Samothrace, at Lemnos, at Thebes (in Boeotia), at Tyre, at Memphis, in the British Isles and in Gaul.

Prometheus was one of the Cabiri, according to the initiate Pausanias; and Anubis Schenouda says that Ptah was the first of the Egyptian Cabiri.

They came to Celtic lands by sea and were worshipped there, as is shown in the text of an ancient Irish glossary, 'Samhandraoic, cadhon Cabur': 'the magic of Samhan-Cabur', that is to say, of the hero-civiliser Samaël, Satan or Seathar, The Cabir.

In another glossary, the name Baäl or Beäl (Belenus, identified with Apollo) is given as a synonym for Seathar, as it is also among Welsh, Gallic and Germanic peoples.

Pausanias refuses to lift the veil of the Cabirian mysteries.

'The forest sacred to Ceres, Cabiria and Core,' he says, 'is 25 stadia (*about 3 miles*) from Thebes; only initiates may enter it. The temple of the Cabiri is some 7 stadia from the

233

wood. I beg the curious to excuse me from telling them what the Cabiri are, or what is done in their honour and that of the Mother Goddess. But there is nothing to prevent me from saying what the Thebans believe to be the origin of the ceremonies. They say that there used to be a town here whose inhabitants called themselves the Cabiraei.

'Ceres visited this place and confided a secret to Prometheus who was one of the inhabitants, and to his son Oetnaeus. What it was that she told them, and what more is known about it, I am not at liberty to reveal.

'The mysteries are, therefore, the personal gift of Ceres to the Cabiri.

'They were driven from their city by the Argives (Greeks), at the time when the Epigoni took Thebes.

'The celebration of the mysteries was suspended for a time, but it is said that Pelarge, the daughter of Potnaeus, and her husband Istmiades restored them.

'If they are offended, the anger of the Cabiri against humanity is implacable, as has been proved on many occasions. . . .

'Some soldiers of the army that Xerxes left with Mardonius, who had remained in Boeotia, dared to enter the temple of the Cabiri—possibly in the hope of finding treasure, or, as I think, because they despised those gods—went raving mad and some hurled themselves into the sea; the rest leapt from the top of the cliffs.

'When victorious Alexander set fire to the city of Thebes and all the country round about, some Macedonians went into the temple of the Cabiri, as being in enemy country. They were all killed by lightning and thunderbolts.'

Quite a number of people believe that the Kabbala derived from the knowledge originally given to the Cabiri by extraterrestrial Initiators.

In Egypt, the seven Cabiri represented the seven planets. Ptah was the eighth. The name of the highest-ranking of the Cabiri was Satan or Saman.

The story of the Cabiri establishes a link between Celtic lands, Phoenicia, Phrygia and Egypt from which came civilisation. The island of Samothrace was formerly named Saon, like the island of Sein, off Brittany, which was in classical times known as Sena or Seon. Sein was inhabited by a community of nine Druidesses, who were in charge of the sacred cauldron in which the initiatory draught was brewed.

The Mystery of Delos

The original cult of the Hyperboreans was established in Greece at Samothrace, Eleusis and Delos.

The cult of Apollo as celebrated at Delos is closely linked with that of the Great Goddess and of the Virgins of the North who inspired the poet Olen. According to Herodotus, Olen was the author of the hymns chanted by the women of Delos.

'The Delian women meet to sing a hymn which Olen, a Lycian, composed for them, and in which they invoke by name the Hyperborean virgins Argé and Opis.

'The Delians say that it was from the Hyperboreans that they learnt to honour these virgins and to celebrate the feasts.'

The link with Celts is evident from an inscription in the cave at New Grange in County Meath, near Drogheda, where, beside the thrice repeated symbol of the Celtic spiral, the following is written in ogham: 'a mor an Ops' (to Ops, the Great Mother), and another one meaning 'to the unknown god'.

The Delian mysteries, therefore, had the same origin and the same significance as all the others, but they kept their original purity longer, because the island lay apart from the main currents of civilisation.

In Persia the cult of Mithra, protector of man, was instituted to combat the 'religion of evil' which, so said the prophets, was about to be established on earth after the forces of light had been vanquished.

Mithraism was derived from a pagan religion in harmony with the laws of the universe, and professed the highest and strictest moral principles.

Of all Greek Mysteries connected with Delos and the Cabiri, the riddle of the Argonauts is the most impenetrable. The exoteric story may be summarised as follows: the Argonauts were fifty Greek heroes among whom were Jason (their leader), Hercules, Castor and Pollux, Orpheus, Telamon, Peleus and others.

They embarked on the *Argo*, a ship specially built for them under divine supervision, to go and steal the Golden Fleece from Colchis in the southern Caucasus. A piece of oak—said to be oracular—from Jupiter's sacred forest at Dodona was built into the prow.

After many adventures, Jason carried off the Fleece and took it back to Greece; he also brought with him Medea, the daughter of the King of Colchis, who had helped him in his quest with her magic.

By her arts she rejuvenated Aeson, Jason's father, but Jason abandoned her, and she took vengeance on him by killing the two children she had borne him, and then fled in a chariot drawn by a flying dragon.

Looking at the story again, one might say that all the best-known people of the period, as it might be Einstein, Rigoulot, the Curies, Cocteau, Picasso, Gagarine and all the Olympic champions, embarked on the fastest known vessel, the *Argo*, to go and look for a sheep skin!

True, it was a *golden* fleece, and gold was very rare, but there must surely have been some other motive, and a wildly exciting one at that, to induce fifty heroes—savants, poets, musicians, sportsmen, etc—all picked men, to set off into the blue.

An important detail is that the golden fleece was that of a *flying ram*, traditionally identified with a flying machine used by Initiators.

This particular relic, which no doubt was the wreck of an airship, was to be located in Georgia or Armenia, not far from the mountain on which the Bible says that Noah's Ark came to land, as did also the intergalactic space-ships of the angels referred to by the Patriarch Enoch.

Were they machines such as those seen by Ezekiel, sort of flying saucers with an outer covering, or 'fleece', of gold?

Four thousand years ago, Europeans did not see jet aircraft in the sky, but flying rams, the Assyrians saw winged bulls, the Phoenicians flying serpents, the Chinese dragons ... in short, everyone gave an unfamiliar machine the name which came into his mind by a natural association of ideas. As will be seen, this story is based entirely on the idea of aerial locomotion.

The Hyperborean north comes into the story, too, and initiation by a woman, the Caucasus where Prometheus, the Atlantean, son of one of the Oceanides, had serious health troubles, and to crown all, there are dragons! Truly an astonishing number of coincidences.

Jason, helped by the magic of Medea, overcomes the dragon who guards the Golden Fleece. Medea is obviously an initiate, as was customary for Hyperborean women who were in the old days taught by 'Angels'. When he returns, Jason dedicates his ship *Argo* ... to whom? To Jupiter? No, to Poseidon, the god of Atlantis or, as Plato says, the King of Atlantis.

As regards the Golden Fleece, nobody seems very sure what happened to it. Nothing more is said about it, unless—which appears probable—it came to be mentioned in the Mysteries at Delos or Eleusis.

Jason deserts Medea who, after all, had played a great part in the affair; so she kills her children as though she disdained to leave descendants of her divine race to an ungrateful country like Greece.

Then she disappears in a chariot powered by dragons, or possibly actually on the flying ram—though in that case it would be distressing for a Greek to have to admit that the exploits of fifty heroes had been brought to naught by the ruse of one woman all by herself!

Undoubtedly some fantastic truth is veiled by the adventures of the Argonauts, so fantastic that it was never revealed, perhaps because it was unbelievable.

237

In the tenth century A.D., Suedas started the alchemists off on the thrilling adventure of making gold, by telling them that the Fleece was a parchment on which was inscribed the secret of the Philosophers' Stone.

According to Pausanias, the voyage of the Argonauts was a part of the ancient mysteries for, he said, the ram at Eleusis was associated with Hermes in a legend which he was not permitted to reveal.

The Kabbala of the Hebrews contains the story of a flying chariot, the secret of which could not be revealed even to 'the few', except with bated breath.

This also was the opinion of the Druids about the serpent, 'the greatest and darkest of all the mysteries', a universal symbol which, apart from its meaning as a flying machine, also signified the primordial creative wave of the universe.

In the *Timaeus*, Plato says: 'Although it is a matter of great difficulty to discover the creator and the father of the universe, it is an impossibility when he *has* been discovered to make him known to everyone.'

No doubt he was right, and the secrets remain almost inviolate in the ancient Mysteries about the Argonauts, the Ark and Agartha, which seems to have the same etymology: argha = a long ship, whence is derived Agartha = an underground shrine.

CHAPTER SEVENTEEN

THE MYSTERY OF AGARTHA
AND OF SHAMBALLAH

Agartha is a mysterious subterranean kingdom that is said to lie under the Himalayas and where all the Great Initiators and the Masters of the World in the present cycle are still living.

Agartha is an initiatory centre, and is understood to function on a principle similar to that of the pyramids, the Himalayas forming the external monument, and the crypt being the kingdom far removed from earthly and cosmic contamination. But how could the higher powers of the spirit, intensity of thought and contemplation, be developed in a neutralised cavity?

All in all, it seems probable that the vast potentialities of the human and supra-human ego can manifest more successfully in a secluded retreat than in the open, exposed to the contagion of its surroundings. On the other hand, one might think that, theoretically, beings who had already reached the highest peak of perfection had no need to evolve further.

Light in Darkness

Traditionally, there are four entrances to Agartha: one between the paws of the sphinx at Gizeh, another on the Mont-Saint-Michel, a third through a crevice in the Forest of Broceliande and the main gate at Shamballah in Tibet.

The idea of a subterranean kingdom is as old as the hills, and no doubt it was thought up by way of contrast to celestial cities inhabited by the gods and invisible cosmic powers. It has nothing to do with the idea of hell, but has a connection with the Greek Hephaestos and the Vedic Yavishtha, both of them personifications of the fire inside the earth, but also of subterranean initiation.

On the human plane, there is in every creature some scintilla of the light which matures the secret forces and drives away the shadows. Let the least chink be opened, and what is hidden becomes visible, the esoteric becomes plain.

Our Mother Earth is subject to constant cycles, ranging from wear and tear of the surface by sun, frost and rain, to reconstruction by internal forces. This is how granite comes into being, the foundation of the earth's crust—a fact that has only recently been discovered.

Work carried on in solitude, silently, unseen, is nearly always the most fruitful; external forces are destructive, demoralizing, but the interior forces will recreate and ensure natural development.

Human life itself first manifests in the mother's womb, and the child first sees the light as it comes from the cavern, the initiatory grotto symbolised in the cult of the Black Virgin.

Jesus resolutely refused the initiation offered him by Mary Magdalene, the sinner, the incarnation of the Venusian Virgin despised by Hebrews. Yet the pagan cult of the Black Virgin and of the grotto was so deeply rooted in men's unconscious ego, that it did not succumb to the assaults made upon it.

In the mystery of Agartha, these considerations have a significance which will not escape occultists.

The Vault of Zalmoxis

According to Professor Doru Todericiu—who was probably quoting from Alcide d'Orbigny—Zalmoxis, a pupil of Pythagoras, came to Alesia to teach what he had learnt from the Master.

This statement must be taken with considerable reserve because it is believed that Zalmoxis, regarded as a philosopher by most people and as a god by some, lived at an earlier date than Pythagoras. He is thought to have been the civiliser of the Getae, a Thracian tribe.

One story says that he had been a slave to Pythagoras in Samos, but was freed by him, and went back to his own people to teach them the immortality of the soul.

Herodotus has a curious account of him:

'He had a house built under the earth, withdrew from the sight of the Thracians, descended into his retreat and stayed there for three years. Everyone wept for him as dead. At last, in the fourth year, he reappeared, and by this stratagem induced men to believe what he had preached.

'I neither reject (Herodotus continues) nor admit what is told of Zalmoxis and his underground dwelling; but I think he lived a good many years before Pythagoras.'

The Getae worshipped him as a god and believed that after death they would join him in another life. Each year, by way of sending a messenger to him in his Other-Worldly kingdom, they tossed a warrior into the air, and caught him on the points of their lances, so as to 'give him a noble death'.

The cult of Zalmoxis is regarded by historians as forming a natural link between the Celtic religions and those of the peoples of the Near East.

In spite of discrepancies in the chroniclers' stories, Zalmoxis was obviously a wise man and an initiate, who lived in an underground hermitage in order to be able to meditate; and he preached the immortality of the soul, most probably before Pythagoras. He was not, therefore, his pupil, but his spiritual master, and it was in his honour that Pythagoras said that Druids were the wisest men in the world.

The Vara of the Iranian Plateau

Sometimes the greatest truths are those which men believe to be unproven, but which come to them through their memory-chromosomes. We are always ready to believe in something that happened a long time ago or that is going to happen in the future. The trouble is only that these are out of touch with the wavelength of the present. Hence, men are willing to believe in a subterranean mystery that might intervene in their destiny and in that of the whole human race.

Think of the pointer on a compass: it shows where the greatest magnetic forces of the earth are concentrated, and yet, these are places where apparently nothing at all happens.

241

It might be, therefore, that Agartha is either at the North Pole or under the Himalayas. In any event, one tends to imagine initiatory centres to exist below the surface and always with some sort of lighting system based on highly technical knowledge!

There is a story in the ancient Persian *Shah-Nameh* (Book of the Kings) which describes how Jam or Yima, the son of Tahmuras, the Master of the World, always lives in a subterranean fortress, called a *vara*, surrounded by the purest-blooded of his own people. The god Ahura, foreseeing the Flood, gave the most precise directions to Yima about the building of his sanctuary-shelter. 'Make the *vara* as long as a race course, and its width equal to its length. Take to it representatives of every species of beasts both great and small, of men, of dogs, of birds, of sheep and oxen....

'Take with you also specimens of every sort of plant, the most beautiful and the most sweetly scented, the most delicious of all fruits. These will never die as long as they remain in the *vara*. Let there be nothing deformed or feeble, nothing foul nor evil, let there be none who are liars or spiteful or envious; admit no one with bad teeth, nor a leper. In the uppermost part, nine avenues must be laid out; in the centre six; in the lowest three. One thousand couples, men and women, will live in the upper part; six hundred in the centre; three hundred in the lower. One window must be made in the *vara* to admit light.'

Henri Corbin, a writer on traditional history, says that the *vara* has doors and windows which themselves emanate light, 'both created and uncreated'.

Shamballah or K.B.L.

It is thought in initiatory circles that the predominance of the yellow races is near and inevitable, and this implies the end of the ascendancy of the white races.

Once again, only those will be saved who have sought refuge in high places.

There is, however, one sect—activated partly by spiritual

242

motives, partly by political—called the 'Grand Lodge of Vril', which is trying to create a sort of fraternal union between West and East, and has for some odd reason installed the old Germanic god Wotan, whom the Scandinavians named Odin, in a sort of Agartha which they call *Kambala* or Shamballah.

It appears that Ferdinand Ossendowski and René Guénon discovered some similarity between Shamballah and Agartha.

According to the author of *Beasts, Men and Gods*, the subterranean people of Agartha have attained the highest degree of knowledge, and number eight million persons, living under the rule of the Master of the World. The Indo-Tibetan occult forces of the East are believed by the Grand Lodge of Vril to be the sole repositories of the most ancient Aryan traditions.

The Master of the Three Worlds enthroned at Shamballah or K.B.L. is named Lucifer or Odin. The forces of K.B.L., the principles of which are set out in the Vedas and the Bardo Thödol, will act as a synarchy 'to unite the yellow races, as the most numerous, with the fair nordic races, as the most capable, in a joint struggle against the forces of evil'.

The K.B.L. forces are of a magical nature and result from the four main traditions of the world—Tibetan, Hindu, Egyptian, Germanic, all of which are polarised on a fifth tradition, that of Shamballah or subterranean Free Masonry.

The external representative on the earth's surface is the Grand Lodge of Vril.

Let it be said at once that the present writer does not agree with the initiatory claims of the sect, and still less with its politics. The Grand Lodge of Vril (G.L.V.) relies on documents which seem doubtfully authentic, and professes ideas that are fundamentally opposed to his own. At the same time, he feels that it is only right to set down the teaching of the G.L.V., if only because it differs so radically from what he himself believes to be true.

The Luminous Race

'The Master of the Three Worlds, whose initials are K.R.T.K.M., reigns at Shamballah over a community of

Magi, the *Green Men*, who constitute the cosmic synarchy Tchun-Yung, or the Direct Middle Way'. These magi are the descendants of Venusian ancestors and claim to be the successors to Zoroaster and Mahomet; their mission is to revive the 'true ritual of the Black Stone'.

The foundation of the sanctuary of Shamballah goes back, according to K.B.L. statements, to the year 701,969 of the era of Lucifer. (The name Lucifer is, of course, used here in its literal sense of 'light-bringer'.)

'The next Buddha will come from the West and from the North, and will be the Kalki-avatar of the Hindus, or Kundaliniavatar, who will wear on his finger the metal ring of Genghis Khan. His coming will mark the return of the Golden Age, and will precede the advent of the *luminous race*, contemporary with the resurrection of Mu or Tao-Land.

'It will be the end of the Kali-Yuga, the casting out of the Jotün and the cacodaemons from the governmental centres of the earth, and of the 100,000 years of evil karma inherited from the darkness of Atlantis.'

It is difficult to find one's way around this maze; it is not easy to see just what part is to be played by the 'masses of yellow men'.

Moreover, if the initiatory centre is at Shamballah in the Himalayas, it must have been chosen with the consent of the Hyperborean Lodges of the North, and also of a place in England, which is invulnerable although no walls surround it.

Paul Grégor, who specialises in esoteric sexual magic, also has something to say about the subterranean people:

'For obscure reasons, they are said to have built tremendous altars, and to have excavated shafts by which to go down into the bowels of the earth, to the core where all the fire and all the water of the earth have their origin, from whence all the streams of lava of all the volcanoes erupt. Down below, among the sombre foundations of the whole universe, the bulk of a people called the Mysterious Builders are believed to have settled.'

Paradoxically, Theosophists, whom one would not suspect of cherishing an ideal devoted to the white magic of spiritual-

244

ism, also believe that the one whom they regard as the Master of the World lives in an Asiatic Shamballah.

'Theosophical Teachers say that the Lords of Venus founded the Grand Lodge of Initiation as soon as they reached the earth; their present dwelling is symbolically called by the ancient name Shamballah, an astral city, said to have existed in the Gobi Desert. This holy city, ruled over by the Master of the World, is invisible to the eyes of the uninitiated.... It is the secret sanctuary, the seat of the occult government of our glove. The legend of the subterranean realm where the Masters and the secret archives of the world are kept in security is a glorious reality.'

Mount Merou

The Agartha of Ossendowski and the Shamballahs of the G.L.V. and of Theosophists—are they the same, or are they different sanctuaries, possibly in opposition to one another? The latter seems the more probable.

According to the Swami Matkormano, the initiatory centre of Asia is Mount Merou; and that is where Shamballah is. In Hindu theology, this is the mountain on which the people from whom they claim descent were bred.

The lamaist cosmology of Tibet says:

'Mount Merou rises in the centre of the terrestrial globe. On the four sides of the peak, which are of crystal, azure, ruby and gold, the four kings of the earth live with their demon peoples.'

The G.L.V. consider that 'Mount Merou is the centre of Shamballah and the point of intersection of two planes of existence which are at the same time both material and immaterial'.

In Russian Turkestan there is a geometrical figure, the geophysical reality of which belongs to supra-conscious or extrasensory perception. It is composed of two pyramids, one of which is reversed. The pyramid pointing upwards is Mount Pamir; and the pyramid with its point downwards is Mount Merou, representing the hyperphysical and geophysical planes.

At the point of intersection is the summit of Merou, a

245

mountain that is sacred to both Aryans and the yellow races, upon which rises the stronghold of the King of the World—the omphalos, the umbilical centre of the microcosm and of the macrocosm.

Four roads lead from this centre to the four cardinal compass points: southward to the pole of Sion, westward to the pole of Lake Sale, northward to the pole of Thule and eastward to the pole of Pamir, the Himalayan extension, its extremity being Darjeeling. These poles are foci of tremendous magnetic energy, periodically affecting nations and their history. . . .

At the summit of Merou rises the Diamond Palace called Glasburg (literally, the glass palace) which is in some sort the dwelling of the sovereign lord of the subterranean world. At its four corners the Palace has towers called Towers of Silence in the Mazdean religion, which enclose accumulator batteries of the magnetic energy generated by the earthly poles. After transmuting it, they deflect this energy towards the galaxies of our siderial world. Thus Glasburg is the centre of energy for the universe. . . .

The towers receive and transmit magnetic earth waves. which are ultra-sonic vibrations reaching a pitch called the *great silence*. These waves of 'weight' are contained for an infinitesimal moment in lead and in the magnetic photons emitted by Saturn's rings that affect the earth every fourteen years. They are derivatives of protons A 1 (sub-atomic energy of the incandescent centre of the earth).

The G.L.V. expects to ensure its domination over the world by control of the force known as *Vril*.

This mysterious force was discovered—more probably invented—by Bulwer Lytton, who describes it in one of his novels named *The Coming Race*; this, according to the G.L.V., will be the *Vril-Ya*.

Vril

The control of Vril is an end in itself, for it will give man the ability to acquire all powers. There are two ways of gaining it. *The scientific way*, which consists in isolating chemically the particles of Proton A 1 contained in lead, to capture them in the photonic magnetism of Saturn or in lava issuing from an active volcano. This was the way followed by Wotan and some alchemists. Under the effect of the radiations so obtained, the male sex glands activate all the *Korlos*, and confirm the ego in its physical centre of gravity.

The mystic way borrows a ritual from higher magic, which demands the following elements: the sound vibrations of the letter K, the sign of Saturn, the colour violet, an amethyst, lead, runes, a mandala centred upon K.B.L., and the Ankh, initiation effecting a symbolic regression in time, the word of life for the resurrection of Tutankhamen, metempsychosis. . . .

Bulwer Lytton, who had been initiated into the Brotherhood of Luxor, saw vril as a kind of magic ring, which would cure disease but might also emit a death-ray. Anyone able to control this energy could cause earthquakes and eruptions, and could reactivate extinct volcanoes.

It is an odd thing that from time immemorial, men have dreamt of becoming Masters of the World and having the power to destroy whole nations, or even the earth itself. Are such ideas a part of white magic? Of course not.

Sorcerers have claimed to possess such powers, but this was no more than wishful thinking. Modern scientists have resolved the problem: nuclear fission is the hellish outcome of the research and the desire-images of ancient magi. Are our scientists working white magic? Unfortunately, no.

Contrary to these destructive inventions, people of a different temperament dream of establishing a new Golden Age, and use their desire-images to rouse forces that will try to keep at bay those of black magicians. The Masters of the true Humanity of Light think and work, no doubt in the invisible which has no such name as Agartha, Shamballah or Mount Merou. The only clue is that members of the Rose Croix have said that the name of the sanctuary of the Masters of the World begins with the letter A.

CHAPTER EIGHTEEN

THE UNIVERSE

The universe is the sum total of everything that exists. It is eternal, infinite, incommensurable; it is beyond the grasp of the human senses or the human mind. But, to give themselves the chance of studying it more easily and of satisfying their curiosity, physicists imagine an infinity of universes and concentrate on exploring as much of these as is perceptible to them. Thus, our universe is said to have a diameter of 20 milliard light-years, and to be between ten and a thousand milliard light-years old.

One may listen to its life-story on the radio-telescope at the Princeton Observatory in America—it is like a mighty breath blowing from the depths of time.

The Law of Hermes

The universe is composed of milliards of astral bodies which make up the groups we call constellations.

A group of constellations forms a galaxy. Ours is the Milky Way. Galaxies appear to be moving away from one another, but some astrophysicists think that the cosmos may be acting as a gigantic lens and by refractions and reflections producing phantom images that confuse us.

Nebulae are masses of galactic or extra-galactic gas or dust. These pieces of elementary information are indispensable to anyone hoping to explore the mystery of the past, the present or the future, whether on a philosophical, historical, social, initiatory or scientific plane.

Man is fundamentally a part of the universe and all his

problems reverberate as the infinitely small to the infinitely great, according to the Law of Hermes Trismegistus: as above, so below. Does that mean that the universe is made in the image of the atom? At present, scientists do not think so, chiefly because they have identified a great many different types of atom, of unstable structure, and buffeted by violent turbulent forces.

A priori, the universe seems to be of a homogeneous nature and, on the whole, more peaceful than atoms, even though its components spend their time in moving away from each other, for no reason yet discovered. To put it more simply, one might say that an atom is an organised complex *before explosion*; the universe is an organised complex *after explosion*.

Time and Speed

The idea of infinity suggests some interpretation of time, space and the measurement of distance.

To give a precise definition of time is impossible. At most one might say that it is a kind of extremely erratic measure of life, differently understood by the intellectual and the intuitive, by philosophers or by scientists. People are increasingly associating it with the concept of space: time, they say, is the fourth dimension. In that sense, time would be the manifestation of the unceasing recurrence of the life of matter.

Astronomers certainly think of it in that way, but they also find it a more useful unit for measuring interstellar distances than miles or kilometres. Sirius, for instance, is so many millions of miles away from the earth, that it is easier to measure the distance in time. By that system, it is nine light years distant.

Stars are 100,000 light-years away, nebulae 200,000; the nearest galaxies are a thousand million light-years off, and the more distant ones anywhere from five to ten thousand million. Not that such figures really mean anything to one's mind or imagination.

In any case, the distances are always wrong, because stars

and nebulae and galaxies seem to repel one another and continually move away from each other in space-time, especially those known as *quasars* or fiery quasi-stars, which are thought to have been projected from the centre of the universe—the primordial sperm, the omphalos of the ancients—at speeds which approximate to 300,000 kilometres per second.

When they attain the speed of light, it is thought that quasars disappear, become 'something else'—unless, perhaps they reach a super-luminal rate? It may be that they turn into a colossal force that sweeps through the universe in a reverse direction and obliges celestial matter to form a universe so small that it is less than an atom—in fact, a nought. But a nought in which all the energy of the vanished universe would be concentrated; an explosive energy beyond space-time, as inconceivable as God, and forming an anti-universe, made of anti-matter, and non-existent in anti-time. This theory is much too neat to have any possibility of approaching the truth which is, quite certainly, wildly fantastic.

The movement of galaxies and quasars might be imagined to be like a line of cars on an infinite road, each one travelling at a different speed from the others. There is no real starting point, only an arbitrary point from which to start calculations —which, for us, is the position of the earth. Distances are calculated by observing the stars whose colour turns redder in proportion as they become more remote from us. This is known as the Doppler Effect. Their speed comparative to the earth is also a function of the approach of their colour towards the red of the spectrum; this is Hubble's Law.

This is what we have to help us in exploring the universe, in the hope of getting a better understanding of that space-time which the ancients thought of as empty and in which they placed the stars much as we might put candles on a Christmas tree.

Euclidean Space: This is three-dimensional, having length, breadth and height, and corresponds to our normal system of life and culture.

Einstein's Space: Experimental scientists came up against

insurmountable obstacles; the great physicist added to Euclid's space the dimension of time and the idea of relativity. For instance, in Euclid's system, two parallel lines are always at the same distance from one another. One must agree with Einstein that it is impossible to measure simultaneously the deviation of two parallels at four points that are distant from each other. In others words, the simultaneity of two events exists only for a single observer; whence proceeds the notion of space-time.

It has also been observed that there are no straight lines in the universe, not even for the path of light; there is therefore no correspondence between the universe and rectilineal geometry. Nowadays the word 'straight' is no longer used in scientific language, but 'geodesic', to mean 'the shortest distance between one point and another, with allowance made for the curvature of the earth'. The universe itself is said to be concave, convex, curved or doubly curved—all of which are really only suppositions.

From the Infinitely Great to the Infinitely Small

The theory of expansion and contraction makes one believe universal creation to be subject to cycles that run from the infinitely small to the infinitely great, and vice versa. Matter, then, would be the basis of everything. It is not dense and persists only apparently. As far as physicists are concerned, it presents itself in geometric form, with little blobs at each of its angles. These blobs are atoms.

The atom, which is the smallest unit of a simple body, consists of: Firstly, a nucleus, made up of protons with positive charges, and neutrons which are neuter. They are all called by the general name of nucleon. Protons and neutrons mutually attract one another, and rotate or spin round one another with a magnetic momentum.

Secondly, a cloud of negative electricity which surrounds the nucleus with a multitude of whirling particles known as electrons. The electrons also have a magnetic momentum and

251

a spin.

The atom as a whole is neuter, because the electric charges cancel one another out and cohesion is maintained by the exchange of particles which act as 'glue': the π mesons.

It sometimes happens, either naturally or intentionally, that there is some disproportion between the numbers of protons and neutrons; in which case some of them escape from the nucleus and form what are called radio-active elements.

The proton–neutron stability of a nucleus can be broken by an artificial bombardment of particles, which causes radiation, which in its turn may produce chain reactions.

The whole mass of an atom is practically concentrated in the central nucleus, the dimension of which is something like 0·000,000,000,000,1 cm.

Imaginary Calculations

It is essential to make it clear that notions such as a concave, convex, curved, finite or infinite universe, an imaginary potential, imaginary intensity, imaginary numbers, fourth dimension, π meson, etc., are purely mathematical terms and have no particular concrete meaning.

The word 'imaginary', in particular, simply designates one method of calculation. It must therefore be understood that the concept of the universe, the totality of matter, occupying a finite or an infinite amount of space, is in reality pure speculation, an abstraction. The same thing is true of contraction and expansion, of the vacuum which contains everything, and even of time.

What faith can one have in science, therefore, if it operates only in the imagination? What certainty can there be in anything if God Himself is no more than a flight of fancy impossible to apprehend, if Truth is inaccessible? The scientist never expects to rely upon a certainty, and Buddha, the wisest of the Sages, always preached that all is *maya*.

(The word cosmogony means the theory of the creation of the world; but nowadays the word cosmogenesis is generally used instead.)

Naturalistic Cosmogony: God is the Universe. The Universe-God is self-created. The forces of nature are gods.

Indo-European Cosmogony: According to the Rig-Veda: 'there was neither being nor non-being, nor ether, nor the canopy of the sky, nothing that was covered and nothing with which to cover; nothing but *That. He* alone breathed, alone with *Her* whose life he sustained in his bosom.'

'Other than He, nothing existed that has since existed.'

'Desire, formed by the intelligence of That, became the original cause; the cause became progressively providence or living souls, and matter or elements.'

'*She* who is sustained in his bosom, is the lesser; and *He* who is cognitive is the greater.'

'Who knows exactly and who in this world can state certainly where and how creation came about? The gods are later than the creation of the world.'

This means that the universe is both created and uncreated, unknown and unimaginable; 'it came into being,' says the Rig-Veda, 'by the power of thought.'

To put it more plainly, creation and the He-She principle cannot be understood, and never will be.

According to the Code of Manu, which is later than the Rig-Veda, the universe was wrapped in darkness, imperceptible, unrevealed, when the Lord, existing of Himself (Brahma, neuter), and who is not to be apprehended by the external senses, made the world perceptible.

He whom the mind cannot conceive created divers substances from his own substance. He first produced the waters in which he placed a germ that became a glorious seed from which the Supreme Being himself was born in the shape of Brahma (male), the begetter of all creatures.

Brahma remained in embryo for a whole year (one Brahmanic year is equal to 3,110,400 million human years), and by means only of his thought, he divided himself in two: heaven and earth.

Hawaiian Cosmogony: From dark chaos, living forms, animal and mineral, emerged by gradual evolution: zoophytes, corals, worms, molluscs, algae, reeds.

From the mud resulting from the decomposition of the earliest creatures, plants, insects and birds evolved, then the higher marine animals, then other animals, the whole in six periods. In the seventh period a series of abstract psychic qualities developed. In an eighth period woman was born, and then man and the gods. (Biologists believe that the first human being was either a hermaphrodite or a woman.)

Cosmogeneses

It has always been thought that it is quite hopeless to try to explain what the universe is.

'Newton, the great physicist,' wrote Arago, 'after having enumerated the vast number of forces that must result from the interaction of the planets and satellites in our solar system, dared not undertake the task of calculating the sum total of their effects.'

Though a good Christian, Newton did not believe in the Bible story of the creation, but thought that 'from time to time a mighty power must intervene to put right the disorder in the cosmos'.

Laplace appears to have been the first physicist to produce a coherent theory. He thought that the universe had created itself, that great forces—explosions—had separated the planets from the original mass.

In the nineteenth century, a nebula consisting of infinitely diaphanous matter, was postulated as the initial source of creation. Lavoisier, at the same period, had a flash of genius and promulgated a fundamental law on which contemporary science is still based: nothing dies, nothing is created, everything changes.

This short description of the main cosmogonies shows that among the ancients only the Indo-Europeans, the Phoenicians and the Hawaiians formulated theories that are in direct relation to the cosmogeneses of twentieth-century scientists.

These cosmogeneses are the ones that have descended from the oldest of the peoples—between 8000 and 5000 B.C.—and thus are nearest to the Higher Ancestors.

Development: The Abbé Lemaitre's Universe

The Abbé Georges Lemaitre, a canon of the University of Louvain, is a creationist as well as a Christian.

He believes that the universe is expanding; at the end of the period of expansion everything will vanish.

Creation is Continuous: The Universe According to Fred Hoyle

The universe fills a limitless space. It is always the same and its density is constant. Galaxies steer clear of one another, nebulae are formed from spontaneously created hydrogen, to fill the voids.

The discovery of quasars, which have nothing in common with any previously known celestial bodies, has challenged Fred Hoyle's theory, and he now adds (and Vishnu Narlikar with him) that some anomalous regions—zones of turbulence, in which we on earth are situated—exist in a uniform and infinite universe.

An Explosion: The Universe of Sir Martin Ryle

The astonomer at the radio-observatory in Cambridge, England, postulates the occurrence of a 'big bang' some thirteen milliards of years ago, when all matter concentrated in a single point in space exploded with inconceivable violence. This primordial explosion illustrates the axiom that energy equals matter.

Quasars, a kind of luminous waves, were the first to emerge. Next came the galaxies. The total mass is spread over an infinite space: at first, at a speed that is gradually diminishing; it will be nought when time coincides with infinity, in thirteen milliards of years. By then all space will be fully occupied, and time will no longer exist.

Or else, secondly, waste matters will slow up progressively, then attract each other, and will shatter themselves in a universal implosion, and that will be the end of the world.

The Oscillating Universe of Allan Sandage

The universe is eternal and complete.

Paradoxically, Professor Sandage, of the Mount Wilson Observatory, is obliged to conceive of an initial concentration of all the matter in the universe. This matter explodes as in Professor Ryle's theory; expansion begins and lasts for forty-one milliard years.

Then everything goes into reverse, and contraction begins: quasars, galaxies, nebulae, all return to the point of departure for a fresh explosion. The cycle of expansion and contraction is eighty-two milliard years.

There has been and there will be an infinity of cycles.

This conception is, actually, the same as that of the Abbé Lemaitre.

All these universes are unsatisfactory, because they are finite and limited.

The Cosmogenesis of Oscar Klein

Initially the universe was a sort of nebula with a diameter of two thousand milliard light-years, in which the Swedish physicist Oscar Klein postulated the existence of a world made of particles and an anti-world made of anti-particles, that is to say of matter and anti-matter. Particles and anti-particles were too widely disseminated in space to have any chance of meeting.

Under the effect of universal gravitation, matter and anti-matter condensed (*contraction*), forming two distinct worlds. Passing them to a cycle of expansion, these worlds developed their galaxies, the speed of whose flight is calculable.

There is no interaction (*explosion*) between the world and the anti-world, because they are separated by a neuter zone called 'ambiplasma', subject to extremes of temperature. Nevertheless, the particles and anti-particles sometimes, very exceptionally, meet in this zone, causing explosions, compared with which those of our atomic bombs sound like peashooters.

Radio-telescopes record the radio-waves resulting from the crash of matter against anti-matter, and not from quasars as had been thought.

The Cosmogenesis of Andrei Sakharov

This Russian scientist thinks that our universe was born of an anti-universe which vanished twenty or thirty milliard years ago. In its initial state the universe was chiefly made up of anti-particles, whose condensation at a very high temperature provoked an explosion that, as in atomic disintegration, produced more matter than anti-matter.

Our world, then, was formed of the excess of matter-particles.

The Cosmogenesis of Gustav Naan

Gustav Naan is Vice-President of the Esthonian Academy of Science; his conception of the universe is much the same as Oscar Klein's. The world and the anti-world of Gustav Naan are of the same nature, but reversed, with perhaps the same solar systems, the same galaxies, and planets inhabited by men like ourselves. Between these two worlds a barrier exists, which cannot be broken by man except under the threat of disintegration: a barrier of nullity.

The world in contraction vanishes at zero point. But from that nothingness, matter may arise if it is balanced in the anti-world by an equal quantity of anti-matter.

Contemporary astronomers who are able to sound the depths of heaven to a distance of thirty milliard light-years, say with proud certainty: 'Quite soon we shall be able to find the time when our universe did not exist!'

The cosmogenesis of our ancestors, described in the Rig-Veda, offers no such opportunity.

The Vedic cosmogenesis is admirable and, like the speculations of the scientists at Harvard, Cambridge and the Collège de France, it allows for imagination and the inconceivable as well as the Nothingness which contains the possibility of Something. It affirms that man will never solve the mystery of the universe.

It agrees, nevertheless, that there is a system of contraction and expansion (or pulsation), since this unknown and unexplored universe is represented by 'the in-breathing and out-breathing of Brahma'.

Anti-matter

The cosmogeneses of Klein and Sakharov do not explain the initial creation of the universe because they start from a given, though hypothetical, point. There remains always the barrier of mystery that baffles our curiosity. Still, the concept of anti-matter calls for an explanation.

Actually, it was always known to initiates, and no doubt it is connected with the indefinite Other Side and the parallel universes that evade our investigation.

'Poetry is truth,' said Goethe, anticipating the anti-world and the 'looking-glass world' suspected by a great seer, Jean Cocteau, who knew how to find the way in.

It is quite possible that the next discoveries about anti-matter will bring a first solution to some of the unknown mysteries that haunt us.

Two French scientists, Louis de Broglie and J. P. Vigier, have for a long time conceived that besides the known universe, there might be a sub-universe in which known particles (electrons, protons, neutrons and foreign bodies) manifest as anti-particles (anti-electrons, anti-protons, etc.).

In fact, our universe might be only the surface of an ocean whose depths were unplumbed.

It is to an English physicist, P. Dirac, that we owe the theory of anti-particles which, in 1928 made possible the discovery of the anti-electron or positon, and the anti-proton, whose mass is equal to that of protons but with a negative charge.

As a speculation, one might say that anti-matter is formed of anti-atoms with negative nuclei, surrounded by positons.

In 1966, at the National Laboratory of Brookhaven (U.S.A.), American physicists created a nucleus of anti-hydrogen by using an anti-proton and an anti-neutron. This discovery at the molecular level makes the theory of anti-worlds admissible.

Contrary to the opinion of Oscar Klein and Andrei Sakharov, the Esthonian philosopher Gustav Naan thinks that an anti-world would not be lost on the confines of the universe, but would exist in our own as, in some sort, a parallel world.

Some scientists even think that photons (particles of light) could result from energy created by a combination of particles and anti-particles. So, from the collision of a world and an anti-world, light would be born. Or, in other words, in accord with secret doctrines light and all creation would be born of God and the Anti-God.

When a universe in contraction reaches zero, which is nullity, it enters the anti-world. Thereby another explosion is caused and a fresh expansion begins; or else the anti-world passes beyond the zero point of non-existence and takes the place of the vanished world. On this theory, if it is admitted that God rules the universe, He would be replaced by the anti-God and the anti-universe at the beginning of each new cycle.

These ideas are not at variance with the esoteric doctrines formulated by the Egyptian Master Anubis Schenouda, who thinks that imperfection is indispensable to ensure perfection, just as the primitive Carnac in Brittany was necessary to balance the sublime Karnak in the Valley of the Nile. For every thing needs two poles that can be called upon to substitute for each other.

'Everything is possible,' said the great scientist Niels Bohr 'so long as it is mad enough!'

In that case one may take seriously the philosophical speculation of the Soviet paper *Pravda Komsomol* about the world of matter and the world of anti-matter: 'In a world where everything is symmetrical there can be nothing except nullity, a vacuum. Space and time themselves do not exist.'

Who Created the Universe?

Whatever the universe may be, it represents matter endowed with dynamic will backed by perfect intelligence.

If matter was created, there must have been a pre-existent creator whom one may call God or Intelligence or Creative Thought or the Prime Mover. If matter was not created, if it has existed from all eternity, the Prime Mover informs creation and is in some sort identical with it.

In the first case, if matter was created by a creator, one question jumps naturally to the mind: how was God or Universal Intelligence or Thought created? And one is back at the beginning of the problem. Reason rejects this explanation: you might as well say that the universe created itself, which is simpler and more logical.

One must therefore reasonably identify God or Thought or Intelligence with the whole universe and not with an intelligent principle existing outside that universe.

Scientists accept the idea of a God or Intelligence or Thought or a Universal Soul, on condition that it is considered to be an abstraction, an imaginary conception of the Unknown, indeed the Unknowable.

God, as the fourth dimension, like the curvature of space, belongs to the realm of the imaginary, of speculation and the non-figurative.

CURIOSITIES

CHAPTER NINETEEN

ODDMENTS AND ODDITIES

It takes all sorts to make the world, and though the horoscope of the present time seems to be dominated by signs of tragedy and madness, we find even now that queer things happen to bring some comic relief to our melodrama. Nature itself sets insoluble puzzles at every level.

The structure of the atom is a mystery, and nobody knows why hops curl round a stake clockwise but bindweed anticlockwise.

A London doctor named Weston has observed that in England people whose names begin with the first eight letters of the alphabet live longer than others.

Why should these things be? There must certainly be reasons, but nobody has troubled to discover what they are.

Bonaparte's Pentacle

Mysteries are often caused simply by ignorance. The question has often been asked why Roman cement was much harder and more durable than modern concrete. The secret was discovered by M. H. Guettard: it lies in the technique of manufacture—the Romans used to leave lime to settle for three years to ensure the highest quality.

Even among thoroughly well-educated people, knowledge sometimes gives way to superstition, as in the story of the pentacle-necklace that is at present owned by the Israeli General Mosche Dayan.

This necklace was once the property of Napoleon Bonaparte. It was sent to him, so it is said, on the eve of the Battle of the Pyramids by some Egyptian priests. The talisman protected him throughout the subsequent campaigns, even during his amazing advance in Russia.

In Moscow he forgot it and left it behind in a chest of drawers; fate turned against him from that moment.

The jewel passed into a Russian family, who, during the 1917 revolution, emigrated to Nice.

This information has been given by the CEREIC, which adds that in 1956, after the first Arab–Israel war, General Dayan was friendly with a French-Jewish journalist, through whom he came to know this Russian family at Nice, who were also Jewish and who still held the talisman.

As a mark of respect to the General, the jewel was presented to him, and it is well known that from that time on, he has enjoyed enormous success.

Napoleon—Breton or Charentais?

In a book of prophecies (*Prophets Across the Ages*) the historian Henry James Forman tells the curious legend of the British–Israel Society.

King Sargon of Assyria, who destroyed the kingdom of Israel in 722 B.C., carried away to Babylon 27,250 families who never returned to Palestine. According to Forman, these Israelites later settled in the British Isles, and a beautiful refugee married one of the Kings of Ireland in 480 B.C.

The English royal family, so says Forman, is descended from this Celtic–Hebrew alliance.

This idea is no more startling than the claim that Napoleon was a Breton. At least, that is what may be read between the lines of *Mysterious Brittany*, a guide book written by Gwenc' Hlan Le Scouëzec.

In 1768 Napleon's mother is understood to have spent several months at Saint-Sève, in Finisterre.

It is not even certain that she left before Napoleon's birth on 15th August 1769, because the relevant page in the register of births has been torn—which gives free rein to the imagination.

Another tradition is current in Charente, where it is said that Napoleon was born on the Isle of Aix, which is also known as the 'Isle of Beauty'. And, far beyond anything that Corsica can show, Aix possesses a statue to *Saint Napoleon* (of Austerlitz), set in the wall of the church by the owner of the island.

Dashing One's Head against a Wall

Charles Hoy Fort was a great collector of curious tales, and it is sometimes interesting to follow in his footsteps.

A youthful Peruvian, Franco Bernaola, aged eight, is passionately addicted to petrol and drinks several glasses of it every day without apparently doing himself any harm. He has all the doctors of the country guessing!

In 1966, donkeys in the district of Gharbieh, west of the Nile Delta, committed suicide in considerable numbers by dashing their heads against a wall. This oddly recalls the epidemic of suicides that startled Ireland in the 'year 3656 of the world'.

A lot of the Irish apparently went mad, and killed themselves by dashing their heads against the stones of the sanctuary erected in honour of the great idol Cromm Cruach (*of the bloody head*).

How can one explain the invasion of Greenwich on 3rd September 1967 by millions of earth worms? The fire brigade had to use hoses to clear the streets.

Kladanj, in Bosnia, is a place blessed by the gods. It contains a spring of water which prolongs youth and acts as an aphrodisiac. Its taste is insipid; but thousands of tourists buy bottles of it every week on the black market.

It must have been useful to an American doctor from Salt Lake City, who preached a doctrine advocating polygamy for people over sixty. This, he said, would satisfy the natural desire for variety, and would free them of frustration complexes.

Americans are much interested in the idea—all except the doctor's wife, who says it's a lot of nonsense.

American Curiosities

One of the most astonishing countries, possibly the oddest and the least well known—at any rate to Europeans—is America, and the United States in particular.

Near Gold Hill in Oregon is a house, in appearance much like the rest but, once inside, the visitor is in another world. It is impossible to stand upright in it, perpendicular to the floor, because there is no vertical. A plumb line, instead of hanging straight down towards the centre of the earth as it does elsewhere, is inclined at an angle of about 26°. To walk, you have to lean well over to one side—in fact a woman wearing high heels is better off if she removes one shoe. Nobody knows the reason for this peculiarity; but it is suggested that it may be due to a meteorite buried in the earth under the house.

Every time it rains near Playa racetrack in Death Valley, California, rocks weighing up to six or seven hundred pounds move of their own accord, leaving clear traces along the perfectly level ground on which they lie. But no one has ever seen them move. It is not the wind which makes them slip, because sometimes rocks which are close to one another slide in different directions.

Ghosts, which are highly esteemed in America, make dates with each other in places called Ghost Towns in the South, and people interested in occultism go there to meet them.

On a mountain road in Colorado there is a path that visitors tend to avoid. It does, in fact, cause an optical illusion. Anyone who passes over a particular ridge and walks along that path appears to be absorbed into the fourth dimension and disappears from view, even if those with him stand on the ridge itself.

In the Isle of Man, a similar phenomenon tricks motorists. There is a certain place where the road appears to lead straight downhill. If a car is stopped without braking, it climbs back up the slope for about fifty yards.

Mazdak, the Communist Prophet

In a few years from now, encouraged by the 'fateful' date of the year 2000, prophets and a Messiah will make their appearance, at any rate among certain sects, although they may possibly also succeed in being accepted by the general public. Everything will depend upon the power of those who are interested in publicising their advent.

About the year A.D. 500, Mazdak, a magus and a reformer, High Priest at Nishabur, took the opportunity given by an outbreak of plague and famine in Persia to proclaim himself a prophet. Actually, he was a man full of ideas and of good intentions; he said that he was sent by God to regenerate humanity, as indeed was most necessary even at that date! He denounced the misuse of power and wealth, the venality of judges, preached equality of rank and fortune and said that goods and women should be held in common.

His popularity was such that Kobad, the King of Persia, sided with him and promulgated an agrarian law to favour small farmers. The time was not ripe for that kind of reform, excellent though it might be in principle, and the kingdom collapsed in total anarchy.

Kobad was dethroned, then reinstated, but his successor, who was not interested in practising Marxism before its time had the unfortunate prophet arrested and tied to a tree, where he was shot to death by archers.

One hundred thousand of his followers were delivered over to torture, for Mazdak's doctrine was firmly rooted in the people.

A Determined Messiah: Sabatai-Sevy

Prophetic books having announced that the Jewish Messiah would appear in 1666, an imposter of the name of Sabatai-

Sevy took the opportunity to declare that he was the one they awaited. A sympathiser, Nathan of Gaza, campaigned for him and announced that very soon Sabatai would dethrone the Sultan Mahomet IV, and that all the Jews in the world would be gathered together. A great number of Jews believed in him, but the Sultan exiled Sabatai, who then married three wives in succession. But they all left him: he was impotent.

However, the wind turned in his favour, for he said he was accompanied, invisibly, by the prophet Elias, which was quickly acclaimed by cranks whose principal gift was the power of falling into trances in public places and preaching signs and wonders.

Quite a number of equally sincere and learned Doctors said that Elias used to come and sit at table with them and share their meals.

Sabatai promised in writing that very soon the Jews would dominate all nations of the earth, but that before this could be accomplished, the Grand Turk must be dethroned.

He went to Constantinople, followed by huge crowds, but was seized and imprisoned immediately, to the great benefit of his gaolers, who made the Jews pay an entrance fee to come and worship their fettered Messiah.

The Sultan finally ordered this odd personage to be brought before him, and asked him several questions in the Turkish language. Sabatai was unable to reply since he spoke only Hebrew, which put his followers out of countenance, as they had supposed that their Messiah would be able to express himself in any language. A mass of believers still remained, however, and for their edification the Sultan had him tied to a stake in readiness for the shots of his archers.

'But,' said the Sultan, 'I promise to become a Jew and the disciple of your Messiah if, by a miracle which should be easy for the son of God to perform, his body proves impenetrable to the arrows.'

Sabatai hastened to assure him of his terrestrial origin.

The Grand Turk offered him the choice: either to become a Mussulman or to be shot instantly. 'I shall become a Mussulman!' the Messiah exclaimed. And he donned a turban and worshipped Mahomet without delay.

In the Forest of Broceliande: Eon de Lestoille

'The business of being a prophet or a messiah is a paying proposition when it comes off. But if it does not, you run every risk of being tortured or burnt at the stake. Which seems a high price to pay for a bit of innocent humbug,' said a nineteenth-century philosopher.

In the second century, the fanatic Montanus said that he was the Paraclete (the Holy Spirit), and that the end of the world was at hand.

His disciples, the Montanists, attached great merit to martyrdom and celibacy, and condemned the love of dress, of pleasure and of science.

Perhaps Montanus really was a holy spirit, a saintly man.

In the twelfth century, a Breton fanatic, Eon de Lestoille, having read the formula '*per eum qui venturus est judicare vivos et mortuos*' in a prayer-book, imagined that he was the one who was to come to judge the living and the dead.

He became a hermit in the forest of Broceliande, then returned to the life of the world and proclaimed himself the Messiah. As he was well versed in magic, it was not long before he gathered round him a crowd of disciples, to whom he showed himself surrounded by a mysterious halo. He performed his wonders near the fountain of Baranton.

Drunk with success, he appointed a cohort of angels and apostles and travelled throughout France, preaching and exacting tribute from cities and castles as he went. He was taken prisoner in Champagne, and was condemned to life imprisonment by Pope Eugenius III; his apostles and his angels were burnt alive in the public squares.

The Baranton fountain, in the heart of the Forest of Broceliande was famed for its magical properties. A thirteenth-century poet wrote the following testimony, which is clearly worthy of belief: 'The fountain of Broceliande is a marvel of marvels! If a few drops of the water are sprinkled on the surrounding stones, heavy clouds, saturated with rain and hail appear. The air is filled with the roar of thunder and it grows dark. So anyone who brings about this miracle repents of his rashness and wishes he had never heard of it.'

There are also charters attesting the truth of these wonders; but the truly miraculous part of it is that the magic no longer works!

Tanquelin, God the Father

In these days, the Christian Church is a reputable institution, honoured and honourable; but in the Middle Ages it terrified the poor, whom it oppressed in alliance with the rich and un-scrupulous. By extortion, torture, burning alive, it made itself so much hated, that the people tried to break free at every opportunity, and welcomed passionately and without the least discrimination anything and everything that was anti-religious and anti-Christian.

This state of revulsion explains the hosts of false messiahs and false prophets who proclaimed themselves and who were followed by hundreds of thousands of unfortunates.

For the same reasons, magic and the devil made a far greater appeal than the Mass and the Saints.

About the year 1100, a Flemish dissident named Tanquelin acquired great celebrity by attacking the most sacred dogmas of the Church. In addition, he preached 'permissiveness' in morals, which at once gained him crowds of proselytes. To increase even more the trust and admiration of the people, he dressed in rich garments of velvet and brocade, wore a plumed hat, and highly-coloured leather boots, and was always moun-ted upon a magnificently caparisoned horse. He recruited an escort of scamps whom he called his apostles, all of them as cunning and rascally as himself but always ready to shout at cross-roads: 'Make way for the Lord of the world, for God incarnate!'

The good people believed in Tanquelin, so much so that

when the ruffian raped a girl, it was looked upon as a divine act! One chronicler went so far as to write: 'When Tanquelin said a word, everybody applauded as if it had been a victory over the devil!'

The water in which he washed was saved by his followers, who divided it among themselves drop-wise, and believed it was a cure for all ills.

Tanquelin finally declared himself to be God in Person and the Father of Jesus Christ. People believed him, because of his fine appearance, his grand manner, his splendid clothes and his persuasive words.

One time, drunk with pride according to some stories—just plain drunk according to others—and to carry the joke as far as he possibly could, he appeared before an assembly with a large picture of the Virgin Mary beside him.

Addressing the picture in a condescending manner, he cried: 'Virgin Mary, today I take you for my bride!'

Then, turning to the crowd who marvelled at being present at so rare and glorious a spectacle: 'I have married the Holy Virgin: now it is for you to contribute to the expenses of the marriage and the celebrations. Two chests have been placed at the foot of the platform. The men will put what they wish to give me in one of them, the women in the other. Then I shall know which sex feels the greater love for me and for my wife.'

It was the women who proved the more generous, and even more so in the evening, when Tanquelin-God, as drunk as a lord, but no less lecherous for that, decided to celebrate his wedding night as the old Romans did in the decadent period— and not with the Virgin Mary!

He propagated his doctrines in Flanders and in northern France, and he even went to Rome, hoping to induce the Pope to recognise him as God.

Actually, he never showed himself in daylight in Italy.

When he returned to Flanders, he tried to persuade a priest that he was an incarnation of the One God; the discussion degenerated into a row, and the priest, to prove to Tanquelin that his pretensions were ill-founded, hit him with a cudgel and killed him.

So died God, the creator of heaven and hell, called Tanquelin in Flanders and Belgium.

His heresy persisted for a long time after his death.

John of Leyden and Robespierre as Messiahs

After being a tailor's apprentice, an inn-keeper and an actor, John of Leyden adopted the profession of prophet. First he became an anabaptist, organised a revolt in 1534 and drove out the Bishop of Münster.

Taking the early Christians as his model, he preached that goods should be held in common; and then, relying upon 'revelations', he had himself proclaimed King of the New Jerusalem.

Finding that the churches were full of riches accumulated by the priests, he took possesion of them and never appeared in public except wearing a gold crown encrusted with diamonds; he dressed as sumptuously as Tanquelin, and was accompanied by the same kind of suite. He called himself King of Justice over the whole world and had coins struck with his effigy.

In imitation of the Hebrew Patriarchs and of Solomon, he commanded that polygamy should be practised in Münster, and for his own part he married fifteen pretty girls. Splendid public banquets, which he called *cena* (supper), stimulated the enthusiasm of his followers.

John of Leyden—or rather, the King of Justice—himself waited on the people as they sat at table, which considerably enhanced his popularity. He sent missionaries into all countries, but the dethroned Bishop gathered a large army, returned to Münster, and slaughtered great numbers of the heretics.

John of Leyden defended himself heroically. When he was captured he was paraded through the streets, shut in an iron cage, then tortured, torn to pieces with red-hot pincers. His remains were hung in the cage from the top of the tower of Saint Lawrence's church.

During twenty centuries over 100,000 Messiahs, prophets or

incarnations of God have tried their luck with credulous people, more or less successfully. There were few sovereigns who were not considered to be divine in secret societies. Even Robespierre, surnamed the Incorruptible, but who was in reality a fanatic 'drunk with blood and glory', according to those who knew him best ... even Robespierre was infected by the virus of messianism.

Having instituted the cult of the Supreme Being, he over-reached himself and lapsed into sheer lunacy, in which Catherine Théot was chosen to be 'the Mother of God', and was to have her own throne erected near the Pantheon on the site of the Law School. It was at this spot that she was expected to liquidate kings and peoples, so that only 140,000 should survive, the elect, who were to live in the earthly paradise.

Mad though she was, she enjoyed real celebrity in the days of the Revolution. The conspirators who organised this farce attached two pretty girls to her, and called them the Enlightener and the Dove; it was their mission to take the place of the Mother of God after her death.

The three women acknowledged Robespierre to be the Messiah, and on 2nd August 1793 the President of the Jacobins, who knew all about the business, spoke at the Party Meeting of 'a Saviour who was to come', though without mentioning any name.

Women, soldiers, generals, carried silver or bronze medals of Robespierre, and the feminine admirers of the Incorruptible had no hesitation in whispering to him at moments of intimacy :

'Robespierre, you are a God!'

The enemies of the Tribune—and they were many in the Committee of Public Safety—took the opportunity to ruin his reputation.

A police raid surprised Catherine Théot and her followers at a meeting one day, and they found hidden in the lady's mattress the draft of a letter addressed to Robespierre in which he was called 'Son of the Supreme Being, eternal Word, Redeemer of the human race, Messiah foretold by the prophets. . . .'

The situation become uncomfortable for the 'Messiah', for the Convention decided to summon his followers before the tribunal, at which the compromising letter was read aloud.

The Incorruptible, thanks to his influence, which was still great, and by bribing certain of the plotters, caused the intrigue to miscarry; but of course it was talked about behind their backs, and Robespierre was made to look a fool.

CHAPTER TWENTY

PREDICTIONS AND THE END
OF THE WORLD

Prophecies are visions of the future described by inspired persons, events which are expected to occur at a later date, and are seen through the intermediary of a diviner, a clairvoyant or an astrologer.

René Guénon, a true initiate, denounced the trickery of prophecies such as those of Nostradamus, or what was supposed to be 'written in the Great Pyramid of Gizeh'.

'The destruction of Paris by fire,' he wrote, 'has been prophesied a great many times, even to giving the exact dates, but nothing happened. Astrology,' he continued, 'or the tarot cards, are the stock-in-trade of numbers of simple experimenters, who are incapable of learning so much as a vestige of authentic traditional science, which might be of real interest, though it also has some very shady aspects.

'The supposed prophecies in the great pyramid have been disseminated in England, and from there all over the world, to serve ends which may be partly political ... but which are also connected with persuading the English that they are descendants of the lost tribes of Israel.'

René Guénon's opinion may be exaggerated, but there could be some truth in it.

False Prophecies

The end of the world has been foretold for the last two thousand years and more by Hebrew Prophets, and especially by the mysterious Saint John of the Apocalypse.

God Himself is believed to have alerted his disciple: 'Blessed is he that readeth, and they that hear the words of this prophecy, and keep those things which are written therein: for the time is at hand.' (Revelation I, 3.)

Fortunately St. John would seem to have misinterpreted the matter, for the time which he thought was 'at hand' is long past, and the end of the world has not come yet.

Predicting the future is a contagious disease which has raged at all periods of history. Between June 1688 and February 1689 some five or six hundred cranks caught it in the provinces of Dauphiné and Vivarais alone.

Misfortune and hope, the second a result of the first, are the chief causes of the malady.

In 1968 Padre Pio, who certainly was a holy man, revealed that a cure would be found for cancer, and this no doubt will come true. Unfortunately he felt it necessary to add that after 1980 there would never be another war like the one in 1940, and that men would enter a Golden Age in the year 2000 ... which is very difficult to believe.

Those whom we call scientists are not luckier in their pronouncements.

In 1966 a Portuguese astronomer said that an asteroid weighing 17 milliard tons would crash into the earth on 15th June 1968.

As for predictions published in newspapers during the past half century, they have all been false, no one of them ever having foretold anything of importance with the exception of things that had a fifty-fifty chance of coming off.

Predictions about the End of the World

The great temple at Benares contains a curious apparatus designed to measure the time between now and the end of the world. Three slender diamond pointers, each about half a yard long, are attached to a bronze dial. At the creation of the world, God threaded sixty-four golden discs of different sizes on to the first of these pointers, the largest at the bottom and the

275

smallest at the top. This is the Tower of Brahma.

The puzzle consists in threading the discs on to the other pointers, in such a way that none of them ever rests on a disc with a smaller radius. All the pointers must be used. When anyone succeeds in arranging the Tower of Brahma on each pointer, the end of the world will have come. Calculations have shown that there are at least one hundred milliard possibilities, which is reassuring.

At the end of each cosmic period or *kalpa*, so the Bhagavata Purana teaches, the world will perish by fire, in one of four possible ways:

—accidental destruction (*naimittika*), resulting from the sleep of Brahma; this occurs at the end of each kalpa.

—natural destruction (*prakritika*) by the elements. At the end of the two periods of the life of Brahma, everything is reabsorbed in him;

—continuous destruction (*nitya*): youth, maturity, old age, the eternal succession of changes that life is heir to;

—final destruction (*atyantika*): individual souls return to the supreme soul from whence they came (Brahma) and enter into *nirvana*, or rather that which will become *nirvana* when the Buddha himself becomes Nothing.

In Scandinavian mythology, the end of the world, or the twilight of the gods, called *ragnarokr*, will come when the earth disappears in a great conflagration. The gods themselves will perish in a desperate fight against their enemies.

This conflagration will be a purification rather than extermination, for a new and better world will arise. This was also the doctrine taught by Zeno, the Stoics and Seneca.

In the Champs des Dolents (Field of the Sorrowful) at Dol-de-Bretagne, is a red granite menhir, which legend says fell from heaven.

It has been thought to be a meteoric stone, and it is buried down to about fifteen feet in the earth; only one end of it is still visible, and that sinks an inch every century. When the stone disappears completely, that will be the end of the world.

The Mess of Pottage

There is a biblical prediction which does not seem to have been noticed by interpreters, but which is of considerable interest at a time when the whole Arab world is in league against the young Israeli nation.

This prediction is contained in a passage in Genesis, which everyone thinks he knows but which, in fact, is one of the greatest mysteries: the story of Esau.

The current version is as follows.

Rebecca was barren, but her husband Isaac prayed to the Lord and she conceived; 'and the children struggled together within her.... And the Lord said unto her: Two nations are in thy womb, and two manner of people shall be separated from thy bowels; and the one people shall be stronger than the other people; and the elder shall serve the younger.'

When her time came, she was delivered of twins. 'The first came out red all over like an hairy garment; and they called his name Esau. And after that came his brother out, and his hand took hold on Esau's heel; and his name was called Jacob. Isaac was threescore years old when she bare them.'

We are told that as the boys grew up, Essau became 'a cunning hunter, a man of the field; and Jacob was a plain man dwelling in tents'. In other words, Esau was a worker, while Jacob took life easily.

Isaac had a real preference for his elder son, but Rebecca, a wily woman, 'loved Jacob', and contrived to have him blessed by Isaac, which would give him the privileges and rights of the first born.

One evening, 'Esau came from the field and he was faint'. Jacob had been preparing a dish of lentils, and Esau sat down at the table and asked Jacob to let him share the meal, which gave Jacob the chance for a mean piece of blackmail.

'Sell me this day thy birthright,' he said. To which Esau replied 'Behold I am at the point to die; and what profit shall this birthright do to me?'

And Jacob said: 'Swear to me this day!'

So Esau swore to him, and thus he sold his birthright.

'Then Jacob gave Esau bread and pottage of lentils; and he did eat and drink and rose up, and went his way; thus Esau despised his birthright.'

This was Act I in the machinations to which Esau fell victim.

Jacob takes another Mean Advantage

Isaac had become very old, and 'his eyes were dim, so that he could not see'. He said that he would bless Esau and pass on his position to him before he died.

But Rebecca was on the watch, and she heard what Isaac said. She decided to substitute Jacob for his elder brother and obtain the blessing for him.

But Jacob said 'Esau my brother is a hairy man and I am a smooth man. . . .'

In short, Jacob was afraid that his father would discover the fraud and would curse him instead of blessing; but Rebecca took the curse upon herself, and told Jacob to dress himself in some of Esau's clothes. She put the skins of freshly killed kids upon his hands and upon the smooth of his neck, and sent him to receive the blessing which would confirm him in the rights primogeniture that he had stolen.

Isaac was to some extent suspicious, and asked: 'Who art thou?'

'Jacob replied: I am Esau, thy first-born.

'And Isaac said unto Jacob: Come near, I pray thee, that I may feel thee, my son, whether thou be my very son Esau or not.

'And Jacob went near unto Isaac his father; and he felt him and said: The voice is Jacob's voice, but the hands are the hands of Esau.

'Isaac asked: Art thou my very son Esau? And he said: I am.'

Isaac also detected the strong smell of Esau's clothes, and

was finally convinced that he really did recognise him, and gave him his blessing, saying particularly: 'Let the people serve thee and nations bow down to thee: be lord over thy brethren and let thy mother's sons bow down to thee.

'And it came to pass, as soon as Isaac had made an end of blessing Jacob, and Jacob was yet scarce gone out from the presence of his father,' that Esau came in; and begged his father to bless him also.

Though he was now too late to receive the rights of the first born, yet Isaac softened the blow by saying: 'It shall come to pass . . . that thou shalt break his yoke from off thy neck.'

Finally Esau was exiled to Mesopotamia.

Four points should be noted in this story:

—First, The Lord permitted a peculiar piece of trickery, and the branch of Israel descending from Jacob found itself entrusted with a mission which began in a more than doubtful fashion.

—Secondly, Esau was abnormally hairy, and had a strong smell, which seems to be connected with the mystery of the seirim.

—Thirdly, the Hebrews were destined to see other nations submit to them.

—Fourthly, the Hebrews who were descended from Jacob would one day be conquered by the descendants of Esau.

The development of these points reveals the hidden meaning of the Bible story and the nature of the Jewish mission; it is particularly interesting in view of recent events in the Near East.

Esau, a Seir

It may be that things fell out as the story says, but actually, according to occult truth, it was necessary, indispensable and right that Esau should not have been chosen to succeed Isaac as Patriarch of the Israelites.

It was a matter of genetics, but the details have been oddly transmuted by time and legend.

279

The mission of the Hebrews was to safeguard the purity of the white races, which was imperilled by monstrous and degrading customs.

All the evidence goes to show that there was a time after the Flood when both men and women used to have sexual intercourse with animals, from which resulted the birth of monsters, as is told in all mythologies, as well as in the Bible, in Chapter XVIII of Leviticus:

'Thou shalt not ... lie with any beast to defile thyself therewith: neither shall any woman stand before a beast to lie down thereto: it is confusion.

'Defile not ye yourselves in any of these things: for in all these the nations are defiled which I cast out before you.'

All the evidence shows that the Lord insisted upon genetic purity.

He was willing to put up with murder, robbery, deceit, to breathe the smell of burnt offerings, even of battlefields where enemy corpses putrified. On the other hand, he was inflexible when there was the slightest risk of biological deterioration: the human race must learn self-control, it must never fall, so that the Jews should be known in future ages as an absolutely pure race.

And it seems likely that the unhappy Esau was not of the pure race.

He had a strong smell, and his body was very hairy, which in itself is suspect at a time when women might have had intercourse with animals.

Translating the *Torah*, the Rabbi Yonah ibn Aharon writes as follows:

'The creatures which interest us particularly are those which spread terror among the Jews when they departed from Egypt and wandered in the Sinai desert.

'They were the Sheidim, or Seirim (destroyers), *hairy creatures*.

'The best description of them may be gained from the story of how Rebecca dressed up her younger son Jacob to make Isaac believe he was Esau. Esau was brought up as a hunter;

he was ashamed of the shaggy red fur that covered him, which had gained him the nickname of Edom (the Red).

'The text implies that though he appeared to be Jacob's brother he was not so in reality; it seems in any case that Rebecca had no very deep affection for Esau. . . .'

It does indeed seem probable that Esau was not the real brother of Jacob. True, they had the same mother, but Isaac was already forty years old when he married Rebecca, and sixty when the children were born. She was, so they say, barren—and it remains for geneticists to explain whether twins born of the same mother could have different fathers. It has also been suggested that they were not actually twins; and that Rebecca had sinned with one of the Seirim, and therefore chose Jacob, as the better of the two, to succeed Isaac, and that she felt no twinges of conscience at having entered into the plot to deceive both Isaac and Esau.

The Chosen People, not Semites in general, nor the Hebrews as a whole, but the descendants of Jacob, surnamed Israel, were to extend their rule over other nations.

Over all peoples? Verse 27 of Chapter XVIII of Leviticus, seems to suggest that their domination was to extend only over people who had fornicated with animals.

The mission of the Jews was, therefore, laudable and beneficent for the whole of the human race, but it was limited in time and was to come to an end with the advent of other Aryan races from the Caucasus, Greece, Gaul, Scandinavia, whose stock was at least as pure as their own. Among Aryans, in this context, are included all those whose ancestors escaped from the Flood via the Iranian plateau—Arabs, Hebrews, Egyptians, Slavs, Celts—in addition to those already mentioned. It is a criminal and unbelievable misuse of words to try to differentiate between the races—particularly as regards the German racial war against Jews.

The descendants of Esau were not Hebrews and still less were they Israelites, since he married a girl from the land of Canaan, which was the hereditary enemy of the Chosen People.

The Canaanites occupied territory to the south of Syria, and were descended from Ham, the second son of Noah. Among Ham's descendants was also Mitsraim, the ancestor of the Egyptians.

When Esau was obliged to go into exile after the blessing bestowed upon his younger brother, he went to the land of Edom, south of Palestine and north-west of Arabia Petrea (Eilat, Akaba), and became the founder of the Edomites, who were traditional enemies of the Hebrews.

This piece of biblical history explains something of the arguments concerning the legitimate territory of the State of Israel and of the Gulf of Akaba, which was never a part of the heritage of the Israelites descended from Jacob nor of the Israelis, their successors, but was in fact the patrimony of Esau and of the Canaanite and Egyptian descendants of Ham. This is the historical point of view; but on the political plane, the Israelites hold the country on the edict of the U.N.O., and have bravely defended their right to it.

If Isaac's prophecy were to be fulfilled, one might think that the Egyptians and their allies would finally overcome the Israeli descendants of Jacob. But it would be perfectly reasonable to object that the whole story is legendary, and that many of the biblical prophecies have not been fulfilled.

The Antichrist of the Hebrews

According to tradition, before the end of the world the Antichrist will appear upon earth and will lead all men astray.

A great many political personalities, emperors, kings, dictators, have been labelled the Antichrist by their contemporaries —Nero, Napoleon, Hitler, Stalin, Nasser, all appear on the list. As far as the Jews are concerned, the Antichrist will bear the name Armilius. Rabbinic mythology says: 'He will be born in Rome, of the union of a number of scoundrels of various nationalities with a creature of exquisite beauty.

'His height will be prodigious, for he will be ten ells tall (about 35 feet); the distance between his eyes will be an ell;

the eyes will be red and fiery, and will be set deep in his head; his hair will be red-gold, his feet green; he will have two heads. He will proclaim that he is the Messiah, and the God whom all men should worship. All the posterity of the Romans will be ranged at his side. Nehemiah, the son of Joseph, the first Messiah (they expect two), will make war on him. He will march against him at the head of 30,000 Jews. Armilius will be beaten, and 200,000 men will be killed in the first battle.

'Armilius will return to the attack and, after losing an enormous number of his troops, will unknowingly kill Nehemiah, whose body will be borne thence by angels, to be interred with those of the ancient Patriarchs. After this the Jews will lose heart and take to flight. All nations will persecute them, more ferociously than ever before.

'But in the end, they will rise again. The Archangel Michael will sound the trumpet three times, and at the first blast the true Messiah will appear, the son of David, together with Elias the prophet. The Jews will gather round him and will make war on Armilius, who will be killed in a battle in which sulphur and fire from heaven will be rained upon his army (? an atomic war).

'This will be followed by the reign of the Messiah, and all Christians and infidels will be wiped out.'

The End of the World as Scientists see it

Two American geophysicists, Keith MacDonald, of the Environmental Science Services Administration, and Robert Gunst, of the U.S. Coast and Geodetic Survey, have calculated that the next end of the world will take place in the year 3991.

These two scientists have established that since the fifth century the magnetic field of the earth has been running down, increasingly so since 1670.

The magnetic field will have disappeared completely by about the year 4000, which will bring disastrous climatic changes and monstrous mutations in living creatures.

This is a resolutely optimistic calculation, for it seems very certain that the increased momentum of discovery and knowledge will bring the breaking point to well before the year 4000. We are consuming the time we have to live in days that are abnormally long, in action and speed, at the expense of conscious living. The rhythm of the advancement of science destroys our grey cells, drowns them, and the chances that we shall destroy the whole globe grow stronger and more probable from day to day. Men are going to other planets, an adventure which looks remarkably like a retreat, an exodus. By the time the first task force of earth-men has settled on the Moon, Venus or Mars, the end of our Earth may well be in sight.

Pioneers for the next cycle would thus be secured, as is predicted in the secret writings.

Then, if one may still believe in tradition, the Cabiri, Prometheus, Azazel, the Nagas, will appear on earth on their flying serpents, dragons, rams, solar barques, airships, which mean that initiators will again be coming from another planet to teach refugees from the Flood who will have returned to primitive conditions. Men from another planet—but they might well be earth-men returning to their own home.

Electronic Astrology

All astrology cannot be put on a level with the ramblings of rhabdomantists, clairvoyants, thaumaturgists, and other magi; some of them are genuine initiates, but most are 'enlightened' only in the most unflattering sense of the word—that is, cranks and charlatans.

In the old days, diviners, astrologers, physicists, mathematicians, Chaldeans, magicians and those who just guessed, were all included under the same heading.

The advancement of science has put mathematicians and physicists in the front rank, and it may be that astrologers will in due course also be advanced to the élite class.

For this to happen, it would be enough for astrology, if it is a science, to undergo internal reorganisation as mathematics,

284

chemistry and physics have done. A science or an art which does not progress is condemned to a more or less short lease of life.

Meanwhile, biologists and electronic scientists, armed with ordinators, organograms, perforated cards and programmers, are beginning to ask an electronic machine to provide a horoscope for any given individual, listing his capabilities, his potentials, his tastes, his health, and the mathematically calculated prospects for his future.

In America experiments with horoscopic machines are already playing a great part on the social side.

To obtain a horoscope within a few minutes, it is only necessary to press a score or so of buttons which adjust the machine: to co-ordinate the geographical place of birth, the year, month, time; length of life of the parents; medical particulars, university degrees, physical appearance, salary. Some of this information is recorded in figures, milligrams and as 0 or 1.

A perforated card, drafted in machine language, is passed into the decoder, and within a fraction of a second, sixty-six million planetary aspects and analytical systems are explored in the magnetic memory.

The horoscope is printed and issued in just over a minute.

To make the 'horoscopitheque' function, a dollar bill must be inserted.

In order to attain the precision reached by this machine, it would be necessary, so it appears, for ten astrologers, deeply versed in astronomy and mathematics, to work for three years on a single case, which would represent 90,000 hours of study.

In less than eighty seconds of effective operation, the machine will deliver a nicely printed horoscope seven pages long.

Undoubtedly, the future of astrology is linked with electronics, which does not exclude the participation of a qualified astrologer, at least insofar as the machine will not be endowed with the power of selection and interpretation for all possible cases.

But there seems to be little doubt that before long biologists will prefabricate human destiny, will interchange genes and will fit people so neatly into the pre-arranged forms of social life, that it will be hopeless for anyone to expect to have an individual fate that differs from the collective destiny.

While awaiting these imminent horrors, the astrologer continues to play his part in the mysterious unknown.

THE SCIENCE OF LUCIFER

CHAPTER TWENTY-ONE

SORCERY

The function of black magic and the cult of evil is to reverse the natural order and, in general, to give a wrong significance to everything.

In principle, the purpose of magic is not to do harm; on the contrary, its aim is to use—empirically—all the forces for good that are immanent in nature and in the physiological make-up of humanity. It is by an aberration that it has only too often come to be associated with fraudulent or unbalanced occultism.

White magic is directly connected with paganism, which takes us back to nature and restores the psychic balance of which some religions have deprived us.

The Bardo Thödol

The reason for describing false spiritualism—which includes black magic—is to show the danger threatening a neophyte when he is faced by ill-understood teaching that is essentially pernicious but is presented in the guise of initiation.

In India there are sects whose members commit suicide by simply refraining from all action, and 'sages' who, according to Strabo, burn themselves alive after long and rigorous discipline in detachment from the self.

In the Andes there are so-called 'thunderstruck men', who may also be considered to be deranged. They are people who have literally suffered shock from electric storms; they are recognisable because they have a diagonal gash across their faces running from the forehead to the chin. They are believed to be clairvoyant.

In Tibet, the *Bardo Thödol* (*Book of the Dead*), gives a whole ritual of black magic, according to the English version made by the Lama Kazi Dawa Samdup.

Where exactly the book originated is not known. It is thought to be a Tibetan adaptation of an Indian original or, more probably, a Buddhist adaptation of a Tibetan tradition, dating from before the seventh century.

The *Bardo Thödol* gives a description of the death of men who may have been Grand Masters and who, though dying, are still fully conscious. It tells how the spirit of the dying man sees infernal visions that shock and horrify him. In the intermediate state between death and rebirth the soul observes the effects of causes due to actions performed during its life on earth. Hell, devils, torments, do not exist objectively; everything is created by the spirit itself.

Next the mechanism of transmigration is shown, and the way in which an individual can decide upon his new parents and upon the sex in which he wishes to reincarnate.

'The phenomena of life may be likened to a dream, a phantasm, an air-bubble, a shadow, a glistening dew-drop, the dazzle of a lightning flash; and they should be considered as such.

'All is *maya*.' (Buddha in the Unalterable Sutra.)

In an even more condensed form, the *Bardo Thödol* treats of the cycle of life intervening between death and rebirth, the ancient law of karma, and the doctrine of reincarnation, all of which are essential to human existence.

Never eat Beans (Pythagoras)

The Egyptians used to think that the soul could migrate in a broad bean. In black magic it plays the same part as a toad—it acts as a sponge to absorb fluid.

In Sicily and in Southern Italy the practice of 'consuming' an enemy is still carried on; the magical ceremony is operated as follows:

A magician attaches to a dried broad bean some of the hair, nail parings or blood of the person who is to be 'consumed'. He places this effigy in a glass of water, to which he adds a few spoonfuls of olive oil, and on this he floats a night-light.

He evokes the victim by the power of his thought and so transfers the person's life into the bean. After a few days the bean begins to germinate, symbolising that life has been transferred. The sorcerer then practises 'sympathetic magic' whereby the light, which burns day and night and is fed by the oil, consumes the life of the person upon whom the spell has been cast.

The rite of blood is probably the oldest form of magic; it was used by alchemical sorcerers who sacrificed children to the fire. Paracelsus knew of the rite, but did not practise it.

It was believed that the red corpuscles of the blood had a neutralising effect upon foreign bodies in the alchemical brew.

In February 1968, the members of a band of sorcerers who lived in a cave in the State of Bahia in Brazil, cut off a man's head in order to sacrifice it, with some of the victim's blood, to an enchanted serpent who lived, so they said at the inquest, in the depths of their cave. If they had managed to satisfy it, the serpent would have reverted to its original shape, that of a wondrously beautiful maiden.

Erotic Inspiration

Serge Hutin is an erudite specialist in magic. The following notes on Tantrism were written by him.

'The ultimate aim of alchemy—actual physical translation from one state of matter to another—might be expressed thus: "To go to heaven without passing through death."

'An adept, freed from all the terrestrial limitations that have resulted from the original Fall, definitely leaves the physical plane of existence and rises to the height of suprasensory vibrations in a glorified body. To attain this result he follows a particular occult course for which he prepares by graduated

290

psychic exercises, with progressively liberating effects.

'But what is the internal force used by alchemists to ensure their ascent to heaven? The great secret of Tantric alchemy is simply this: to reverse, to turn inwards, the physical sexual energy, so as to awaken the tremendous divine force which slumbers in the ordinary course of existence. This is *kundalini*, pictured in Tantric iconography as a coiled snake, which must be roused to work its way up the whole of the spinal column. One by one, each of the psychic centres—called *chakras* in Sanskrit—will be stimulated, the state of ecstasy (transitory at first, later permanent) will develop when the force reaches the higher centres (the thousand-petalled lotus) in the top of the cranium.

'Two paths are open to the adept: that of the *right*, in which the magical liberation is effected by solitary discipline; and that of the *left*, in which the alchemical result is achieved by inverting the method, that is to say by consummating a 'chemical marriage', symbolised concretely by a man and a woman.

'The two paths do not appear only in the Hindu and Buddhist forms of Tantrism, but were also developed in the western tradition of alchemy. There are two types of adept: those who work alone, like the alchemist monks, for example; and those who work in couples, the best known of them, in western countries, probably being Nicholas Flamel and his wife Pernelle. Aleister Crowley was a contemporary "magus", who indulged largely in "left-hand" magical practices, in England and elsewhere.'

The Witches' Weighing Machine at Oudewater

Oudewater is a small holiday resort in southern Holland. It has a weighing machine in the Office of Weights and Measures, that was famous in the old days for extreme precision.

The balance is ten feet high and its platforms, on one of which Queen Juliana was once weighed, are about three feet across.

In the Middle Ages trial-by-weight terrified anyone suspected of dabbling in the black arts. The mechanism was called the 'Witches' Balance'.

It was in use until the seventeenth century.

Christians of those days claimed that witches, who had the power of flying astride a broomstick to attend their Sabbaths, weighed less than honest women. People with swarthy complexions, with frizzy hair, dark skins, flashing black eyes, or twisted limbs were reputed to be creatures of the devil. Nor, indeed, has the belief died out altogether yet.

In addition, it was believed that the Evil One always put his brand on the bodies of his people—the 'devil's mark', which usually showed as tufts of hair, birthmarks or other blemishes shaped more or less like a cloven hoof or a claw-like hand.

Five or six centuries ago, to have the reputation of being a witch or to be suspected of having peculiar marks on one's body was enough to send many an innocent person to the stake. That was why from all over Holland, also from France, England and Germany, thousands of poor wretches, male and female, flocked to ask for a trial-by-weight at Oudewater, to establish the purity of their bodies and souls.

Most of these people were women. They had to get on to the balance stark naked, with their hair unbound, so that they could not conceal any extra weights about their persons.

If the weight was judged to be satisfactory, all that remained was for the Jury of the Balance to inspect minutely that anatomy of the 'patient' and to hand out a certificate to say that he/she was no diabolist—fortunately this was the most usual outcome. The ceremony was not free, by the way—it cost three florins per acquittal. And as it took place in public it always attracted large ribald crowds.

Magic and sorcery take on a more sinister aspect when, instead of being indulged in by cranks with peculiar tastes, they become a criminal practice carried on by people one of the least of whose sins is to believe in the efficacy of their lucubrations and in the inspiration of their unbalanced minds. The evil lies not in magic itself but in those who believe in it.

Ghosts may know the Future

In olden days everyone believed that the spirits of people who died by violence haunted the earth in search of peace or of another body in which to reincarnate.

The belief is still held by spiritists, sorcerers and those practising black magic, who think that the body has a double, a shade, which lingers in an indeterminate zone after death, somewhere between this world and the Hereafter, or in the anti-world.

Scientists have given evidence that life really does persist in another world which, without absolutely proving the beliefs of black magicians, at least provides them with some substance. So it has of late years been shown that the magical practices of necromancers and old-time physicists were based on empirical knowledge of a science whose laws we are only now beginning to understand.

How far is it true, one wonders, that doubles or ghosts have the power to foresee the future, to prophesy? To the extent that it is possible to enter into communication with them, that it is to say to make them speak, it is highly probable that we are at the same time listening-in to the future; the world in which ghosts live has really no common dimension with ours, and especially not as regards time. This makes it understandable that the practice of black magic, in one of its disciplines, was aimed at inducing phantoms to speak, either with the help of mediums, which is harmless, or by fixing the soul of a dead person in a magic oracular statuette, which is linked directly with ritual crime.

Necromancy

From the very earliest times men have tried to call up the spirits of the dead, either out of curiosity or for some other reason, and have used magical rites to do so.

Syrians and Hebrews were great necromancers; The Bible quotes the case of the Witch of Endor, who raised the ghost of

Samuel at the request of Saul.

Isaiah says that spirits evoked in this way manifest their presence by a gentle murmur or by words spoken in a low voice.

Georg Horn (or Hornius), a German historian and geographer, says that the Hebrew word *nephilim*, meaning giants, shining ones, mighty ones, is derived from the word *nephi*, a cadaver, and means necromancers. It is also possible that nephilim could mean powerful, brilliant, erudite men, in fact magicians in the sense that to the unlearned every scientist is a magician.

What makes one suspect that there was apt to be trickery in the business is that the Greek version of the Septuagint calls them *engastrimyths*, which means ventriloquists.

Jews and Syrians, say chroniclers, 'used to kill a child by wringing its neck, then they cut off the head, salted or embalmed it and stood it on a metal plate marked with the name of whichever spirit or deity they wished to evoke.' Black magicians who indulged in these horrible practices acted without malice or intentional cruelty, but solely, one might say, in a spirit of scientific enquiry, with the fine detachment of a biologist doing a piece of vivisection.

Often, indeed, they submitted themselves to fasting and other mortifications in order to lend an even greater solemnity to the sacrifice. On the other hand, there were some who gave themselves up unreservedly to demonology or to erotic sadism.

In the fifteenth century at Toledo—Toledo was at that time the centre of Arabian magic—there were schools of necromancy housed in deep caves, which were walled up on the orders of Queen Isabella the Catholic. We are told that, given a corpse, Arabic magicians could make a body materialise, imponderable but visible, having no living organs, yet able to suffer in spirit, but also to enjoy the pleasures of love.

Since the Middle Ages, true satanic black magic has been based on ritual murder, either for the purpose of using the victim's last breath in alchemical work, or to operate a transfer

of life from the victim to a statue or statuette, which was later
to be used for prophecy.

Ritual Sacrifice by Alchemists

Whatever may have been the aim of alchemical research—and
it was generally claimed to be a spiritual quest—it was but
rarely that practitioners of the art were led into perversions
and crime. On the other hand, they certainly used methods
that would seem most peculiar to anyone not familiar with biological laboratories, and that were not at all orthodox even in
the eyes of alchemists themselves. They evidently suffered
pangs of conscience, and if hard-pressed would take refuge
under the 'oath of initiation', so as to avoid talking about it.

Fulcanelli, in his book *Le Mystère des Cathédrales**, writes
as follows about *boiled dew*:

'I wish I could say more on this subject, which is one of
immense importance, and show how the *Dews of May* (Maia
was the mother of Hermes)—the life-giving fluid of the month
dedicated to Mary, the Virgin Mother—is easily extracted
from a particular body, base and despicable though it may be
(of which the characteristics have already been described), were
it not that there are limits which must not be overstepped. . . .
This touches upon the deepest secret of The Work, and the
vow must be kept.'

Errors and omissions excepted—the jargon of amateurs trying to give the impression that they are saying everything, but
carefully avoiding anything that might be understood—the
Dews of May seem to have a certain similarity with the hor-
monal secretions of a woman. If so, why not say so?

Complete absence of sunlight is a sort of dogma in alchemy
while on the other hand one of its principles is to 'give birth to
a new creature' by using 'the blood of two children born of
different mothers'.

Undoubtedly these words are meant to be taken symbolically, at all events by properly initiated alchemists, but the

* Published by Neville Spearman.

295

metaphor might have been chosen more delicately.

Unless one branch of alchemists chose quite traditionally to anticipate ritual human sacrifice as a preparation for the Great Work?

The Great Work of Gilles de Rais

Gilles de Rais, Lord of the manors of Machecoul and Tiffauges, of Laval, of Montfort and others, first made his name by outstanding courage, and his loyalty to Joan of Arc. Then, in about the year 1435, he became an alchemist, surrounded himself with sorcerers and magicians, began the search for the Philosophers' Stone and tried to solve the mystery of the Great Work.

Although he was reasonably well educated, he could not disentangle the symbol from the literal meaning of what he was learning, and believed that the active principle of the Stone must derive from the actual life of a man or, still better, from that of a child.

La Meffraie, an old witch, was ordered by him to go all through the countryside of Brittany and La Vendée, to look for shepherd boys, beggars, lost children, whom she beguiled into accompanying her to Gilles' mansion, where they became the victims of ritual murder. Ultimately rumours reached the Duke of Brittany; Gilles de Rais was arrested, brought to trial and executed at Nantes on 25th October 1440.

Before his execution he saw François Prelati, his master alchemist, and said to him amid tears: 'Farewell, François my friend, we shall not meet again in this world. I pray to God that He may give you patience and knowledge; and be sure that if you persevere and have faith in God, we shall meet again in Paradise with great joy.'

Unfortunately for so excellent a Christian, he had not always lived up to these proper sentiments, as was shown at the trial.

In a tower in one of his houses—though it was said that he had never lived there—a huge box was found full of charred bones, that appeared to be the remains of about forty children. Almost as many were discovered in the attics of four or five other houses; the total number of his victims was calculated to have been 149.

He appears also to have killed seven or eight women, to several of whom he had been married—but that is another story.

Michelet said that the Sire de Rais used to raise demons and that he sacrificed young children to the devil, praying to be granted gold, wisdom and power. The normal ritual in this form of crime is to make a sacrificial holocaust in honour of some reputedly infernal deity—Satan, Beelzebub, Moloch, Lucifer or the terrible Kali, the Hindu goddess of hell.

Rais strangled the children with his own hands, used their blood and the principal vital organs in the preparation of hideous brews which, after being mixed, boiled and re-boiled, would, it was hoped, lead to the discovery of The Stone.

After all this, he attended church devoutly, joined in sacred processions and was a delightfully kind and thoughtful friend in all circumstances.

Oracular Figures

Necromancy has different aims, one of which is to cause the transfer of a human life into the substance of a statuette which used to be called an 'oracular figure'.

It does not appear that in those days any concrete result was achieved. Nowadays, it is theoretically not impossible that some mentally disordered person with an elementary knowledge of physics and electronics might think that a transfer had some chance of being effected in certain conditions.

One may imagine what a magician, possibly not realising the criminal nature of the enterprise, could be induced to do if his mania drove him to try practical black magic in the hope of creating an oracular figure.

What is called white magic is more often than not really black magic; and since there is no barrier between the edge of

297

the cliff and the abyss, it is probable that some wretched lunatics, visionaries, paranoiacs or criminals might descend to depths of horror from which reason recoils.

The operation is understood to consist in raising a ghost, one of the 'doubles' that persist after earthly life is extinct, and attaching the apparition to a body of natural matter such as clay.

Electric fixation would be operated by a sort of induction from the ghost to a magnetic torus controlled by a transistor; or, at a pinch, to the tape of a magnetophone, though this last would not be a very sure method.

The figure would have to be made, according to ritual magic, of clay mixed with the blood, hair, nails and if possible the vital organs of a particular victim. For, clearly, there must *be* a victim, a human being, preferably young, so that the glands, the hormones and the breath should be in a state of development and growth. This was why Gilles de Rais sacrificed young children.

Egyptian books on sorcery spoke of the mode of transference by means of the *Ka* or *Kraa* (this last being an onomatopoeic word for the last breath of a dying person) as the soul leaves the body.

Sorcerers in olden times used to try to catch the *kraa*, either in order to resuscitate another dead man or to enclose it in something like a knob of butter or a bean. A modern magician —if such there be—might in his turn try to embed the soul of his victim in a torus, a magnetic strip, a mandrake root or a piece of amber attached to a statuette made of natural matter.

A lunatic might believe in the miracle; even a scientist might, since the soul is traditionally credited with entering into places that are electrically charged, or into objects that have been impregnated by a living body.

The statuette would be constructed on the same principle as that which made people gather mandrake roots grown underneath a gibbet in the old days—but in a more scientific way, if one may use the term.

There would remain only the problem of making the figure

298

speak and give oracular answers to questions. This would require the performance of at least two ceremonies:

—a rite of homage, such as the dedication of an altar to the statue and the celebration of services in its honour;

—a magic rite of stimulation by means of vigils, prayer and meditation, to create a force powerful enough to give the figure the ability to remember and to express itself in sound and words.

To ensure the necessary psychic concentration, magicians invoked the help and protection of some entity believed to be malefic, such as Satan, Beelzebub or Kali.

Actually, it would be equally effective in black magic to transfer the *kraa* to a young plant which, if carefully tended, would act as support for the statuette by providing the raw material of life. In this way the spirit would be attached to a living body capable of prolonging its existence.

Ritual crimes are still committed, even today. In May 1966 two sorcerers were condemned to death in Tanzania for killing a boy of twelve, who was actually their own nephew and grandson.

They had cut off his sexual organs, his tongue, his eyelids and his right ear (touch, speech, sight, hearing) which they had dried in the sun and then reduced to a powder that they believed had magical properties.

Other ritual crimes have been reported from the Indies, Chile, Central Africa, Brazil and even from Europe, where magic is not always of a pagan, sacred character—white magic, in the current use of the words.

To draw attention to the dangers, it seems useful to give these grisly details, even if only to put sorcerers' apprentices on their guard.

Black magic is never practised with impunity. It always, and unavoidably, leads to mental and moral deterioration in anyone who indulges in it; it is rarely that it escapes worldly justice, and never can it escape that of the Beyond—the appropriate *karma* that no charm can ward off.

299

MYSTERIES OF THE SKIES

CHAPTER TWENTY-TWO

EXTRA-TERRESTRIALS AND THE
JOURNEY TO BÂAVI

When civilisations begin to crumble, men raise their eyes to the heavens and see strange things. Moses saw a burning bush, John the Baptist saw the Holy Spirit, prophets and people saw flying ships, fiery wheels and UFOs. Will beings from another planet soon land on earth? It all seems to add up to the probability that these 'visions' are somehow due to the premonition of a fantastic future awaiting us; mankind is searching for new gods and is growing increasingly sure that they will appear.

Professor André Bouguenec writes on the subject of UFOs: 'It matters little whether flying saucers exist or not. On the other hand, the phenomenon in itself is of great importance because it actually influences governmental budgets when money is allotted to this form of research. Flying saucers are capable of liberating intelligent if dogmatic minds, of suggesting new theories about our origins and making us accept new ideas about history and vanished civilisations.

'The flying saucer is a miraculous phenomenon in the sense that in spite of ourselves we are transported in time and space into the past, towards our human beginnings, which we suspect were somehow linked with extra-terrestrial life.'

The twentieth century is placed under the sign of Aquarius by most occultists, but that means little to the truly esoteric enquirer.

Grégori B. . . . calls our epoch the *Age of the Condor*.

Incontestably, our age is an age of science, of space-rockets, of eccentration, not to say eccentricity, in every sphere of life.

A physicist, a chemist, a painter, a poet, a mathematician who is not eccentric, out of the ordinary, is a back number.

Of course there are still some old-fashioned artists who might paint a bottle, a glass and an apple on an oak table, to express to all and sundry the state of their souls—but the future is not for them; they are doomed to perish unnoticed.

The live man looks at the heavens, explores the universe, seeking an answer that his own subconscious suggests to him. He probes even the infinitely small, the atom, in which he discovers, as though seen through the other end of a telescope, what happens in the immensities when they are invaded by foreign bodies.

Do they really exist, these 'foreign bodies' that come from the skies, and flying saucers which may mean the same?

Man has a vague feeling that truth is coming or will come from the stars, not only to explain his past history but also to foretell the future, to give some meaning to civilisation, to enrich his inheritance and help him to know his earliest ancestors.

For this reason, UFOs have a role to play.

The Paris Observatory, 1 December 1967

In October 1967, with mythology in mind, also the fact that 1st May was a sacred date among Celts, and that the gods of the Incas and Mayas had a Venusian quality, a note was sent to M. Jean François Denis, head of the Paris Observatory, containing four questions:

1. Is May, either on 1st or at any other time in the month, of importance in the gravitation of Venus towards the earth?

2. Has Venus a satellite?

3. Do you think that Venus might have entered the solar system as a comet and have remained as a planet, some five thousand years ago? (Notes enclosed on the subject.)

4. The Tirvalour Astronomical Tables mentioned in these notes were deposited at the Navy Office in the eighteenth century by Sylvain Bailly, Astronomer Royal and Mayor of Paris.

Is it known where these Tables are now?

A month later, the following answer was received, from which much may be learnt:

'R. Forgo, Astronomer at the Paris Observatory to M. Robert Charroux:

Sir,

1. The month of May appears to have no particular importance as regards the position of Venus relative to the earth; but it was noted that on 17th May 1966 Venus was at the aphelion (the point farthest from the sun in its orbit). In 1967 it reached its greatest heliocentric latitude on 15th May; that is, it was at its highest point in the sky.

2. Venus has no satellite.

3. The theory that Venus was an intruder into the solar system will have to be examined.

4. The Tirvalour Tables are not at the Paris Observatory....'

A list of addresses was added, at which enquiries had already been made fruitlessly.

All the same, this gave some useful information, for undoubtedly, rightly or wrongly, the planet Venus is often referred to in the matter of extra-terrestrial migrations.

The head of the Paris Observatory evidently thought it wiser not to write an answer himself, but probably Monsieur Forgo reflected the official opinion in his reply.

It is clear that the month of May is very important in the Venus–Earth relationship. Both in 1966 and in 1967 Venus was nearest to our globe in May.

Officially, the *possibility* that Venus arrived in our planetary system four or five thousand years ago is admitted (it is implicit in all traditions), and that it actually occurred at the time when the last extra-terrestrial initiators came here. It is worth noting that the Initiators of the Celts all arrived on 1st May.

But this point is of no interest to astronomers. And neither, it seems is the place where the Tirvalour Tables are hidden.

This is not to say that political governments in the modern

world are concealing anything that has to do with contact thought to have been made with space people. There is nothing to prove this. But it is a fact that the Establishments of all countries seem to be hiding any documents of historical value that run counter to accepted Judeo-Christian history. The sequestration of the Tirvalour Tables is only one incident among many. And this forbidden history smacks strongly of Venus, of Sirius or of some other astral body.

Life on Mars

The conquest of the moon by American cosmonauts seems to have put an end to the theories of people who thought of it as a sort of half-way house for space-ships, or a satellite inhabited by strange creatures, Selenians or Lunarians. Yet there is no doubt that life does exist on other, more salubrious planets.

'UFO Contact Bufoi', a Belgian paper, writes:

'According to an American astronomer, there must be at least 100 million planets in the universe that are covered with vegetation and inhabited by beings much like earth-men.

'Dr. P. Morrisson, of the Institute of Technology in Massachusetts, thinks that beings living on other planets are much more like ourselves than we are apt to suppose.

'Professor Harold Urey, Nobel Prize winner for chemistry, is convinced that the chemical elements forming the basis for living creatures are the same throughout the cosmos, and he argues from this that life itself will manifest identically on all planets governed by physical conditions of the same kind.'

Life most probably exists on Mars, says Dr. Richard Young, of N.A.S.A., even if only in rudimentary form.

Purely as a hypothesis, a French Review called *Unknown Phenomena*, has published the study of a possible correlation between UFOs and earthquakes, which have been unusually frequent in the last few years.

'It has been proved,' says the periodical, 'that phenomena are engendered by these machines, ranging from the jamming of engines to the calcination of organic matter. They are,

305

therefore, causing some form of magnetic disturbance.

'During most earthquakes, people see showers of black or fiery particles, lights in the sky and other manifestations of this type.'

It is an interesting theory, but would surely demand investigation in reverse: could it not be that earthquakes produce these mysterious phenomena in the sky rather than the other way round?

Extra-terrestrial Alphabets

A French journal, *Phenomènes Spatiaux* (*Space Phenomena*) published a letter from R. P. Reyna, astronomer at the Observatory of Adhara de San Miguel in the Argentine Republic, from which the following passage is taken:

'I know only two men who say that they are in communication with individuals from UFOs, and one of them writes a cosmic language called *varkulets*; I went to see him with several other people, and we were shown something like a dozen books written in this script. He went on to tell us that he had seen their cities and had had their form of government explained to him. . . .'

These statements have been confirmed with Dr. Reyna.

A reproduction of the *varkulets* characters including some ideograms, appears between pages 240–41.

According to the translation which Dr. Reyna sent, the E is like a question mark with a dash over it; the O looks like the figure 4 in our script; the Y is a trident; the A is like a small f written backwards; and so on.

The periodical *Space Phenomena* very properly and understandably has considerable reservations on the authenticity of this form of writing:

'Are the men whom R. P. Reyna met really anything but mystagogues or lunatics? And the meetings they claim to have had with extra-terrestrials—are they pure invention or are they the result of delirium? On the other hand, could there be a modicum of truth in their assertions and their documents?'

What Dr. Reyna asks herself is what we are all asking our-selves. . . .

If the documents she refers to are the work of a mystery-monger, one must at all events grant that the inventor did not spare himself, for he filled a dozen volumes with the unknown characters, when he might have been content with a great many fewer.

And if he was a practical joker or a visionary, one must admit at any rate that he had some talent and that his dreams were far from ordinary. . . .

Mn. Y. returns

It was in very much the same state of mind as R. P. Reyna's that the present writer and a friend heard statements made by Mn. Y. in 1966 about his journey to the planet Bâavi in the Alpha group of Centaur A and B.

After some years of silence, Mn. Y. renewed contact. No doubt he had thought things over, possibly he had received certain orders, and this time he brought substantial documen-tation which was, not to put too fine a point on it, wildly exciting.

'Five years ago,' he said, 'the extra-planetary beings who look after us manifested themselves officially.'

Like R. P. Reyna's mysterious personage, Mn. Y. produced so compendious a documentation, that the life of one man would not have been long enough to invent it all. For ex-ample:

—The story of the journey to Bâavi.

—An almost complete grammar of the Bâavi (or Bâal) lan-guage, which was submitted to the criticism of an expert in linguistics at a College in Algiers. This man said that it could certainly be the grammar of some language unknown to him, but that it contained anomalies, which led him to suppose that the grammar had been copied or written by someone who was not an expert, because there was a good deal of confusion and imprecision, and probably the writer did not know the Bâavi

307

language himself.

To which Mn. Y. replied that indeed he was not familiar either with the language or the grammar, and that he had made the copy as best he could.

—Descriptions of inter-galactic space-craft, constructed on a system which in some particulars was entirely different from any terrestrial science.

—Invention of a system of timing, a philosophy.

—Documents written in Armenian and stating the fundamentals of Bâavian science.

One could only wonder whether anyone would take the trouble to work out anything so complete simply for the sake of taking a rise out of people.

True, it would not be the first time that somebody had invented a new form of writing.

But it would also mean that Mn. Y. had gone to the further trouble of inventing a science, a system of timing, of weights and measures, of philosophy, and ethics.

In short, all this would involve a tremendous amount of work for a single individual, whose personality would be worthy of great respect if he were what he claims to be—and whose inventive skill must be admired if he were an impostor.

For these reasons, it is proposed to publish some of the astonishing revelations contained in Mn. Y.'s files:

A man went from Earth to the planet Bâavi, and tells the story of his adventures on the interplanetary journey.

He explains the principles of the construction of a vaïd (a space-craft).

The reader is left to form his own judgment of the extraordinary revelations contained in the narrative.

Parchments in a Pottery Container

The documentation presented here did not come direct from the constellation Centaur. In part the papers were written down from memory and plans were drawn from originals which the present writer did not see. The Armenian manuscripts—whose authenticity is extremely doubtful—came from another source in a way that is reminiscent of the discovery of the Dead Sea Scrolls.

In 1934 Mn. Y. was in southern Algeria in the highlands between the Ighargharem Valley, near the Tassili of Ajjer (Azdjer), and the Issaouan Valley.

While there, he came across an old Saharan nomad who had a fund of strange tales, but who was never taken seriously either by the local people or by the few Europeans who passed that way.

Mn. Y. managed to get on to good terms with the old man, who one day took him into a cave where the two of them dug up a flat pottery dish covered with sand that had apparently blown in from the desert. In the dish was a parcel sewn into an animal skin, which appeared to have been packed fairly recently. Mn. Y. undid the stitches and saw that the parcel contained a manuscript book of aphorisms and religious texts; and between two pages of the book were two parchments written in a language that seemed to be Armenian and which, as was shown by what followed, gave five Bâavian maxims.

The guide did not ask for any monetary reward for his trouble, which interested Mn. Y.

How had the parchments come to be buried in this place, why did the old man tell about them—and by what miracle did an archaic Armenian text come to be the transcription of documents about the planet Bâavi? Not even Mn. Y. himself could say, let alone anyone else.

But perhaps the apparently fortuitous discovery was somehow a line cast by Initiators to bring Mn. Y. into contact with them.

Text of Document No. 1: 'Space in a galaxy and in a galactic group is not absolute space in the accepted sense. It is the womb of three-dimensional worlds.

'In absolute space, time-movement does not exist.

'The extra-cosmic present is the essence of absolute space.' (That is to say, it is the essence of a universe which is neither elemental nor vital.)

309

M. Samuelian, an erudite philologist, who was consulted about the manuscripts, declared them to be of no value. They are, he said, either simply a fraud or they are written in a code in which the letters in French words have been replaced by the corresponding letters in Armenian.

In the first of these cases, therefore, Mn. Y. had been cheated by a pretended discovery; the second might have been designed to bring an earth-man into contact with extra-terrestrial emissaries. The mystery and these considerations raise quite justifiable suspicions.

Text of Document No. 2: 'So-called external space is axiomatically possible only in a limited cosmos.

'In a three-dimensional world, the important thing is for the elemental to be constant: thus immobility is made apparent by comparison with movement and remains independent of it though not immaterial to it.'

'I went to Bâavi'

Mn. Y. came to see us at Vienne.

This was not his usual custom, and we had a presentiment that he was going to tell us something important. Perhaps he was coming on an official mission? That, in fact, was more or less the case.

About dusk, it was on 10th November 1968, and might have been about 6 o'clock in the evening, when twilight predisposes to confidences.

Mn. Y. began to talk, at first with some hesitation, but in the end we heard the essentials of the adventure.

During the War, at some date between 1940 and 1945, Mn. Y. disappeared for two months. Times were difficult, and nobody went willingly to the commissariat or to the police station; in short, his family thought he was dead and went into mourning.

'I had gone to meet some people,' said Mn. Y. 'The ones I met inspired confidence, and they too showed confidence in me. They took me to Bâavi with them.'

310

'Look here,' we objected, 'it can't have happened just like that. You must have left home, have taken your car or a taxi, or a train. Transport was either non-existent during the war, or very precarious. How did you get to the meeting place?'

'By train as far as Cosne-sur-Loire. Then I was in a covered cart, horse-drawn, in which I travelled for a couple of hours. Although it was dark and the cart was covered, I noticed one name—Villaine; but that wasn't the end of the journey.'

'Did you see the next vehicle you were to travel in?'

'Of course.'

'Did you touch it before you got into it?'

'I touched the part where I got in, which was nearly five feet off the ground. I had quite a job to climb aboard.'

'When you were doing so, did you feel as if you were in a different state, were you in full possession of your senses, or did it all seem like a dream?'

'I was excited, but perfectly conscious. The most curious part was that as soon as I had got in, I had a feeling of weightlessness. The whole thing rose vertically, and flew in a direction running approximately from Auxerre to La Rochelle.'

The aim of this sort of interrogation is obvious: to find out if Mn. Y. had really been on this journey or if he had only imagined it, if he had dreamt it or if he had undergone hypnotic suggestion.

The various possibilities had to be investigated, ranging from lies to truth and including hallucination.

How can we make our feelings understandable?

To all appearances the man is balanced and sensible, taciturn rather than garrulous. He has no wish to make a splash, to impress, to be the centre of attention. He is cultured, intelligent, serious-minded. Honestly, from our knowledge of him, we were prejudiced in his favour. Everything about him seemed open and sincere, but there was the immensity of the whole affair—to visit a planet which is three and a half light-years distant. That may be 'just next-door' to an astronomer, but is rather a different matter for a cosmonaut!

Mn. Y. had already told us secrets about other things, things

311

to do with prescience, intuition and even 'revelations'. We reminded him of it:

'As far as we are concerned, we do not believe in revelation, as you know. You are different; the state of mind of someone who believes in revelations is not far removed from the kind of credulousness of a bigot or a fanatic. Anyone who sees and hears miraculous things may easily believe that he has taken a journey in Time. Do you see what we mean?'

'Certainly I do. But it is something of an exaggeration to say that I believe in "revelations"—any more than I believe in God, at least what people think of as God. I understand your hesitation and your doubts; and I think you are right. One can't easily believe in anything of that sort. All the same, I am talking about an adventure that I lived through while I was fully conscious, and which lasted for two months. Yes; I spent two months on Bâavi. The journey took an hour and a half. Everything happened very quickly, and as far as that is concerned, I must say that consciousness did not come into the question. The machine—the vaïd, I mean—flew at more than gravific speed, and then we were in anti-time. I also know that the vaïd accelerated even more before turning and that it changed course three times on the way from Earth to Alpha Centaur.'

Guessing at the World

When Mn. Y. told us in detail what his life and adventures had been while he was on the planet Bâavi, we knew exactly what the state of mind of Rusta Pisan must have been when Marco Polo—who was in prison at the time—dictated to him the incredible tale of his travels in Asia.

Marco Polo's book was at first called *Guessing at the World*, and was treated with so much incredulity in Italy, that he was called 'Signor Million', just as Christopher Columbus was dubbed 'Señor Fabuloso'.

Just imagine: Marco Polo told people that the Chinese used wooden blocks for copying their books—and that was a century and a half before the 'invention' of printing by Gutenberg!

In the same way, it will probably only be in the future that the story of Mn. Y.'s voyage will find a public sufficiently intellectually conditioned to take in the extraordinary story that he told in 1968.

Of course the truth or otherwise of the story cannot be checked. However, we can go so far as to say that on Bâavi all human activity is concentrated in a metropolis, the rest of the planet being left to nature and to the animals which inhabit it. Men and women are on a footing of absolute equality, and have a life-span which, though not unlimited, runs to several centuries. Their age is, so to speak, arrested when they attain their majority.

Before becoming full members of society, young people, as soon as they reach the proper age, are expected to make their genetic contribution, whether they are male or female; after that they are sterilised.

There is no marriage among the Bâavians; love is free in the physical sense, but the fact of indulging in it one or more times a day with one or several women, does not imply any particular feeling of affection or tenderness. The Bâavians all love each other, without any special preferences. Exceptions are rare—a state of affairs very difficult for us to envisage. They foresee that a great cataclysm will occur on earth within a comparatively short time, and it seems that the Bâavians want to save some part of the human race, possibly with the idea of repopulating the earth afterwards.

'Operation Noah', as one might say.

This is all we are allowed to publish.

There remains the great, the agonising, the burning problem: Is Mn. Y. speaking the truth? Did he have his adventure purely in imagination? Has he been tricked by phantasms as perhaps Enoch and Ezekiel were?

'Did you bring back anything, photographs, or a film, or some object that would be evidence of your stay in Bâavi?,' we asked when he had finished speaking.

313

'No. I was naked when I got into the vaïd; and I was naked when I came down again.'

'Then how on earth can you expect anyone to believe what you have been saying? You know very well that nowadays you have to show some proof if you want to be taken seriously.'

'Fair enough,' said Mn. Y. 'You should not believe what I say on my word alone. But I can tell you the secret of anti-gravitation, and of the construction of a vaïd. You can have the papers examined by any expert you like or who wants to see them. If the documents turn out to make sense, you will be obliged to believe me. If, on the other hand, they are only gibberish, you will draw the obvious conclusion.'

'Would you authorise us to submit them to any scientist we choose?'

'With pleasure. The privilege of truth is to be able to stand up to examination.'

Conclusions of Mn. Y.

Here follows a faithful transcription of the conclusion of our interview with Mn. Y.

'Have you never had the feeling that twentieth-century man no longer lives in harmony with universal laws? The direction of its evolution is turning the planet Earth into a sort of infernal machine destined for a tragic fate.

'In our society, the individual human unit will soon be replaced by another sort of unit, a kind of robot, whose ideals and behaviour will be expected to conform to the artificial criteria dictated by the masters. At every social level, from the labourer to the intellectual, people's minds are troubled, and this anxiety is expressed in anarchic agitation, violence, confusion, the negation of art and denial of the divine. In the vehemence of the natural desire for survival, our civilisation resorts to techniques in which the machine is superior to the man who invented it.

'One can no longer believe that any thinking being will be able for much longer to keep his freedom of choice, or even his

314

right to life, so imminent does the cataclysm seem that will destroy our planet.

'These ideas are not intended to introduce a new philosophy according to which everything must be destroyed so as to make possible a fresh beginning. The results of violence are always abortive. Only one decision is immediately essential—to make certain that *somewhere* free will, the right to choose, will always exist. Men who are of this mind should get to know one another as quickly as possible. Mn. Y.'

Mn. Y. sent a detailed plan for the construction of a vaïdorge, *which will not be communicated to anyone at all.*

The design has been examined by competent engineers, sworn to secrecy, who thought the ideas showed genius, but pointed out that there were technical impossibilities, no doubt due to the nature of our scientific system.

The brief description which follows is by the hand of its author, and the present writer admits that he is not qualified to judge of its merits.

Vaïdorges: Mn. Y.'s Description

A vaïdorge is made of anti-gravitational metal.

A mass is regarded as positive in a gravitational field because it can be expressed in conventional weight.

Once it leaves that gravitational field it becomes neutral or 'a-gravitational'.

Intrinsically, however, it retains an autonomous force of gravity which will attract any body smaller than itself, in proportion to its volume, that is to say, according to the amount of space it occupies.

But if this same mass acts as a repellent within the gravitational range of a planet, if it repels instead of attracting objects in space smaller than itself that come within its orbit, one may say that it is anti-gravitational and that its weight is negative.

In the centre of the disk, with a domed cover above and below, is the navigation cabin.

This may be compared to a large ball-bearings system, with

315

about a quarter-inch play in its movement. It can, neverthe-less, remain absolutely stationary except for the continuous giratory movement of the disk itself.

Its reliability depends on the one hand upon the gravita-tional galactic waves (gravific waves) that vibrate in resonance with the lenses of the disk; and on the other hand upon a belt of radio-active material surrounding the central cell of the cabin that emits unstable nucleons.

The navigation cabin is spherical, transparent from within, but opaque from the outside; it is isothermal and resistant to both light rays and radiation; light can be seen from the in-terior, but this interior is itself dark.

Inside is a central sphere some five feet in diameter, which contains only the ship's instruments, the navigational aids and protosynthetic machinery. This central sphere is also the actual stabilising mechanism; it prevents the ship from react-ing to any giratory movements of the disk which may be caused by cosmic forces of turbulence.

There are four radius vectors which are connected to the remote-control apparatus that keeps the sphere in the exact centre of the navigation cabin.

It should be noted also that everything in this cabin is weightless, so seats etc. would be of no use. It contains nothing but mooring ropes stowed all around its circumference, to act as stabilisers while the ship is at rest. A hand-rail surrounds the machinery, so that all manoeuvres can be carried out while the navigator steadies himself with one hand.

A vaïd cannot stand on the ground, but it can be made to hover steadily at four or five feet above ground by making certain adjustments at the gate-lock.

Observers have noticed three marks on the ground after the departure of the vessel; this is due to the fact that it uses three floating magnetic hawsers.

The three ropes do not touch the ground, but their mag-netism attracts minute particles of earth to the loose ends, and this small amount of ballast is enough to prevent the vaïd from drifting laterally.

Modification of gravific waves is effected by twenty-four lenses (twelve on either side of the disk) that switch on the apparatus. The various evolutions—starting, sudden stoppage, enormous acceleration—are controlled by a titanium ring 'swimming' in a tube.

Gravific power, when used, acts simultaneously on every part of the ship and on everything within its sphere of influence.

If a vaïd is to be brought down from a height to less than about 14,000 feet, an artificial electrical charge produced by the rotation of its disk is brought into action. The autonomous electricity is adjusted to the gravitational field of the planet that is to be visited.

A vaïd can travel at more than the speed of light, at even more than the speed of gravific waves, although these move seventeen times faster than light.

The vaïd is said to function in 'negative' time, because this is equal to 0 in our mechanical time-system; but inside the navigational cabin the personal biological time of the occupants remains normal. Above 300,000 kilometres a second, speed as a function of energy no longer has the same meaning.

The vaïd possesses energy greater than so-called 'absolute' speed; yet when it reaches this limit it develops a force which might itself become absolute but for the fact that its passage into negative time is comparable to the transit of an electron converted instantaneously from one orbit to another when its potential energy is changed.

Stabilised at a new space-time point, it has only to carry out the same manoeuvre if the light-distance to be covered demands it.

This short explanation is not aimed at teaching readers the technical details of a vaïdorge. It is meant only to impress on them the vital fact that space-craft are not powered by engines in the usual sense of the word, or by any mechanism intended to counteract the pull of forces within one's normal experience.

The traditions of every continent are agreed that Initiators came to Earth from the skies, apparently in interplanetary space-craft.

'Certain occultists tell us,' writes Maurice Magre in *The Key to Hidden Records*, published in Paris in 1935, 'that beings who have reached a state of development superior to our own and who live on the planet Venus, sent messengers to Earth to teach men the elements of their knowledge. These messengers are believed to have imparted the knowledge to disciples who in their turn passed it on to others.'

Certain Indian sects think that *yetis* ('abominable snow-men') were prototypes left on earth by the inhabitants of heaven, to see if they could be acclimatised. Space people would be assured of the chance of procreation through them if all went well.

Science is, we know, hostile to the idea of flying saucers and space travellers; but in all traditions, in the history of every civilisation, and in the mysteries of space which exercise such a fascination over our contemporaries, there are too many positive elements, and too many coincidences for any open-minded person not to be impressed. Scientific discoveries, all we have learnt about the past and the stresses and strains of the present, have made life so fantastic that nothing now seems fundamentally impossible. One hopes to be able to face it all in an unbiased way, to recognise that the best and the worst run side by side, the reasonable and the unreasonable.

One's ambition must not be to set bounds, to define and delimit, but to accustom the mind to think in a way that will oust preconceived ideas, psychoses, prejudices, even if the new images with which we are confronted are no more than a different expression of the same truth.

We do not know whether extra-terrestrials wish to contact us, whether Initiates still hold the key to tremendous secret knowledge, whether ghosts live in a parallel world. . . .

There is a vast deal that we do not know; but what we can

conceive of is wonderful and rouses an intense, a burning, thirst for knowledge; and the wonders that we can imagine are necessary to help us to see beyond the distorting mirror, beyond the illusions that are the prelude to the imminent time of the apocalypse.

An unsuspected universe exists in our secret selves; behind the confusion of the objective world there must be another, more radiant world, towards which all our vital forces are striving: our faith in the existence of an ideal.

THE END

A SELECTION OF FINE READING AVAILABLE IN CORGI BOOKS